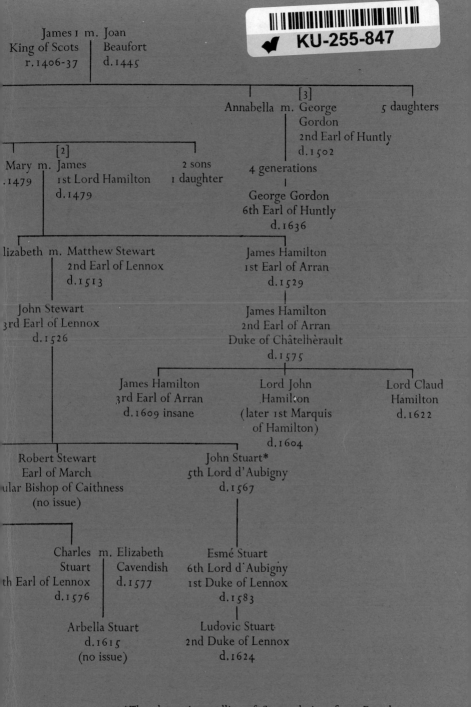

James I m. Joan
King of Scots | Beaufort
r. 1406-37 | d. 1445

[3]
Annabella m. George   5 daughters
Gordon
2nd Earl of Huntly
d. 1502

[2]
Mary m. James   2 sons
.1479   1st Lord Hamilton   1 daughter
d. 1479

4 generations
|
George Gordon
6th Earl of Huntly
d. 1636

lizabeth m. Matthew Stewart   James Hamilton
2nd Earl of Lennox   1st Earl of Arran
d. 1513   d. 1529

John Stewart   James Hamilton
3rd Earl of Lennox   2nd Earl of Arran
d. 1526   Duke of Châtelhèrault
                              d. 1575

James Hamilton   Lord John   Lord Claud
3rd Earl of Arran   Hamilton   Hamilton
d. 1609 insane   (later 1st Marquis d. 1622
                      of Hamilton)
                      d. 1604

Robert Stewart   John Stuart*
Earl of March   5th Lord d'Aubigny
ular Bishop of Caithness   d. 1567
(no issue)

Charles m. Elizabeth   Esmé Stuart
Stuart   Cavendish   6th Lord d'Aubigny
th Earl of Lennox d. 1577   1st Duke of Lennox
d. 1576   d. 1583

Arbella Stuart   Ludovic Stuart
d. 1615   2nd Duke of Lennox
(no issue)   d. 1624

*The alternative spelling of Stuart derives from French usage.
Mary, Queen of Scots spent her formative years in France, and
Matthew and John Stuart took French nationality. The Kings of
Scots preceding Mary were therefore 'Stewarts', and James VI and I
and his descendants were 'Stuarts'.

JAMES VI

of Scotland

Caroline Bingham

WEIDENFELD AND NICOLSON
London

Printed in Great Britain by
Willmer Brothers Limited
Rock Ferry Merseyside

Contents

Illustrations

Author's Note and Acknowledgements

READERS of my earlier book on King James VI, *The Making of a King: the Early Years of James VI and I* (1968) will notice that some opinions expressed in it, and some interpretations of characters and events are different from those in *James VI of Scotland*. The explanation is not inconsistency, but changing views, which are the natural products of continuing interest in a particular period, and in the lives of its *dramatis personae*.

In this book almost all the prose quotations from Scots, except for very brief ones, have been translated into modern English. I have translated them reluctantly in deference to readers (Scots among them) who have told me that they find the language of sixteenth-century Scotland laborious to read. Verse quotations retain their original orthography, without which I feel too much of their flavour would be lost.

The different spellings of the surname Stewart/Stuart are explained in a note at the foot of the genealogical table on the front endpaper of the book.

No author completes a book without incurring debts of gratitude which it is a pleasure to repay in the form of acknow-ledgements. I would like to offer my most profound thanks to Graaf W. C. van Rechteren Limpurg Almelo, for his kindness in allowing me to use his portrait of James VI as a youth (plate 16), as an illustration to this book, and for his generosity in having the picture re-photographed for the purpose.

I am also very grateful to the owner of the miniature of James VI as a child (plate 6), who provided the photograph, but who wishes to remain anonymous.

I wish to record my gratitude to the other private owners and to the institutions who have given their permission for the reproduction of the illustrations detailed as follows: plate 1 (the parents of James VI) by kind permission of Sir David Ogilvy, Bt, and the National Library of Scotland; plate 2 (detail of portrait of Lord Darnley and his brother by Hans Eworth), by gracious permission of Her Majesty the Queen; plate 3 (coin of Mary, Queen of Scots), by courtesy of the Hunterian Museum, University of Glasgow; plate 4 (detail of the Darnley Memorial picture by Livins de Vogelaare), by gracious permission of Her Majesty The Queen; plate 5 (James VI as a boy by Arnold Bronckorst), by courtesy of the Scottish National Portrait Gallery; plate 7 (the Palace Building, Stirling Castle), by courtesy of the Department of the Environment; plate 9, (The Regent Mar), by courtesy of the Scottish National Portrait Gallery; plate 11 (drawing of Esmé Stuart), by courtesy of the Trustees of the British Museum; plate 15 (Mary, Queen of Scots and James VI, by kind permission of His Grace the Duke of Atholl and the Scottish National Portrait Gallery; plate 17 (James VI as a young man), by gracious permission of Her Majesty the Queen; plates 18 and 19 (James VI and Anne of Denmark), by courtesy of the Scottish National Portrait Gallery; plate 20 (Queen Elizabeth I), by courtesy of the Victoria and Albert Museum; plate 21 (King James VI) by courtesy of the Scottish National Portrait Gallery. Plate 10 (drawing of the Regent Morton) is of unknown provenance. Plate 12 (portrait of Esmé Stuart) is in the possession of the author. Plates 8, 13, and 14 (views from *Theatrum Scotiae*) are not subject to copyright, but the book from which they were photographed is in the possession of the London Library.

Finally, I would like to thank Miss Alex MacCormick of Weidenfeld and Nicolson, who has been a most patient and helpful editor of this book, and Miss Elspeth A. Evans of the National Portrait Gallery, who gave me valuable assistance with the illustrations. Mrs Sheila Collins typed the manuscript with admirable expertise.

CAROLINE BINGHAM

PROLOGUE

The Metamorphosis
of a Kingdom

Now is Protestantis risen us amang
Sayand* thay will mak reformatioun. . . .

Sir Richard Maitland of Lethington,
Papistis and Protestantis

ON 14 December 1542 James V, the last King of pre-Reformation Scotland, died at the age of thirty. His two legitimate sons had died in infancy. He left seven acknowledged bastards, and the heiress of his kingdom was one week old.

Mary, Queen of Scots was born in the Palace of Linlithgow, half way between Edinburgh and Stirling, while her father lay on his deathbed many miles away, at Falkland Palace in Fife. He never saw her, and the news of her birth was the last bitter blow to a dying man who had hoped for a son. She inherited not only his kingdom but also the gathering storm of troubles which had contributed to the lassitude and despair that led him to welcome death.

Scotland was on the brink of one of the greatest ideological crises of history, the Protestant Reformation, and the Catholic Church was in no condition to resist the fervour of its opponents. James V, paradoxically orthodox and immoral, had bullied Scottish prelates to reform their lives, while at the same time he petitioned the Pope to bestow rich benefices on his illegitimate sons. The hierarchy was inevitably weakened by such flagrant abuse of the proprieties of ecclesiastical preferment, especially as it was practised not only by the King but by many noble families over-endowed with sons. In consequence the lower ranks of the clergy suffered from lack of direction or example. Satirists derided the luxury and laxity of bishops, the

*saying

I

illiteracy of parish priests, the sybaritic lives of monks, the unchastity of nuns. Devout Catholics, of whom there were many, looked to the future with ever-growing alarm.

Marie de Guise, the French widow of James V and the mother of Mary, Queen of Scots, was determined that when her daughter grew up she should rule a Catholic kingdom. But the success of her ambition grew less and less probable as Calvinist ideology infiltrated Scotland, influencing the greatest of the aristocracy, the lesser lords and the lairds (or gentry), and the populace of the east coast towns.

In accordance with Scottish custom, the Regent for the infant Mary, Queen of Scots was not her mother but her nearest male relative, James Hamilton, second Earl of Arran (see genealogical table at front). Marie de Guise contemptuously described him as 'the most inconstant man in the world', but he added greatly to her difficulties by inclining to Protestantism at the outset of his regency and concluding with Henry VIII of England a treaty by which Mary was to marry Henry's son, the future Edward VI.

The treaty was swiftly repudiated when Marie de Guise and her astute adviser Cardinal Beaton concerted their influence against Arran. Henry, who had hoped to make Scotland an English province through the projected marriage, expressed his frustrated fury by two invasions of Scotland, in 1544 and 1545, which the Scots with dour humour called 'the Rough Wooing'. Henry VIII died in 1547, but the Regent for the boy-king Edward VI continued his policy and in the same year inflicted a heavy defeat on the Scots at the battle of Pinkie.

In this extremity Marie de Guise appealed for help from France, which was granted on condition that the little Queen of Scots should be sent to receive her education at the French Court and should be married in due course to the Dauphin François, the eldest son of King Henri II and his Queen Catherine de' Medici. So it was that in 1548 Mary sailed for France and ten years later married the heir to the French throne.

In the meantime Marie de Guise became Regent of Scotland in 1554, and the Earl of Arran received the French dukedom of Châtelhèrault as a reward for making way for her. The Queen-Regent spent the rest of her life struggling to defend the Catholic inheritance of her daughter with the assistance of French arms. A long tradition of friendship between Scotland and France had

2

given the name of 'the auld alliance' to a time-honoured bond, but the increasingly Protestant complexion of Scotland made the presence of many Catholic Frenchmen less welcome than of old, and the prospect of help from England, the recent enemy, seemed a feasible means of ousting them and of achieving the official religious conversion of the country.

Further encouragement came with the death of Henri II of France, who was accidentally killed at a tournament in 1559: the young husband of Mary, Queen of Scots became King François II, and it appeared improbable that the Queen-Consort of France would ever wish to come home to rule her native kingdom. The prospect of an absentee sovereign seemed to offer the Scottish Protestants their best hope of success, and the great reformer John Knox returned from his exile in Geneva to fire their enthusiasm. Suddenly Marie de Guise faced an armed rebellion, in which her illegitimate stepson Lord James Stewart, the ablest of James V's bastards, played a leading part.

The Queen-Regent was already a dying woman when the Reformation Rebellion broke out. Her death in June 1560 saved her from humiliation, for the rebels triumphed, with the assistance sent by the young Queen Elizabeth I of England, who had been on her throne for eighteen months. The rebels summoned a parliament of dubious legality, which forbade the saying of Mass in Scotland, repudiated the authority and jurisdiction of the Pope and adopted a Protestant 'Confession of Faith', the official foundation of the new Kirk. The metamorphosis of the kingdom, long in preparation, seemed to have been brought about almost overnight.

One more dramatic event concluded this *annus mirabilis*: in December François II died of an abscess in the ear. Mary, Queen of Scots, discovered that she was of no further importance in France. She was no longer the cynosure of the Court but a superannuated *reinedouairière*, whose presence was merely tolerated by her unloving mother-in-law, Catherine de' Medici. Gallantly she resolved to return to Scotland and take up the challenge of ruling the kingdom which had turned Protestant in her absence.

On 19 August 1561 she landed at Leith, and John Knox, to whom her religion was anathema and the very idea of a woman ruler was repugnant, reported that, 'The very face of heaven, the

3

time of her arrival, did manifestly speak what comfort was brought into this country with her, to wit, sorrow, dolour, darkness and all impiety. . . . The sun was not seen to shine two days before, nor two days after. . . .'[1]

When the damp veil of the Scottish *haar* cleared, Mary saw her country cruelly marked by the scars of recent war, her capital and her palace and its adjoining abbey of Holyrood still damaged after the English invasions. Ecclesiastical buildings especially, throughout southern Scotland, had been maltreated by the English soldiery, and during the rebellion mobs of Protestant iconoclasts had wrought yet more destruction. Monks and nuns, mercifully permitted to continue living in their sometimes ruinous monasteries and convents, were forbidden to perform the duties of the religious life. At the same time the ministers of the new religion forbade the laity to observe the festivals of the liturgical year. There was to be no more rejoicing at Christmas or Easter, and certainly no processions on saints' days.

Partly as a result of the grim influence of Calvinism, partly as a consequence of the recent years of warfare, a mirthless spirit settled upon Scotland. Some people inevitably felt nostalgia for the past. A poignant recollection of the brilliant Court of James v and the vivacity of his subjects is captured by the poet Sir Richard Maitland of Lethington, who wrote:

> Quhare is the blyithness that hes been
> Baith in burgh and landwart seen?
> Amang lordis and ladyis schein,
> Dauncing, singing, game and play :
> Bot now I wait nocht quhat thay mein –
> All mirriness is worn away.[2]

Mary, Queen of Scots no doubt saw 'sorrow, dolour, darkness and all impiety', though from the opposite viewpoint to that of Knox. But whatever her first impressions of her kingdom, she wisely accepted the *fait accompli* and began her reign circumspectly by granting official recognition to the reformed religion, while insisting on the practice of Catholicism as her sovereign privilege.

Fortunately not all her subjects were as unwelcoming as Knox. The poet Alexander Scott, who was himself a Protestant, greeted Mary with a stately ode which glorified both her and the Scottish monarchy:

> Welcum, illustrat ladye and our Quene:
> Welcum, oure lyone with the floure delyce:
> Welcum, oure thrissill with the Lorane grene:
> Welcum, our rubent rois upoun the ryce:
> Welcum, oure jem and joyfull genetryce:
> Welcum, oure beill of Albion to beir:
> Welcum, our plesand princes maist of price:
> God gif thee grace aganis this guid New Yeir![3]

It must have lifted her spirits to hear these joyous lines, among which, in another verse, the poet expressed the hope that in the 'good new year' of 1562 the Queen would 'get a gudeman' (a husband). And in this respect Mary could feel that the world was at her feet, for she was nineteen years old and a sovereign queen: a great match for the 'gudeman' who could give her the surest means to secure her position, an heir to Scotland – a son who would quite possibly be the heir to England also.

CHAPTER ONE

The Royal Child

This is the son whom I hope shall first unite the two kingdoms of Scotland and England.

Mary, Queen of Scots, 1566

ALEXANDER SCOTT, in his *New Yeir Gift to Quene Mary quhen scho come first hame* (1562) prophesied that ambassadors would hasten to Scotland to seek the Queen's hand in marriage on behalf of princes, dukes and kings. The prophecy was correct, but more than three years passed before the most eligible widow in Europe went to the altar with her second husband. On 29 July 1565 Mary, Queen of Scots, married her cousin Henry Stuart, Lord Darnley.

Very early, between five and six o'clock on that summer Sunday morning, Mary, Queen of Scots entered the Chapel Royal in the Palace of Holyroodhouse, escorted by Matthew, Earl of Lennox, the bridegroom's father, and John Stewart, Earl of Atholl. She was dressed in black, as a last tribute to her late husband the young King François II of France.

Mary, Queen of Scots was an elegant, auburn-haired young woman, twenty-three years old and almost six feet tall. She had the aquiline features, delicate brows and heavy-lidded eyes which characterized her family; but her beauty must be taken on trust, for her portraits do little to convey its elusive quality.

Contemporary artists served her bridegroom better, and it is easy to understand the dazzling first impression created by Lord Darnley, a yellow-haired, grey-eyed youth of rather epicene beauty, taller than the Queen by two or three inches and her equal in elegance.

The bridegroom had previously received the titles of Earl of Ross and Duke of Albany – titles traditionally associated with the royal House of Scotland – and by his marriage he became officially 'King Henry'. Perhaps the fact that he cut so poor a figure as a king was the reason why historians, with almost perfect unanimity, have referred to him as 'Lord Darnley'.

Darnley had already shown himself to be a somewhat erratic character, not least in religion. His religious practices were a bewildering mixture of Catholicism and Protestantism; but if he thereby intended to make a politic appeal to men of both persuasions, he utterly failed. On his wedding day he surprised everyone by marrying the Queen by Catholic rites and then withdrawing from the chapel and leaving her to attend the nuptial Mass alone.

Nothing daunted, when the whole ceremony was over, Mary took off her mourning and was dressed afresh in brilliant clothes and jewels. The rest of the day was given over to festivity, and it was only after supper, when many hours of feasting and dancing had passed, that the Queen and her King-Consort retired to bed. They lived happily for a short time afterwards, before the Queen, who had made a love-match in the face of strong opposition, suffered bitter disillusionment.

Despite the notoriously bad effect of love upon judgment, the Queen's choice of a husband had much to commend it. Her ambition in the early 1560s was to gain recognition from Elizabeth I of England as heiress presumptive to the English throne. She had a claim to it: in the eyes of Catholic Europe she had a better claim than the Protestant Elizabeth.[1] Her cousin Darnley also had a claim, and the union of their two claims in marriage strengthened hers and gave an immeasurably stronger claim to a child born of that marriage.

Mary and Darnley were both grandchildren of Margaret Tudor, daughter of Henry VII (see genealogical table at back). Margaret had been married in 1503 to King James IV of Scotland, and their only surviving son became King James V. (James V was twice married, first to Madeleine de Valois, then to Marie de Guise, who became the mother of Mary, Queen of Scots.) After the death of James IV, Margaret had married Archibald Douglas, sixth Earl of Angus, and the only child of their marriage was a daughter, Lady Margaret Douglas, who married Matthew Stuart, fourth Earl of Lennox (who was a descendant of King James II of Scotland), and their elder son was Henry Stuart, Lord Darnley. Mary and Darnley were thus first cousins, and as a scion of the

8

royal blood of both Scotland and England Darnley was a worthy choice as King-Consort of Scotland.

Politically he had less to commend him, and the Queen's marriage caused dangerously inimical reactions in both kingdoms.

In England no marriage made by the Queen of Scots could be regarded with equanimity. Elizabeth, though she entered many marriage negotiations, in the end chose not to marry at all; yet she could not readily accept that her kinswoman and neighbour-sovereign should play her part for her in providing an heir to the English throne. This aspect of the situation apart, had Mary married otherwise than she did, the history of England might have been less peaceful: had Mary married a foreign Catholic prince – for example, Don Carlos, the son of Philip II of Spain, who was one of her many suitors – she would have had the resources, and might have had the encouragement, to press her claim to the throne of England by force of arms.

Elizabeth was well aware of this danger, and she successfully foiled Mary's negotiations for a foreign marriage; but so long as Mary remained unmarried, the danger continued to exist. To permit her marriage with Lord Darnley may well have appeared to Elizabeth the lesser evil; for Elizabeth might have prevented it by the direct exercise of her authority.

Darnley's father, the Earl of Lennox, was a renegade Scot who had been forfeited and exiled for his treasonable dealings with England during Mary's minority. He had lived in England since 1544, and Darnley had been born there. Darnley was therefore technically an English subject, and possibly it was with the thought that this fact might retain her some control of his future actions that Elizabeth, in the full knowledge that he intended to woo the Queen of Scots, allowed him to go to Scotland in 1565. In characteristic agonies of indecision, Elizabeth subsequently ordered him home again, but the Queen of Scots had already made up her mind. The strong imperatives of passion added their decisive influence to the reasonings of dynastic policy, and Darnley remained in Scotland to marry the Queen.

But within Scotland itself there was as much opposition to the Queen's marriage as there had been in England. The very facts which commended Darnley in England condemned him in Scotland: his father's record and his English birth. And conversely, his position in the Scottish succession also militated against him. If he had a reversionary claim to the succession, after the Queen herself, there were others of the royal blood who considered that they had a better one and viewed his advancement with resentment.

The regally-connected family of Hamilton (see genealogical table at front) was descended from a grandson of King James II, whereas the Lennox family was descended only from a grand-daughter. Darnley's marriage to the Queen might well cancel out that disadvantage. The Queen's kinsman James Hamilton, Duke of Châtelhèrault, the erstwhile regent, had hoped to see her married to his son, the young Earl of Arran.* Her preference for Darnley put an end to his hopes, which had grown increasingly futile as the unstable young Earl declined into insanity.

The Hamiltons, ambitious as they were, were not Darnley's strongest opponents in Scotland. Since the beginning of her rule in 1561, Mary's chief adviser had been her half-brother, Lord James Stewart, whom she had created Earl of Moray. Mary had been wise to seek the support of her half-brother, for at the outset of her personal rule he could have been her most dangerous enemy – as indeed he was to prove in the end. He was the son of King James V by his favourite mistress Margaret Erskine, whom he had at one time aspired to marry. But for papal opposition to that marriage, to which James V had yielded, Moray could have been legitimately born, and King of Scots. No one knows to what extent he thought himself a man thwarted by fate, but he had found some fulfilment for his ambitions through his supremacy in the Queen's counsels, and he could scarcely be expected to brook displacement from them by the sudden elevation of her young consort.

So the Queen of Scots made her love match in the face of Elizabeth's coldness and the enmity of the Hamiltons and the Earl of Moray. Elizabeth watched and waited while Châtel-hèrault and Moray made common cause.

The two of them made a 'band', or agreement of mutual support, as early as March 1565. But although Moray showed his disapproval of the Queen's intended marriage as early as May, by withdrawing from her Council, he was slow to make another

*The third Earl of Arran had inherited his father's former title.

move. A rebellion, which evidently had been for some months in preparation, broke out in August, after the marriage had taken place, and it is hard to see what Moray, Châtelhèrault and their confederates expected to gain by it. Possibly they intended to illustrate to the Queen that her position would be very vulnerable without their counsel and support, and thus bring her once more – and increasingly – under Moray's influence. The rebellion was the more dangerous because the great magnates of Scotland commanded the loyalty of many supporters. For example, every man who bore the surname of Hamilton looked upon the Duke of Châtelhèrault as his chief. If Châtelhèrault rebelled, all the Hamiltons followed. In Lowland Scotland the 'name' was as powerful a binding force as was the clan in the Highlands.

Moray, in the hope of making the rebellion yet more formidable, appealed for English help and did his best to make political capital out of religious differences, by stressing his own staunch Protestantism and the Queen's suspect Catholicism. If Elizabeth had supported him, he might have regained his former position, and perhaps much more; but Elizabeth preferred to remain a spectator and to choose her own moment for intervention in Scottish affairs.

The challenge of rebellion displayed Mary's resolute spirit to the best advantage. On 22 August she commanded a muster and pawned her jewels to raise her soldiers' pay. Then, on 26 August, she rode out from Edinburgh to meet the rebels who had gathered at Ayr. Darnley, riding beside her with his gilded armour and bright hair, must have made a gallant figure; but the Queen of Scots herself provided the impetus and the inspiration of her army. Even her dour enemy John Knox wrote in grudging admiration that, in the action which ensued, 'Albeit the most part waxed weary, yet the Queen's courage increased man-like, so much that she was ever with the fore-most.'[2]

The Queen rode west, but the rebels gave her the slip and re-entered Edinburgh on 31 August. There they received so cold a welcome that they withdrew again on 2 September, and by the 5th they were back at Dumfries. The Queen returned to Edinburgh to recruit a larger force and renew the pursuit. But by the end of the month all was over. Elizabeth saw that Moray enjoyed little support in Scotland; she refused English help, yet she allowed him to claim asylum. On 6 October Moray fled across the Border to an English refuge.

In the midst of this stirring episode, on or about 19 September, the only child of Mary and Darnley was conceived. It is curious to reflect that James VI and I, who in later life proved to be so great an advocate of peace, should have been conceived in the midst of a small-scale war. Yet perhaps the fact is less incongruous than first appears, for in later life James was a noted lover of the chase, and 'the Chaseabout Raid', as the action was subsequently named, had indeed little of the nature of warfare about it and much more of the character of a hunt. Mary and her army as huntress and hounds pursued Moray like a hart: it was her last untramelled triumph.

Several times during the autumn the English ambassador in Scotland, Thomas Randolph, reported rumours of the Queen's pregnancy. By the end of 1565 or the opening of 1566 it was common knowledge. At the same time it also became generally known that the Queen and her consort were no longer on the best of terms. Their love had grown cold with the season, and they entered upon a winter of bitterness.

The causes were not obscure. Darnley was not a level-headed young man; he was one who had had greatness thrust upon him, and the strong wine of greatness turned his head. The kindest things that can be remembered about him are that he could play the lute extremely well and write courtly Scottish verse. This, reputedly, to the Queen:

> The turtour from hir maik
> mair dule may nocht indure
> nor I do for hir saik,
> evin hir, quha hes in cure
> my hart, quhilk salbe sure
> in service to the deid
> unto that lady pure
> the well of womanheid.[3]

He had beauty, and when he was on his best behaviour his manners were engaging. But he had not been equipped for kingship: he had no concept of responsibility, no understanding of politics, no grasp of diplomacy, no interest in administration.

All too soon after he became 'King Henry', he revealed himself as a 'young fool and proud tyrant'.[4]

The Queen became aware of her consort's shortcomings before she had given him too much power to be curtailed. She had not, when she bestowed on him the title of 'King', granted him 'the Crown Matrimonial' which would have given him the right to reign should she predecease him while they were childless. He naturally desired it, if only for reasons of prestige, though he did nothing to prove himself worthy of it. He demanded it, and the Queen refused; bitterness grew between them.

While Darnley found in low company the only audience willing to reassure him of his greatness, the Queen witnessed, at first with distress and then with disgust, his decline into drunkenness and vicious temper and his indulgence in indiscriminate sexual adventures. Under these circumstances, his lack of interest in government was perhaps rather a relief to the Queen than otherwise. A metal stamp was used to imprint the name of King Henry on state documents, and the young man himself was left to pursue his pleasures.

The Queen, who had hoped to receive advice and support from her husband, sought it instead from the secretary who dealt with her French correspondence, David Riccio. This unfortunate man might have enjoyed the Queen's confidence and yet have remained as obscure as his modest appointment presupposed, but for the brief drama which ended his career.

He had arrived in Scotland in 1561, in the entourage of the ambassador of Savoy. He had then entered the Queen's Household, first as a singer – for he had a fine bass voice – and later he had become a secretary. Mary appreciated his conversation, for she was, as the courtier and memoirist Sir James Melville of Halhill put it, 'curious to know and get intelligence of the estate of other countries and would be sometimes sad when she was solitary, and glad of the company of them that had travelled in other parts'.[5] Mary was affable and sometimes familiar with her servants, in the style of the earlier Stewart kings; it was a style well suited to a king, but one which in a queen could give rise to misunderstanding. By the beginning of 1566 Mary, Queen of Scots did not lack enemies ready to misunderstand and willing to compromise her.

That she, in the early months of her pregnancy, with its

accompanying physical discomforts, should suddenly have em-barked on a sexual intimacy with an ugly little man who had been in her service for some years, was extraordinarily un-likely. But even had she done so, it is beyond dispute that James had been conceived before the Riccio scandal was even thought of. Unfortunately for James, it occurred soon enough after his conception for a slur on his paternity to be an easy slander for his detractors. In his later life he was often complimented or flattered as a modern Solomon; but the wise King of the Old Testament had been the son of David, and it was an easy and cruel jibe to suggest that the new Solomon was the son of David too. Indeed, on one of the most disagreeable and alarming days of James's life a hostile mob, catching sight of him in a window, shouted at him, 'Come down, thou son of Seigneur Davie.'

However, upon the irrefutable evidence of the date of his birth, James was Darnley's son. There was also a strong family likeness between them, though somehow similarity of features did not bestow on James his father's good looks.

While Mary awaited the birth of her child, she became increasingly enmeshed in political difficulties, resulting both from the impossible behaviour of Darnley and from the reper-cussions of 'the Chaseabout Raid'. In these circumstances Riccio was a secondary figure and a luckless victim.

Moray and his associates had the sympathy of a group of lords who had not participated in the rebellion which followed the Queen's marriage. These men desired to see the recall and re-instatement of Moray, and they resented he intrusion of Riccio into the Queen's confidence since they despised him as an upstart and a foreigner and suspected him, though probably ground-lessly, of being a papal agent.

To obtain the reinstatement of Moray and his supporters, the assistance of Darnley was required, for by the authority which he already possessed as King-Consort he could cancel the session of Parliament in which the formal trial of Moray *in absentia* was to take place on 12 March 1566.

The Queen would have to be put under restraint while Darn-ley exercised his authority, and to arouse Darnley to a sufficient pitch of excitement to coerce her – he seems to have been some-what in awe of her except when he was extremely drunk – the supporters of Moray worked upon his resentment over the

Crown Matrimonial and also hinted to him that Riccio was the Queen's lover and the father of her child.

When accusations of infidelity are bandied about, few people are prepared to listen to the voice of reason, and Darnley certainly was not one to do so. Having aroused him to a fever of resentment against the Queen and of murderous fury against Riccio, the conspirators promised to secure the Crown Matrimonial for Darnley as the reward for his assistance. The murder of Riccio was planned as the occasion for putting coercion on the Queen.

The dual plan had a quality of cynical savagery that might have aroused the suspicion of anyone less naïvely arrogant and self-regarding than Darnley. Apparently he seriously believed that men who had never shown him much reverence would suddenly support his claim to the Crown Matrimonial, and that Moray, who had even rebelled against his elevation to the position of King-Consort, would suddenly acquiesce. No doubt they were very specious with him. They were, moreover, his kinsmen. They were the Earl of Morton, Lords Lindsay and Ruthven and the latter's son.

James Douglas, fourth Earl of Morton, of whom more will be heard, was the nephew of Margaret Tudor's Earl of Angus and therefore Darnley's cousin (see genealogical table at front), and Lords Lindsay and Ruthven were both married to Douglas ladies. Darnley could think that his claim to the Crown Matrimonial enjoyed family support.

The murder of Riccio, a mere stepping-stone towards the reinstatement of Moray, took place on the evening of 9 March 1566. The Queen was sitting at supper with her half-sister Janet, Countess of Argyll, in a little room which opened out of the Queen's Bedchamber in the James IV Tower of Holyroodhouse. Riccio was in attendance. The first intimation of trouble was the arrival of Darnley. He came in, apparently friendly but perhaps neither perfectly sober nor perfectly at ease, and sat down beside the Queen. Then, shortly afterwards, the ringing tread of steel-clad feet announced the arrival of Lord Ruthven. The Queen looked up, 'stranglie amazed', to see his gaunt figure, like a personification of Death, filling the doorway. Lord Ruthven had been long sick and lately believed to be dying but had risen from the sickbed which everyone had supposed to be his deathbed to participate in a murder. He entered the Queen's supper-room clad in complete steel, beneath a dressing-gown.

This macabre apparition was followed by the rest of the conspirators and an assortment of secondary participants, including George Douglas, a half-brother of Morton, and one Andrew Ker of Fauldonside. They surged in, overturning the table and plunging the room into flickering half-darkness, relieved only by a candle which the Countess of Argyll managed to save from the wreck of the supper.

Darnley clasped the Queen round the waist and held her down, while Fauldonside 'held a pistol to her breast, which refused to give fire'.[6] This account of the event suggests a deliberate attempt to assassinate her, though in fact Fauldonside may not have pulled the trigger but may only have used the pistol to terrorize her.

Riccio, in the realization that he was the intended victim, flung himself at the Queen's feet and clutched her skirts, shrieking linguistically-garbled entreaties in his terror: 'Justizia! Justizia, Madame! Save ma vie! Save ma vie!'

The Queen, who was surrounded by the conspirators, believed that the first blow was struck over her shoulder by George Douglas, using Darnley's dagger.[7] Riccio, whose fingers were bent back to make him loose his hold upon the Queen, was dragged bleeding from the room and dispatched outside it with a total of fifty-six dagger thrusts. Darnley's weapon, to advertise his participation, was left stuck into the corpse.

When the butchery was done, Lord Ruthven returned, collapsed in a chair and called for a drink. The Queen, no terrified woman but an outraged sovereign, confronted him in fury demanding how he 'durst presume to commit that unreverence?' But the half-dying murderer may have been in no condition to answer. 'Well, my lord,' the Queen is reported to have said, 'it is within my belly that one day will avenge these cruelties and affronts.'[8]

If the Queen did indeed make this prophecy, it proved correct, for in the years to come James VI exacted the lives of three members of the Ruthven family. However, he had his own quarrels with the victims and may not have been troubled by his mother's wrong. Poetic justice is not always meted out through the conscious will of its executants.

It has often been remarked that James VI's notorious physical cowardice, especially his obvious shrinking from naked steel, could have had its origin in his pre-natal experience on the night of Riccio's murder. The Queen was almost six months pregnant, her unborn child already quickened, and there seems nothing fanciful in the supposition that it could have been affected by the shock of terror which must have run through her when the muzzle of Fauldonside's pistol was pressed against her and when Riccio knelt clutching her skirts and shrieking his entreaties.

The shock of such an experience, which might well have affected the child, might equally well have caused the Queen to miscarry. Such a result could have been the conspirators' hope and intention. Darnley especially might have hoped for it, if he had been convinced that the Queen's child was not his. Mary herself believed that her own life had been sought, though it is difficult to see what would have been gained by killing her with the child unborn; Darnley needed her alive to bestow the Crown Matrimonial on him, and the rest of the conspirators had nothing to gain by her death, which would have been followed by bitter strife, if not by civil war, between rival claimants. It seems obvious that if anyone's life was sought, besides Riccio's, it was that of the child.

The Queen, however, possessed more than common resilience. She did not lose the child, and she soon turned her apparently desperate situation to her advantage.

Immediately after the murder, Mary was a prisoner, and Darnley cancelled the Parliament which was to have tried Moray and his associates in 'the Chaseabout Raid'. On the very day following the murder Moray entered Edinburgh and received the pardon which the Queen had no power to refuse. But that was the limit of her yielding to the force of circumstance. She turned her attention upon Darnley and so infected him with fear of his erstwhile allies that he was willing and indeed eager to take the opportunity of escaping with her.

Successfully they made their escape from Holyroodhouse and rode to the Earl of Bothwell's castle of Dunbar, where they were joined by the Earls of Atholl and Huntly and Lords Fleming and Seton. With their support, and that of the newly pardoned Moray and his associates Argyll and Glencairn, Mary made a triumphal return to Edinburgh. Morton, Lindsay and Ruthven, with their adherents to the number of sixty, in their turn fled to England.

The final victim of this dramatic turn of events was the treacherous and altogether culpable Darnley. He had betrayed the Queen and then betrayed his allies. He was an object of contempt to every powerful grouping and it is difficult to see how he could have recovered his position. He had forfeited the only strong asset which he had ever possessed – the Queen's love – for he had irreparably alienated her by insulting her character and her sovereignty and by endangering her life. The murder of Riccio was the effective end of the relationship between the Queen and her consort, but for the sake of appearances a reconciliation was effected, until it should be seen whether he had fulfilled his dynastic purpose by begetting an heir.

An uneasy peace, which proved to be the proverbial calm before the storm, settled upon the Scottish Court, while the Queen awaited the birth of her child.

Midsummer 1566 approached, and Lord Herries recorded the Queen's *accouchement* in his memoirs: 'The kingdom and Court was at quiet . . . the Queen, growing great with child . . . retired her from Holyroodhouse unto the Castle of Edinburgh, where, upon the nineteenth day of June she brought forth a son, betwixt nine and ten o'clock in the morning.'[9]

Later in the day, the Queen forced Darnley to fulfil the purpose for which she had been reconciled with him: to acknowledge his paternity of the child.

It was two o'clock in the afternoon when Darnley came to the small closet-like chamber in which the Queen had endured her difficult labour. Lord Herries, situated, fortunately for posterity, close enough to hear the exchanges between the Queen and her consort, reported the grim little scene which ensued:

'My lord,' says the Queen, 'God has given you and me a son, begotten by none but you.' At which words the King blushed and kissed the child. Then she took the child in her arms, and, discovering his face [i.e. unwrapping him to reveal his face], said, 'My Lord, here I protest to God and as I shall answer to Him at the great day of judgment, that this is your son and no other man's son. And I am desirous that all here both ladies and others bear witness: for he is so much your own son, that I fear it will be the worse for him hereafter.' Then she spoke to Sir William Stanley [an English servant of Darnley]. 'This' says she, 'is the son whom I hope shall first unite the two kingdoms of Scotland and England.' Then Sir William answered, 'Why, Madam? Shall he succeed before Your Majesty and his father?' 'Because,' says she, 'his father has broken to [i.e with] me.' The King was by and heard all.[10]

The Queen had spoken twice in prophetic vein : of her son's revenge upon the Ruthvens and of his ultimate succession to the crowns of Scotland and England. Was she also prophetic in her fear that James was so much Darnley's son that it would be the worse for him thereafter? It is difficult to see much resemblance between James's intellectual interests and his father's frivolous ones; but one pursuit which they had in common was that of beasts of the chase. For the rest, James like his father wrote verses and like him also showed an ultimately deleterious fondness for the bottle. In one respect James grew up to resemble neither of his parents: he had a solid foundation of common sense and an extremely strong sense of self-preservation.

His slightly non-regal canniness arose from the type of upbringing to which he was in due course subjected; his scant resemblance to either of his parents from the fact that he had scarcely any contact with them. The myth that he was a supposititious child, substituted for the Queen's son who died at birth, is relatively recent in origin and wholly groundless. Unfortunately, the appeal which 'historical mysteries', as opposed to their solutions, have for a certain type of mind, makes it unlikely that this particularly unnecessary 'mystery' will be eliminated altogether. Some account of its origin and basic absurdity may, however, help to weaken its credibility.

In the *Glasgow Courier* of 14 August 1830 a curious discovery in Edinburgh Castle was reported :

On Wednesday last, as the masons were knocking off the loose lime, previous to recasting the old palace in the Castle, they discovered a hole in the wall. The workmen described it as being three feet and a half long, one foot two inches high and one foot in breadth. Between the end of the opening and surface of the wall (it is in the front of the palace) there was a stone about six inches thick and about the same length, which was supposed, from the thickness of the wall, to be between the extremity of the opening and the inner surface of the wall or room. In this cavity were found several human bones, some pieces of oak supposed to have been parts of a coffin, and bits of woollen cloth, in all probability the lining of it. On the lining the letter J was distinctly visible, and some of the masons said they saw the letter G also. The bones appear to have been those of a young child. Some of them are in the possession of the person from whom we received this communication. It is right to add that the opening was across the wall.[11]

The story of this discovery which, though interesting in itself, had nothing to connect it with Mary, Queen of Scots or her son, began to grow in the telling. The principal guilty party to its distortion was a Mr P. H. McKerlie F.S.A. Scot., who claimed to have been present in the castle as a boy at the time of the discovery, though he did not claim to have witnessed it. He did not write an account of it until 1883, when he described the discovery as taking place as a result of a fire: 'An examination of the chimneys and walls caused the discovery of the coffin to be made. It was of oak and good workmanship. The materials in which the body had been wrapped were of the finest description, conveying that the child was of high origin. The men immediately reported the discovery, but the action of the air caused all to crumble into small fragments.'[12]

It will be noticed that the pieces of oak had become a coffin, the several human bones the body of a child, and the woollen cloth material of the finest description. Mr McKerlie subsequently wrote three more accounts of the discovery, each differing in detail from the previous one.

In 1900 a Mr John Geddie, in an agreeable guide-book entitled *Romantic Edinburgh*, made a passing reference to 'the discovery in 1830, in a recess of the outer Palace wall, close to the entrance of the Royal Apartments, of the remains of a male infant wrapped in decayed cloth of gold bearing the letter "I" . . .'.[13]

But the final metamorphosis of story into myth was the work of a Mr Walter B. Woodgate, who in 1909 wrote a book called *Reminiscences of an Old Sportsman*, in which the original unassuming find had become 'an infant skeleton, wrapped in a gold-embroidered cloth, on which could be traced, "I.R." '[14]

The author of this book described his own contribution to the mythology of the discovery as follows:

In 1884 a National Portrait loan exhibition was organized for Edinburgh. In September that year I was staying at Alloa House. The then Dowager Elise, Countess of Mar and Kellie, told me that she wished me to go and see this exhibition: for special reasons, and to tell her what I thought of it. I forget whether or not she previously named any special portraits for my study; or whether she only lent me her catalogue, and that in it I observed marks directing attention to certain pictures.

Anyhow, I went, and inspected; and returned by dinnertime to Alloa.

Later, the lady and I conferred, and I was cross-examined by her . . . To condense: the conclusion at which we had independently arrived was that James VI of Scotland and 'I' [sic] of England was a changeling, and not the son of Mary, Queen of Scots; also that he was the second son of the Earl of Mar. . . .[15]

Building upon the flimsy substructure of previous writers' exaggerations concerning the discovery in Edinburgh Castle, and upon the hypotheses of himself and the Dowager Lady Mar and Kellie, Mr Woodgate constructed an edifice of nonsense which proved to be more enduring than its materials merited.

It was not unduly surprising that there was a resemblance between James VI and John Erskine, first Earl of Mar, and John Erskine, second Earl of Mar (his father and brother according to Mr Woodgate's theory), for the first Earl had a Lennox Stewart grandmother. But upon the frail basis of this resemblance and Mr Woodgate's comments upon it, the existence of a 'Mar Tradition', that James VI had been in fact a member of the Erskine family, was invented.

However, Lady Antonia Fraser re-examined the matter when researching her biography of Mary, Queen of Scots, and wrote: 'The tale is backed by no contemporary reference, and the present (13th) Earl of Mar and Kellie has told the author that he can find nothing in his extensive family archives to support the theory of an Erskine family tradition.'[16]

The child who had been begotten by Darnley and borne by Mary, and who survived to reign, was placed in the care of the first Earl of Mar and his Countess not because they were his natural parents but because the fosterage of royal infants was an established tradition and because the Erskines had some claim to be regarded as hereditary guardians of child royalty. Previous Lords Erskine had been among the guardians of James V and of

Mary, Queen of Scots herself. Mary, who created the sixth Lord Erskine first Earl of Mar, was confident of his capacity to bring up her child creditably and to safeguard him in the fastness of Stirling Castle. Mar acquitted himself honourably towards the young James, but less so towards the Queen his mother.

Once the Prince of Scotland had been born and the discredited King-Consort had acknowledged his paternity with an embarrassed kiss, Darnley himself became dispensable. By the autumn of 1566 Mary was seeking an 'outgait' from her intolerable marriage. In November the problem was the subject of a conference at Craigmillar Castle between the Queen herself, the Earls of Moray, Bothwell and Argyll, and the Secretary of State, William Maitland of Lethington. The Queen rejected the suggestion that she should seek a divorce, for fear of putting her son's legitimacy in question. Her counsellors therefore assured her that they would devise some 'outgait' for her which would not be detrimental either to her son's position or to her honour. There, for the present, the matter rested, while the Queen planned the last splendid spectacle of her reign: the baptism of the son whom she hoped would unite the two kingdoms of Scotland and England.

The baptism took place on 17 December 1566, in the Chapel Royal of Stirling Castle, a building now vanished, which was demolished and rebuilt before the end of the sixteenth century for the baptism of James's own eldest son. At her own cost the Queen provided suits of cloth of gold and silver and of rich colours for the most favoured of the lords. The ambassadors of the Prince's godparents came to preside like characters in a fairy tale, bearing costly gifts. The young King of France, Charles IX, Mary's brother-in-law by her first marriage, sent rich jewels; the Duke of Savoy sent a jewelled fan trimmed with peacock feathers; Elizabeth of England outdid the others, sending a font for the christening made from 333 ounces of gold.

James, though he may not have cared to remember the fact in later life, was baptized by Catholic rites. The occasion was one of much splendour, though there were rumbles of political thunder in the background. The Queen of England's proxy, the Earl of Bedford, who was a Puritan, refused to enter the Chapel Royal. His place beside the golden font was taken by the

Countess of Argyll, who deputized for him and held the child – a participation in a 'popish' ceremony for which she was subsequently obliged to do penance. Darnley did not appear at all. Either he was kept out of the way or else he sulked in anticipation of the scanty reverence which he might receive.

After the baptism James remained at Stirling in the care of the Erskine family, aware, as a young child is, of physical comfort or discomfort, and oblivious of the *dénouement* of his mother's reign.

The Queen's downfall was swift. The story is well known, and the details provided her enemies with their best weapons. In brief, she succumbed to an infatuation with James Hepburn, fourth Earl of Bothwell, who had loyally supported her after Riccio's murder. On 24 December she pardoned the murderers, who would not have forgotten that Darnley's betrayal had enabled the Queen to turn the tables on them and send them into exile. She would have appreciated that the 'outgait' suggested by her counsellors at Craigmillar might well be an act of vengeance perpetrated by one of those victims of treachery, and as such, in no way detrimental to her honour.

The pardoned murderers of Riccio returned to Scotland in January 1567, and the murder of Darnley took place at Kirk o'Field on the outskirts of Edinburgh in the small hours of 10 February. Darnley had been staying with his father in Glasgow, where he had suffered from an illness which is thought to have been syphilis. Mary, unfortunately for her later reputation, rode to Glasgow, brought him back to Edinburgh and took him to convalesce in the house where he met his death. On the night in question, Kirk o'Field was blown up with a massive quantity of gunpowder, and Darnley was found dead in the garden, uninjured by the explosion but killed by strangulation.

Whether Mary was a participant in, an accessary to, or totally ignorant of the plot which led to her consort's death, has been hotly debated ever since. 'The Casket Letters' and accompanying poems, supposedly written by Mary to Bothwell and containing evidence which incriminates the Queen, are dubious in themselves and do nothing but confuse the issue.[17]

For the rest, two of Darnley's enemies, Moray and Morton, made themselves conspicuously absent. Moray, it was subsequently revealed, went to St Andrews the day before the murder and thence sailed for France; his talent for diplomatic absence and timely return must have been as obvious to his contemporaries as it has been to later observers. Morton, years afterwards, admitted foreknowledge and concealment of the crime. Before his death, he confessed that Bothwell had taken him into his confidence at Whittinghame Castle, where he had gone to meet Morton on the latter's return to Scotland. Morton, on being invited to join a conspiracy to murder Darnley, answered with brutal practicality that, having been pardoned for one murder – that of Riccio – he was not going to court trouble by involving himself in another.[18] But he did not divulge his knowledge of a plot against Darnley's life. Darnley had many enemies, and it has been postulated that more than one plot came to a head on the fatal night. The principal suspect, however, both at the time and thereafter, was the Earl of Bothwell.

Public outcry obliged Mary to bring Bothwell to trial, but the Crown did not act as prosecutor. The prosecution was left to Darnley's father, the Earl of Lennox, who did not dare to enter Edinburgh on 12 April, the day of the trial, since the city was thronged with Bothwell's followers in arms. Predictably, Bothwell was acquitted; but there was a sensational sequel when the Queen married him on 15 May. The wedding took place in the Chapel Royal of Holyrood, by Protestant rites. To add to the unseemliness of the proceedings, Bothwell had hastily divorced his wife, Lady Jean Gordon, the sister of the Earl of Huntly, to whom he had been married only the previous year.

Mary is traditionally supposed to have sacrificed her principles and ultimately her kingdom itself for the sake of her passion for Bothwell. If her third marriage had represented the fulfilment of passion, it is unlikely that on the day following it she would have been threatening – as she did – to kill herself.

Mary, Queen of Scots, though undeniably impetuous, was neither the slave of passion nor utterly devoid of political sense. Passion had played its part in driving her into the arms of Darnley, but dynastic logic had supported her choice. Impetuosity had led her to yield to an infatuation, probably a brief one, for Bothwell. In July 1567 she miscarried to twins, which could only have been begotten by Bothwell, since Darnley was a sick man when she brought him to Kirk o'Field, and it was public knowledge that she had not slept with him there.

In this context it seems obvious that Mary's marriage to Bothwell was an attempt to safeguard her personal reputation. The recognition that such a marriage might also purchase her political ruin provides perhaps the best explanation of the Queen's threat of suicide. So much is conjecture, but it was harsh fact that if Darnley had been barely acceptable as King-Consort, Bothwell was even less so. Mary did not, indeed, give him the title of King, but she created him Duke of Orkney which gave him a sufficiently intolerable pre-eminence. He did not long enjoy it.

If the birth of James had made his father dispensable, it had also, in the eyes of a certain faction in Scotland, had the same effect upon his mother. A strong confederacy was formed, with the avowed intention of 'liberating' the Queen from her undesirable husband. But the true purpose was made clear on 15 June – exactly one month after the Queen's wedding – when Mary and Bothwell faced the confederate Lords on the field of Carberry Hill, near Musselburgh.

Fortune had abandoned the Queen; as the two armies stood arrayed in opposition her troops began to desert. At her instance Bothwell was permitted to make his escape. Then the Queen surrendered, to be escorted to Edinburgh, where she endured the indignity of being abused by the mob with shouts of 'Burn the whore! Burn the murderess of her husband!' From Edinburgh she was taken to the island castle of Lochleven, and there, on 24 July, she was forced to abdicate in favour of her son and to nominate the Earl of Moray as his regent.

On 29 July 1567 King James VI was crowned in the church of the Holy Rude, the parish church of Stirling. The occasion was one of immense significance, for it was the first Protestant coronation in the history of Scotland.

In the sixteenth century the rule of a sovereign of one religion over a people of another was an anomaly which could scarcely be accepted. Therefore the triumph of the rebellion of 1567 was followed by the logical step of adjusting the religion of the infant monarch to conform with the religion of his kingdom. The baby who had been baptized as a Catholic was crowned as a Protestant, and the reign of his Catholic mother was shown to have been a parenthetical interlude in the progress of the Reformation in Scotland.

The ceremony of the coronation was devised to meet the demands both of tradition and of innovation. The King was crowned and anointed by Adam Bothwell, Bishop of Orkney, a bishop who had been duly provided to his see by the Pope and consecrated in 1559, yet who had prudently accommodated himself to the Reformation. The coronation oath was taken on behalf of the King by the Earl of Morton, acting for the absent Moray who was tactfully lurking in France, whence he returned on 11 August. Morton swore for the King to rule in the faith, fear and love of God, and to maintain the Protestant religion; prayers were said in the vernacular, and a sermon on the subject of Joash and Athaliah – thin disguises for James VI and Mary, Queen of Scots – was preached by John Knox.

After this triumph of compromise had been enacted, a salute of cannon was fired from the castle, fireworks were let off, and the lords of the victorious faction feasted in celebration. The thirteen-month-old infant who was the cynosure of the occasion was returned to the care of his nurse and the four young women who rocked his cradle, in his apartments in Stirling Castle. That fortress was to be the centre of his world for more than a decade.

CHAPTER TWO

A Pattern for Princes

He must believe that as King he exists for his subjects and not for himself. . . . His life must be the pattern for every citizen. . . . His mind he must cultivate with sedulous care, his body as reason demands. . . .

George Buchanan, tutor to James VI

STIRLING CASTLE, like a town in itself, crowning its great crag, shelters the town which grew up in its shadow. To the east, the River Forth flows in sinuous curves towards the sea, holding the Abbey of Cambuskenneth in the crook of one of its bends. To the west lies the plain called the Carse of Stirling. In the distance, north-westwards, rise the mountains which mark the Highland Line, sometimes apparently brooding in their closeness, at other times seemingly withdrawn into an unreal region of mist. The highest peaks which march upon the boundary of sight, from south-east to north-west, are Ben Lomond, Ben Venue, Ben Ledi and Ben Vorlich of Loch Earn.

The castle was already resonant with the echoes of a turbulent past when James VI grew from infancy to childhood within its walls, and no doubt he became familiar with its outward prospects and its inward character long before he knew anything of the events which shaped his childhood and set their influence upon his future.

When his cradle had served its purpose, he graduated to a great bed with black damask hangings; on the wall of his bedchamber was a portrait of his grandfather James V. The presence of this king and his other immediate ancestors would probably have seemed very real to their small successor, for much of the castle had been built by them during the last hundred years.

The Palace, which contained the royal apartments, had been begun by James IV and completed by James V. Its exterior was covered by a diversity of lively statues. James V had visited

France and seen the splendid *châteaux* of François, I, which he desired to emulate; his translation of what he had admired into Scots idiom was rich and vigorous. The ceiling of the King's Presence Chamber was ornamented by the renowned 'Stirling Heads' – oaken medallions carved with portrait busts of men and women in classical and renaissance costume. James VI was perhaps confidently assured that one of them was in the likeness of his grandfather, another of his great-grandmother Margaret Tudor, and so on; echoes of these traditions remain to furnish material for controversy, but which decorative roundel bore the face of which Scottish king or queen has been in the main forgotten; only here and there a carving and a portrait hold a hint of resemblance.

The Great Hall of Stirling Castle, in which the Parliament sometimes met, though still less than a century old, antedated the Palace by about sixty years. It was an austere building, impressive in its uncluttered lines and noble proportions, traditionally ascribed to the architect Cochrane, the detested favourite of James III. To the same reign belonged the Chapel Royal, in which James VI had been christened with all the splendours of Catholic ritual; but after the fall of Queen Mary the Chapel began to suffer from neglect, for with the triumph of the reformed religion the parish church became the centre of worship. The coronation of James VI in the church below the castle was symbolic of the shift of emphasis.

The following year, 1568, the new establishment was dramatically threatened by Mary's escape from Lochleven Castle, and influential opinion was shown to have veered in her favour when a surprisingly strong group of supporters, of whom not even a majority were Catholics, gathered to her cause, under the leadership of the Hamiltons. Nine earls, eighteen lords, nine bishops and twelve commendators, whose combined followings made up an army of five or six thousand men, met the forces of the Regent Moray on 13 May at Langside near Glasgow.[1]

There, a brief but hard-fought contest ended Mary's hopes of regaining her throne. She evaded capture, and a ninety-mile ride south from the battlefield brought her to Dundrennan Abbey on the shore of the Solway Firth, where she spent her last night on Scottish soil. Next day, 16 May, she boarded a fishing boat at nearby Abbeyburnfoot and crossed to England, never to return.

In her choice of refuge Mary, Queen of Scots made the decisive error of her career. Had she forced herself to accept the humiliation of returning as a fugitive to France, or had she gained another possible refuge in Spain, the end of her story might have been very different. It is interesting to speculate how much support a Spanish Armada might have won from English Catholics, with the establishment of a legitimist Catholic claimant instead of the imposition of foreign domination as its avowed aim.

As it was, Mary pinned her hopes on Elizabeth, who had expressed sympathy for her during her imprisonment at Lochleven but who, on her arrival in England, offered her the hospitality of a spider's web.

While Mary was held in courteous detention, Elizabeth summoned a conference to decide her future. Moray rode south to attend what purported to be a trial of himself and his supporters for their rebellion against their Queen, before her commissioners. In reality, it was a trial of Mary, Queen of Scots herself for the murder of her consort, and it was made to appear that upon the question of her innocence or guilt hinged the righteousness or otherwise of Moray's rebellion.

The result, after tortuous and protracted negotiations, was a declaration by Elizabeth that nothing had derogated from the honour of either party : nothing had been proved against Moray, who returned to Scotland to resume his regency with his position strengthened by limited English support; nothing had been proved against Mary, whose reputation had been smeared by the Casket Letters and poems, of which Moray had produced copies. Significantly perhaps, the originals were never seen.

Mary remained in her English confinement, which grew more severe as the years passed and the storm clouds of a darkening European situation gathered around England. Religious conflict in Europe hardened Protestant opinion against the Queen of Scots, but until the day of her death it was never beyond possibility that a Catholic *coup d'état* might place her on the thrones of Scotland and England. Despite this spectral fear, her life served a purpose in Elizabeth's diplomacy : so long as she lived, she was a hostage who assured the alliance, or at least the nonenmity, of the Scottish government. The implied threat of her presence in England was the background of James VI's life from infancy to early manhood.

In this context it was essential to the Regent Moray and his supporters that James should be brought up in unquestioning acceptance of the régime which had been imposed upon his kingdom, that he should learn to regard his mother as an enemy and as the representative of an inimical system of government and worship, and that he should never question the righteousness of her deposition.

To this end, as soon as James's mind was capable of receiving formal education, a rigorous religio-political training began. His tutors were appointed during the summer of 1569, soon after his third birthday, though his education did not begin in earnest until the following year.

Moray's chosen instrument for moulding James VI to become an exemplary Protestant monarch was George Buchanan, one of the leading classical scholars of his time, whose fluent pen and consummate latinity won him an international reputation as a poet, satirist, reformer, political theorist, tragedian and historian. Douglas Young's dry comment, however, yields a suspicion that his reputation may have been inflated: 'Taking verse and prose together, Buchanan may be thought the finest Latin stylist of all time, for his verse is much better than Cicero's attempts at poetry, and his prose far surpasses that of Seneca.'[2]

In youth Buchanan had been tutor to the eldest of James V's brood of bastards. Then conversion to Protestantism had led him to discreet emigration during the stormy preliminaries of the Scottish Reformation. In 1561 he returned to Scotland to enjoy the favour of Mary, Queen of Scots, and in 1566 he became Principal of St Leonard's College in the University of St Andrews. He was sixty-three years old when Moray appointed him tutor to the King; his health was failing and his temper was uncertain. His success as an educationalist had been considerable and had brought him yet more laurels; but it was probably too late for him to make contact afresh with the mind of a child of three or four years old.

Buchanan was clear in his own mind about what he wanted to achieve with the King. He set it down in a Latin poem addressed to Thomas Randolph, here quoted in a prose translation:

You often urge me to paint for you what manner of King I should wish, were God to grant me one according to my prayer. Here, then, is the portrait you want. In chief, I would have him a lover of true piety, deeming himself the veritable image of highest God. He must love peace, yet be ever ready for war. To the vanquished he must be merciful; and when he lays down his arms he must lay aside his hate. I should wish him to be neither a niggard nor a spendthrift, for each, I must think, works equal harm to his people. He must believe that as king he exists for his subjects and not for himself, and that he is, in truth, the common father of the state. When expediency demands that he shall punish with a stern hand, let it appear that he has no pleasure in his own severity. He will ever be lenient if it is consistent with the welfare of his people. His life must be the pattern of every citizen, his countenance the terror of evil doers, the delight of those that do well. His mind he must cultivate with sedulous care, his body as reason demands. Good sense and good taste must keep in check luxurious excess.[3]

This 'portrait' contains the kernel of Buchanan's thought on kingship; this was the image in which he intended to make his pupil. He had a more equivocal task in forming James's view of the immediate past – that task was necessarily the presentation of the events of his mother's reign not as modern history but as anti-Marian propaganda.

When Mary first returned to Scotland, she had employed Buchanan to read Livy with her in the evenings at Holyrood. This glimpse of the young Queen refreshing her Latin with the ageing scholar offers one of the pleasantest vignettes of Mary in her pre-Darnley days. Buchanan, in the flush of admiration induced by acquaintance with a queen who cared for such important matters as the maintenance of her classical education dedicated his Latin translation of the Psalms to her:

> Lady, whose sceptre (yours by long descent)
> Gives Scotland now a happy government,
> By beauty, virtue, merit and sweet grace
> Queen of your sex, star of our age, our race –
> Accept (light task) done in the Latin tongue,
> The glorious Psalms the prophet-king once sung. . . .[4]

Later his opinion of her underwent a violent change. He was a 'Lennoxman', a hereditary adherent of the earls of Lennox, and therefore a partisan of Darnley and his father. The murder of the unfortunate King-Consort, for which Buchanan firmly believed the Queen responsible, turned his admiration of her to hatred. Probably he hated her the more because he had first admired and praised her. The fall of the idol made his words seem like the rankest flattery; he detested flattery, yet he could not call back his printed words. Later James could have read them for himself, but he was brought up on Buchanan's revised opinion of Mary, expressed in a book written specifically to traduce her, *Detectio Mariae Reginae Scotorum* – an unpleasing collage of scurrility, much of which Buchanan must have known to be untrue, if he did not himself invent it. Few men, without personal animus to impel them, would relish the task of teaching a boy to believe his mother an adulteress and a murderess; but Buchanan had such animus, and he performed his task with satisfaction.

Fortunately the King had a second tutor, a young man who enjoyed Buchanan's liking and approval, yet possessed a very different character. Peter Young, twenty-seven when he was appointed Buchanan's assistant, had recently returned from his studies in Geneva under Theodore Beza. He was still young enough to have easy contact with a child, and he respected the fact that the child in question was the King of Scots. Sir James Melville contrasted the characters and attitudes of the two tutors. Having observed that the King's foster-mother, Lady Mar, was 'wise and sharp, and held [i.e. kept] the King in great awe', he continued:

... So did Mr George Buchanan. Mr Peter Young was more gentle, and was loath to offend the King at any time, and used himself warily as a man that had mind of his own weal, by keeping of His Majesty's favour. But Mr George was a stoic philosopher, who looked not far before the hand: a man of notable qualities for his learning and knowledge in Latin poesy, much honoured in other countries. ... He was also of good religion for a poet, but was easily abused, and so facile that he was led by every company that he haunted for the time, which made him factious in his old days; for he spoke and wrote as those who were about him for the time informed him ... following in many things the vulgar opinion; for he was naturally popular, and extremely revengeful against any man who had offended him, which was his greatest fault.[5]

That shrewd summing-up of the two men was probably correct

in its main outlines, but there are indications that Young deserves a somewhat more generous testimonial than Melville gave him; he refused English subventions when other members of the King's Household accepted them, and that, if nothing else, would make him worthy of respect in an age which was not over-scrupulous in those matters. But he had the prospect of a long career before him, and it would have been surprising if he had not kept the King's future favour in mind.

The small boy whose kingship made his education a matter of such high seriousness had his portrait painted in or around the year 1571. This is probably the earliest authentic portrait of the King, and it shows a sturdy boy dressed in unrelieved black, with a sparrowhawk on his gloved fist, and a black cap sewn with a band of pearls set aslant on his fair red hair. His round face, framed by a narrow white ruff, closely resembles that of Darnley as a boy or a youth, and even more closely that of Darnley's younger brother, Lord Charles Stuart, an uncle whom the young King never saw. Despite these resemblances, his grey-blue eyes, bleak as twin glimpses of a winter sea, look out from beneath heavy lids and faint arched brows very like his mother's. Such was his appearance during his early years of lessons with Buchanan and Young.

James's formal education lasted slightly less than a decade. Between the ages of four and thirteen, in addition to his native Scots, he learned perfect Latin, Greek and French. It may have been later that he acquired fairly fluent Italian. He received a thorough grounding in Calvinist theology and achieved an intimate knowledge of the Bible, especially of Old Testament history. That his biblical studies were linked with the study of languages is illustrated by the account of him written by the English ambassador Sir Henry Killigrew, who saw him in 1574, when James was eight years old:

His Grace is well grown both in body and spirit since I was last here [1572]. He speaketh the French tongue marvellous well; and that which seems strange to me, he was able extempore (which he did before me) to read a chapter of the Bible out of Latin into French, and out of French after into English, so well, as few men could have added anything to his translation. His schoolmasters ... caused me to appoint what chapter I would; and so did I, whereby I perceived it was not studied for. . . .[6]

James's own childhood comment on his education is well known: 'Thay gar me speik Latin ar I could speik Scottis' – 'They made me speak Latin before I could speak Scots.' The child who was capable of such a shrewd comment had the precocity characteristic of an only child; he was also a lonely child, starved of the company of his contemporaries and constantly observing the adult world.

The little world of Stirling Castle was peopled by the Erskines, who provided the King with a surrogate family, by his tutors and the members of his household.

In the King's early childhood the presiding figure was the Earl of Mar, supported and perhaps sometimes rivalled by his formidable Countess. They were honourable and careful foster-parents to the King, but there is no indication that they gave him personal affection. In this respect, however, he was probably no worse off than many other sixteenth-century children; most parents of the period were more concerned to instil into their children learning, godliness and discipline than to show them affection.

After the Earl of Mar's death, his place as the King's guardian was taken by his younger brother, Alexander Erskine of Gogar, 'a nobleman of a true, gentle nature,' in Melville's opinion, 'well loved and liked by all men for his good qualities and great discretion, no ways factious nor envious, a lover of all honest men, and desired ever to see men of good conversation about the Prince, rather than his own nearer friends, if he thought them not so meet'.[7]

After Buchanan and Young in the hierarchy of the King's preceptors came two more members of the House of Erskine: David and Adam Erskine, commendators or lay-abbots respectively of Dryburgh and Cambuskenneth. These two, the Rosencrantz and Guildenstern of James's Court, were jointly described as 'wise and modest'. Their part was to teach the King manly sports, including perhaps archery and golf, for he received presents of bows, arrows and golf clubs. His inborn fear of weapons limited his enthusiasm for any sport with a martial element, but he rode like a centaur, and the sporting commendators infected him with a lifelong passion for hunting. Cambuskenneth is on record as having given him a book called *La Chasse du Loup* by Jean de Clamorgan.

The Master of the Household was John Cunningham, Laird of Drumwhasel, who was, according to Melville, 'ambitious and greedy, his greatest care was to advance himself and his friends'. He also had a tiresome taste for political intrigue.

The chief concern of all these people, whatever their qualities or failings, was the personal safety of the King, on whose life their own lives and advancement depended, for kingship did not confer security in the tumultuous conditions which followed the flight of the Queen of Scots to England.

Mary's partisans did not regard her defeat at Langside as final, and Elizabeth from time to time allowed her liberation to be canvassed for purposes of diplomacy. After Langside Moray had a minor civil war on his hands, in which his principal enemies were the Hamiltons, who had received the Queen after her flight from Lochleven and rallied to her cause. Following her defeat, Châtelhèrault remained her supporter for reasons of his own ambition; he, once Regent of Scotland, was not prepared to submit to the authority of Moray.

Besides the Hamiltons – actively represented by the Duke's sane younger sons, the Lords John and Claud Hamilton, and his half-brother the Archbishop of St Andrews – the Queen's party still included the Earls of Argyll, Atholl, Huntly, Eglinton and Cassillis. But it was the enmity of the Hamiltons which proved fatal to Moray. On 22 January 1570 he was shot by James Hamilton of Bothwellhaugh, with the cognizance of the Duke and his sons, from the forestair of the Archbishop's house in Linlithgow.

The most interesting and also the most charitable view of Moray is Archbishop Mathew's: 'He was like the great *bâtards* of the fifteenth century in France and the Low Countries, who gave their lives to supporting the stock which fathered them. . . . Like his French prototypes it was his House that he served and not its members. His genuine attachment to the House of Stuart went with a readiness to jettison the Queen of Scots.'[8]

If this judgment is correct, Moray's death was a loss to the latest representative of his House to occupy the throne. His place as Regent was taken by the King's grandfather, Matthew, Earl of Lennox, whose anglophile views made him particularly acceptable to Elizabeth. His Countess, Margaret Tudor's daughter, was, however, held as a hostage in England, to secure the direction of his policy.

During Lennox's short regency, the position of the King's party was materially strengthened, for he took Dumbarton Castle from the Queen's supporters and hanged Archbishop Hamilton, who was captured in it. There was a resulting defection of several of the Queen's Lords, including Argyll, Cassillis and Eglinton, and the remnant of the Queen's party was left with only one major stronghold, though that one was the castle of Edinburgh itself, which was held for her by Maitland of Lethington and Kirkaldy of Grange. The latter had received Mary's surrender on the field of Carberry Hill and had been won to her cause by the sight of the humiliations to which she had been subjected that day.

The capture of Edinburgh was the obvious objective of the King's party, and during the summer of 1571 the campaign was opened, with the Earl of Morton in command, his forces based at Leith. The resulting 'War between Leith and Edinburgh' dragged on without apparent gain to either side, though in the long run the advantage was with the King's party, which by now had the greater resources.

The King's first public appearance immediately preceded the last attempt of the Queen's party to regain the initiative. In August a Parliament was held at Stirling, and James was brought before the assembly, 'being clad most magnificently with robe royal' and with a makeshift crown, sceptre and sword of state borne before him, since the Honours of Scotland were in Edinburgh Castle. He had been given a small speech to learn by heart. Standing beside Lennox on the steps of the throne, he said: 'My Lords and other true subjects, we are convened here as I understand to do justice, and because my age will not suffer me to do my charge by myself, I have given my power to my goodsire [grandfather] and you, to do; and you will answer to God and to me hereafter.'[9]

However, he had not a great deal of understanding of what was going on. While his grandfather made a long speech, which began to bore him, he sat fidgeting and staring at the ceiling, where a pale gleam of daylight peeped between the slates. 'I think ther is ane holl in this parliament,' he said loudly. Perhaps there was a ripple of amusement at the time; a few days afterwards he was thought to have spoken as an oracle.

The defenders of Edinburgh Castle decided to recoup their position by a surprise attack on Stirling and the capture of as many as possible of the King's Lords. The intention of Grange and Lethington was that the hypothetical prisoners should be brought to Edinburgh and compelled to come to such terms as the Queen's party should determine.

The Earl of Huntly, Lord Claud Hamilton and the Lairds of Ferniherst and Buccleugh, who gave their services to Grange's stratagem, made a hopelessly incompetent attempt to carry it out.

Initially successful in capturing some of the King's Lords, who were lodged about the town, they delayed their departure by pausing to loot the booths of the Stirling merchants. The Earl of Mar led a sally from the castle, and the prisoners, who included Morton, were rescued, with the unfortunate exception of the Regent Lennox, who was shot in the back before the rescuers could reach him. He was carried into the castle, in the early morning of 4 September, bleeding from his mortal wound, and by chance his grandson saw him – a horrific experience which James probably never forgot. The Regent's death caused that hole in the Parliament which James was supposed to have foreseen.

Parliament met again to elect a third Regent from three candidates, the Earls of Mar, Morton and Argyll. The choice fell upon Mar; the direction of the war remained with the Earl of Morton. Fighting continued throughout the winter and the spring of 1572, but when the summer came a temporary truce was arranged. During the next few months Châtelhèrault, Lord Claud Hamilton, Huntly and Lord Seton, who had been lodging in the castle, took the opportunity to leave it; the ship of the Marian party was clearly sinking. The King's supporters were able to re-occupy the town of Edinburgh. Grange and Lethington were thenceforward doomed, but a drama which occurred in the autumn deferred the bitter conclusion of their story.

The Earl of Mar died on 28 October 1572, utterly spent, in the opinion of a contemporary, 'because he loved peace and could not have it'. But there were other whispers at the time, which are perpetuated in Melville's account of his death:

... The Regent went to Edinburgh to convene the lords of council, to show them the calamities that civil wars produced. . . . In the meantime, until the appointed council-day, he went to Dalkeith, where he was nobly treated and banqueted by the Lord of Morton: shortly after which he took a vehement sickness, which caused him to ride suddenly to Stirling, where he died, regretted by many. Some of his friends and the vulgar people spoke and suspected he had gotten wrong. . . .[10]

No doubt Morton's reputation suffered because it was he who assumed power after the death of Mar, as the fourth of the Regents who governed Scotland for James VI. Morton had benefited from the gradual strengthening of the King's party during the regencies of his predecessors; consequently, he was able to begin his own with an impressive show of strength.

In February 1573 the Hamiltons capitulated and by 'the Pacification of Perth' acknowledged the sovereignty of James VI. In the spring Morton negotiated English assistance in the reduction of Edinburgh Castle. Sir William Drury, Marshal of Berwick, brought an English siege-train, and on 29 May the last Marian stronghold fell. Grange was publicly hanged in Edinburgh, and Lethington died so opportunely that it was believed he 'took a drink and died as the old Romans were wont to do'.[11]

With the establishment of Morton as Regent, the procession of men raised to authority and cut off by death was halted. Morton was the survivor of that political generation which had participated in the great upheaval of the Reformation, and he was the ultimate beneficiary of the power struggle which followed it. As Regent, his isolation in power gave him strength for a few years and then left him vulnerable when the King passed from childhood into adolescence. But for the remaining years of the King's childhood Morton ruled Scotland with a strong hand; and while he ruled, an uneventful daily routine regulated the King's life.

Peter Young left a record of the King's day. It began with prayers, followed by Greek, which, at the time when Young wrote (unfortunately undated), James was learning from the works of Isocrates and Plutarch and the New Testament. In a list of the King's books made by Young is noted a Greek Testament in folio, which is described as 'manfully and clerkly won fra' me'. The Greek lesson over, James would have gone to his 'disjoone' or breakfast, which at this period was a sustaining meal of meat or game washed down with ale or wine, and doubtless very welcome after hard work on an empty stomach. Latin, learned from Cicero or Livy, followed breakfast, then the rest of the morning was spent on Scottish or classical history. Dinner was taken at midday, and the afternoon was given to composition. If James completed his task, Young turned to other subjects: arithmetic (at which James did not excel), geography, astronomy, dialectic or rhetoric. Supper, which was the main meal of the day, brought work to a close.[12]

Some of this lesson time was shared by other boys, including the young Earl of Mar, son of the late Regent, who was a few years older than the King; Walter Stewart, later Lord Blantyre and Lord Treasurer of Scotland; and William Murray of Abercairney, a nephew of the Dowager Countess of Mar. There is no suggestion that they were expected to endure the same long hours of hard work as the King.

It was a gruelling régime of education, made the more so by James's fear of Buchanan, who did nothing to soften the effect of his formidable presence upon his pupil. Years later, when James was King of England and in middle age himself, he once admitted that he involuntarily trembled at the approach of one of his Court officials, for he 'so minded him of his pedagogue'.

Yet, whatever his misery at the time, James boasted of the result: once, having been praised for his command of Latin, he replied, 'All the world knows that my master, Mr George Buchanan, was a great master in that faculty. I follow his pronunciation both of the Latin and Greek, and am sorry that my people of England do not the like; for certainly their pronunciation utterly spoils the grace of these two learned languages.'[13]

While it was Buchanan who forcibly fed the King with learning, perhaps Young should receive the credit for inspiring him with a genuine love for it. It was Young who was chiefly responsible for collecting a library for him. A letter survives, written by Young to the Lord Justice Clerk, requesting him to use his influence with Morton to ensure that money was forthcoming to purchase books for the King:

The causes wherefore I have taken the boldness to trouble your Lordship herewith are sundry, but chiefly the great affection I am assured ye bear unto our Master's furtherance in learning, and also in case any person should say, as the fashion of the most part is, 'What needs his Majesty so many books, has he not enough already?' – that in that case your Lordship would show them their error and persuade my Lord's Grace always to grant.[14]

The resulting collection, built up by both purchases and gifts, by 1578 numbered some six hundred books. It was a total which probably exceeded that of any other private library of the time in Scotland. Its contents give a guide to the King's reading-matter and to the formative influences which he enjoyed apart from his actual lessons.

Bibles, psalters and the standard works of Protestant theology – such as Calvin's *Institutes of the Christian Religion* – made up a large proportion. Since they were presented by ministers of the Kirk and other Protestant zealots, the King possessed more than one copy of the *Institutes* and innumerable Bibles and psalters. Theodore Beza himself dedicated a book to James: it was the *Icones*, a collection of brief lives of the Protestant heroes, martyrs and reformers. James was a specially suitable dedicatee, as he was the only king, apart from Henri of Navarre, who accepted the Calvinist doctrine. After Henri had become King of France and decided that 'Paris was worth a Mass', James was the only one. The *Icones* had as frontispiece an engraving of James in his character of the Joash of the Calvinists, crowned and armed, wielding a sword and an olive branch, with the motto '*In utrumque paratus*' – 'In all ways prepared' – for peace or war. The design derived from his coinage.

Treatises on the theory and practice of ruling made up another representative section of James's library. This literary *genre*, which flourished in the sixteenth century inevitably figured largely in the library of a child king of whom so many hopes were nourished. Agapetus' *De officio Regis*, Budé's *De l'Institution du Prince*, Guevara's *The Dial of Princes*. Elyot's *Governour*, Foxius Morzillus' *De Regni Regisque Institutione* and Chelidonius Tigurinus' *L'Institution des Princes*, all had a place in the library of James VI, and so did Buchanan's famous contribution to political theory, *De Jure Regni apud Scotos*.

The principal Greek and Latin authors were well represented, as also were ancient and medieval historians. The chronicles of Froissart James possessed in French, but not in Berners' English translation.

The same preponderance of French over English books was to be observed in the poetry which the King's library contained. There were many volumes of modern French poetry which James had acquired from the library which his mother had abandoned on her flight from Scotland. It was fortunate that these books were gathered together for him and not permitted to become dispersed among the casually acquisitive.

Du Bellay's *L'Olive Augmentée* and *Musagnoemachie*, Ronsard's *La Franciade*, *Elégies*, *Mascarades et Bergeries*, passed from Mary to James. He also made the acquaintance of the works of Marot, Mellin de Saint-Gelais and Salluste du Bartas, some of whose poems he later translated and who visited his Court. Strangely, James possessed neither the works of Chaucer nor those of the greatest of Scottish poets, Robert Henryson and William Dunbar, nor yet those of his ancestor James I of Scotland, who had been an outstanding courtly poet of the fifteenth century. When James VI began to write poetry himself, it was to French and Latin models that he returned for inspiration. However, he experienced the influence of the great Scottish 'Makars' or courtly poets of the late Middle Ages through his intimacy with the poet Alexander Montgomerie, who taught something of the art of verse-making during the 1580s.

Books on sport leavened his literary diet: *La Chasse du Loup* has already been mentioned. James also possessed *La Façon de Tirer de l'Arc*, and in English he had that model of English prose Ascham's *Toxophilus*. On the whole, however, James's library creates the impression that English was a foreign language to him, while French was more familiar: he had sixty-eight original works in French and only nineteen in English. Latin, Greek, Italian and translations from these languages and from German made up the balance, together with a few original works in Spanish, which suggests that the King may have had, or may have intended to gain, some knowledge of that language. Lord Glamis gave him Calepino's *Septilingual Dictionary*.[15]

In no sense should Young be seen as functioning in opposition to Buchanan, but the contrast in their methods of treating the King suggests that Young deliberately sought to build up his confidence, which he must have recognized that Buchanan's harsh authoritarianism tended to undermine.

Buchanan, for instance, did not scruple to beat the King, when he thought that James's childish misdoings warranted it, whereas Young skilfully nourished James's self-esteem by keeping a list of his jokes, dicta and smart retorts. The resulting collection of *Apophthegmata Regis* reveals James as having a penchant for bilingual puns and a rather sharp tongue. A priest (*'un prestre'*), said James, must be called *'pour de qu'il est preste à malfaire'* (the pun being on *'prestre'* and *'preste'* – 'ready to do evil'). On being told that Absalom was false and fair, James remarked that, 'The *unus ille naevus* made him a *knaevus'* – 'one blemish made him a knave.' But an unfortunate man named Captain Cockburn, who told a long, would-be funny story in French, 'with many gestures and earnestness', received the crushing retort, *'Je n'ay pas entendu ung seul mot de ce que vous disiez, et me semble estre vray que Mons. le Regent disoit, que vostre francoys ne valoit rien et vostre escossois gaires mieux'* ('I have not understood a single word that you have spoken, and it seems to me true what my lord the Regent says, that your French is worth nothing and your Scottish scarcely more') – though he added by way of reparation, *'Si est que j'estime le conte fort bon seulment en veoire vostre mine et grace'* ('If I esteem the story told well though, then it is only by your mien and grace').[16]

As time went on, the King possibly saw more of Young and less of Buchanan. In the later 1570s Buchanan was at work on his *History of Scotland*, which he dedicated to the King in 1580 with the following words: '... An incurable distemper having made me unfit to discharge, in person, the care of your instruction committed to me, I thought that sort of writing which tends towards the information of the mind, would best supply the want of my attendance. ...' He had resolved therefore, '... to send your Majesty faithful counsellors from History that you might make use of their advice in your deliberations. ...'[17]

Buchanan was concerned to imprint upon the King his own political views, which he embedded in his *History of Scotland*, illustrated in his play *Baptistes* and crystallized in his *De Jure Regni apud Scotos*. He was in the *avant-garde* of political theorists of the time, with a contractual theory of monarchy and a vindication of the rights of the subject to resist tyranny and in extremity to slay a tyrant.

James, who represented the ninth generation of sovereignty in his own dynasty and was the latest of a succession of Scottish kings which the Scots believed to number over one hundred, could not be expected to accept Buchanan's views.

When he came to formulate his own, James laid stress upon the Divine Right of Kings. A king, in James's view, 'acknowledgeth himself ordained for his people, having received from God the burden of government, whereof he must be countable'. It was not an irresponsible view, and James would have agreed with Buchanan that a tyrant, who 'thinketh his people ordained for him a prey to his passions and inordinate appetites', would justly be punished by the wrath of God; but whereas Buchanan would have allowed the people to constitute themselves the scourge of God, James would have required them to wait for the divine punishment to fall in due season.[18]

In this respect, James was not an *avant-garde* political thinker; he spoke for the majority of the men of his period who recognized the divine sanction upon all lawfully-constituted authority, monarchy included. In childhood James was an obstinate and intelligent boy, who could be intimidated by Buchanan yet could refuse to be indoctrinated by him. James, as King of Scots, in fact had the ultimate advantage. In 1584, which was his earliest opportunity, he banned *De Jure Regni apud Scotos*, and subsequently he made his own contributions to the literature of political thought with *The Trew Law of Free Monarchies* and *Basilikon Doron*, to which detailed reference will be made in their context.

The religious ideas which Buchanan and Young sought to inculcate into the King he received with a much more accepting spirit; theologically he became a convinced Calvinist, a persuasion from which he never wavered. It was in the area where he considered that religion interacted with politics that James deviated from Calvinist orthodoxy. The theory of Divine Right here influenced him to resist the theocratic tendencies of the more extreme of Calvinist divines, exemplified by Andrew Melvill, who inherited the mantle of John Knox after the latter's death in 1572. Between a Kirk and a King each of whom claimed to be the channel of divine authority, a power-struggle was bound to develop. It had its origin in the years during which James was learning his lessons in Stirling Castle, and developing his personal brand of 'regal Calvinism'.[19]

By the time he was eleven years old, James was an earnest, self-consciously intellectual boy, ostentatiously learned and endued with a curious, wry sense of humour. In 1577, the Privy Council, acknowledging the onset of maturity with the King's entry into his twelfth year, ordered that '... Our Sovereign Lord the King's Majesty, whom God preserve.... Being come to the twelfth year of his age and daily increasing by the favour of God to greater perfection and activity, as well in his person and ability of body as in his spirit and learning ... in time coming shall be served and attended upon in his chamber with men, committing the care thereof to Alexander Erskine of Gogar....'[20]

From 1572 to 1578, while the King progressed from early childhood to puberty, the Regent Morton ruled Scotland, in the main successfully, though with decreasing popularity.

Morton was the King's second cousin (see genealogical table at front), and his regency has been described as 'the last great showing of the Douglas blood'.[21] In the past the House of Douglas had been wayward, but the marriage of Margaret Tudor to the sixth Earl of Angus had to some extent brought the Douglases more into line with Stuart interests: if Morton began as a murderer of Riccio and a too knowing spectator of the murder of Darnley, he ended as a conscientious Regent for James VI (even though he paid for his earlier misdeeds with his life). He was not a prepossessing man. His portrait by Arnold van Bronkhorst shows a bulky, black-clad figure with sandy hair and a great bush of a beard; a face pouched and puffy with good living, and cold blue eyes which look as though they missed little of importance which passed within the kingdom.

Morton's domestic policy was grounded in an intention to restore to Scotland the rule of law, which it had scarcely known since the death of James V in 1542, and his success, by necessarily heavy-handed methods, was considerable. His foreign policy was based on the maintenance of a firm alliance with England, in which, despite the hostage status of Mary, Queen of

Scots, he managed to prevent Scotland from sinking to the condition of an English satellite.

In religion he was a staunch political Protestant and a contemptuous anti-clerical. He had no patience with Andrew Melvill, a pure product of Calvinist Geneva, who returned thence to Scotland in 1574 and set about influencing the Kirk to accept the Genevan doctrine of the parity of ministers and a system of ecclesiastical polity based on a hierarchy of Church courts: Kirk Sessions, Presbyteries, Synods and ultimately the General Assembly of the Kirk. This system left no room for episcopacy, which the first generation of reformers had sought to suppress but which had shakily survived, only to be officially reimposed on the Kirk by 'the Concordat of Leith' in 1572. Morton had had a violent quarrel with John Knox over a simoniacal appointment to the bishopric of St Andrews, so that it was not surprising that he sourly remarked to the even more vehemently anti-episcopal Melvill, 'There will never be quietness in this country till half a dozen of you be hanged or banished.' But he left Melvill and his followers a free hand to develop the substructure of their chosen system, confident that the position of bishops was secured by law; for though the General Assembly might propose an anti-episcopal polity, only Parliament could lawfully impose it. The General Assembly defiantly condemned episcopacy in 1578, but it was the King not Morton who eventually took up the challenge. Morton's disregard for the development of Presbyterianism left James a difficult legacy.

He would find another inherited difficulty in the economic situation which worsened during Morton's regency and later proved beyond the power of James and his ministers to recoup. It was a familiar enough situation, with the value of the pound Scots falling in relation to that of the pound sterling: in 1560 there were four pounds Scots to one pound sterling; in 1600 there were twelve. However, if Morton could do nothing to protect the pound Scots, he did what he could to protect and restore the resources of the Crown. Casually he made bitter enemies of the Earl and Countess of Argyll, by forcing them to disgorge some magnificent jewels which had been entrusted by Mary, Queen of Scots to Moray and given by Moray to his wife, who after his death married the sixth Earl of Argyll. The Countess complained vociferously, but her diamonds and rubies were indisputably the property of the Crown.

Morton's disregard of enmity was the consequence of a lifetime of conflict in which he had usually worsted his opponents, but it was the trait of character which led directly to his ruin.

He did not consider the wisdom of establishing a relationship of mutual trust with the young King; it appeared to him sufficient to rule Scotland in the King's name but superfluous to pay court to the boy himself. This neglect on the Regent's part left James vulnerable to the opinions of the royal Household, in which Morton was not well liked.

Morton had been firmly allied with the Regent Mar, and he remained on friendly terms with the young Earl his son. But Erskine of Gogar disliked Morton, and Drumwhasel 'became his great enemy' apparently because he felt that Morton did not use the advantages of his position to enrich the right people; George Buchanan had a personal grudge against him, which was probably particularly unfortunate in view of Buchanan's talent for sustained enmity; and a newcomer to Stirling, an ambitious soldier of fortune, Captain James Stewart of Bothwellmuir, the younger son of Lord Ochiltree, made a point of telling the King tales against Morton.

Peter Young had once overheard the King say to Morton, 'Would to God that you were as young as Lord Angus [Morton's nephew] and yet as wise as you are.'[22] James may have spoken with fulsome insincerity to a man of whom he stood in awe – it was not long before he came to pride himself on his talent for 'dissimulation' – but if he once held such a high opinion of Morton, the Regent fell in his esteem under the influence of the ill opinion of the Household.

The first attempt to unseat Morton occurred in 1578, a few months before the King's twelfth birthday. It was occasioned by a feud between the Earls of Argyll and Atholl. Morton proceeded to discipline them with his customary rigour and summoned them to appear before the Council to answer the charges of levying private war and of ignoring a previous summons to lay down their arms. Argyll and Atholl immediately dropped their feud and made common cause against the Regent. They concerted a simple and successful plan. Argyll went to Stirling, sought an audience with the King and requested him to summon a meeting of the nobility, to which the two Earls would present their cause for judgment.

The King was complimented by the measure of responsibility offered him and by the deference of Argyll, who spoke for himself and Atholl. He readily agreed. Morton, as the two Earls had doubtless prognosticated, took exception to these illegal proceedings and wrote to James from Edinburgh requesting him to allow his Regent a properly untramelled use of his powers or else to accept his resignation. Argyll and Atholl were ready to urge the King to take the resignation, which he did.

The King's 'acceptance of the government' was proclaimed in Edinburgh on 12 March 1578. The moment was shrewdly chosen, for James v had been similarly declared of age to rule when he was twelve, two years before the official majority of a king of Scots; and Queen Mary in her twelfth year had been declared of age to nominate her own Regent, and had nominated her mother to replace Châtelhèrault.

'. . . As soon as ever His Majesty shall think himself ready and able for his own government,' Morton had once written, 'none shall more willingly agree and advance the same nor I. . . .' Clearly Morton did not think that his previous words applied to the present situation, for he swiftly organized a counter-coup and occupied Stirling Castle with the assistance of the young Earl of Mar, who had been persuaded that his uncle Erskine of Gogar was withholding from him the post of King's Guardian, which should lawfully be his. Mar's immaturity, for all his few extra years, was as easily imposed upon as the King's.

Morton recovered his power, though he did not regain the regency. Since the fiction that the King was of age to rule was maintained, he became first Lord of the Council, with Atholl officially next in dignity. The King was admitted at least to an appearance of a share in the government, and he turned to Atholl, to whom he took a sudden warm liking, for advice and support.

In the spring of 1579 Atholl died unexpectedly, and as in the instance of the Regent Mar, the rumour circulated that he had been poisoned by Morton. The strength of Morton's regained ascendancy was revealed by the ease with which he was able to shrug off the whispered accusations of a second political poisoning. But the effect upon James's mind can be easily imagined: his resentment at Morton's recovery of power would have become tinged with fear as a result of the rumours; his eagerness to be freed from the shackles of regency would have become an earnest desire to be rid of the sinister figure of the Regent himself.

Morton, continuing to disregard the threat of emnity, occupied the summer of 1579 in supposedly securing himself by destroying what remained of the influence of the Hamiltons. He invoked 'the Pacification of Perth', which had conferred a general pardon upon all who had fought against the King's party in the civil war, and then declared that the pardon did not refer to any who had been implicated in the assassination of the Regent Moray. In consequence, an act of forfeiture was passed against the Lords Claud and John Hamilton, both of whom prudently left Scotland in disguise. The death of the powerful but lethargic Châtelhèrault had left his family vulnerable to just such a stroke. Morton took the Duchess, who was his own sister-in-law, into custody, and then began systematically blowing up the strongholds which belonged to the Hamilton kindred.

No doubt Morton had the impression that he had secured his power, but in fact he had inadvertently signed his own death warrant, for the position of the Hamiltons in the Scottish succession had arguably been taken by the Lennox Stuarts, whose claim was improved by the forfeiture of Châtelhèrault's sons. After the death of Darnley's younger brother, Lord Charles Stuart, who had held the title of Earl of Lennox from 1572 until he died in 1576, the heir of the House of Lennox was the next brother of the Regent Lennox, Lord Robert Stuart, titular Bishop of Caithness, who was childless. The next in succession was the son of the Regent's youngest brother, John Stuart, Lord d'Aubigny, who had inherited the estates of the Franco-Scottish Stuarts of Aubigny and settled in France, where he died in 1567. The forfeiture of the Hamiltons and the prospect of the Lennox inheritance encouraged d'Aubigny's son, Esmé Stuart, to visit Scotland, to assert his rights to both the Lennox title and to his place in the succession (see genealogical table at front).

Drumwhasel, ever ready to initiate a new intrigue against Morton, may have incited the King to write and invite Esmé Stuart to Scotland. At all events, he arrived in the late summer of 1579, to illumine James's hitherto austere existence.

CHAPTER THREE

'My Phoenix Rare'

> . . . I complain not of sic common cace,
> Which diversly by divers means dois fall :
> But I lament my Phoenix rare, whose race,
> Whose kynde, whose kin, whose offspring, they be all
> In her alone, whome I the Phoenix call;
> That fowle which only one at onis did live,
> Not lives, alas! Though I her praise revive.
>
> from *Phoenix*, James VI

LOVE came early into the young King's life. At the age of thirteen he fell in love with his cousin Esmé Stuart d'Aubigny, who
was a man in his middle thirties.

James's experience of women was slight and not encouraging.
In the circumscribed world of Stirling it must have included
only the female members of the royal Household and the ladies
of the Erskine family, headed by his formidable foster-mother
Lady Mar, who, though she had objected when Buchanan beat
him, had nonetheless 'held him in great awe'. Buchanan himself,
a celibate misogynist whose detestation of Mary, Queen of Scots
was extended in diluted form to women in general, taught the
King to hold them in contempt. This aspect of Buchanan's teaching James appears not to have rejected.

In adolescence James took to writing poetry, and he was
probably still a youth when he wrote the following verses in
condemnation of women :

> As falconis are by nature faire of flicht,
> of kynde as sparhalkis farr excellis in speid,
> as martronis haif in springing greatest micht,
> as gooshalkis are of nature gevin to greid,
> as mavvisis of kynde are gevin to sing,
> and laivrokkis after candlemess to spring. . . .

As skoles of herring flees the quhaile for feir,
as great alde pykes will eat the young and small,
as remorae will stopp ane shipp to steir,
as kynde makis seahors to be creuall all,
as kynd makis crevisses to swimm abak,
as troutis of nature fischaire baitis will tak. . . .

Even so all women are of nature vaine,
and can not keip no secret unreveild,
and quhair as once thay do conceave disdaine,
thay are unable to be reconceild,
fulfillid with talk and clatteris but respect,
and oftentymes of small or none effect.

Ambitious all without regaird or schame,
but any mesure gevin to greid of geir,
desyring ever for to winn a name
with flattering all that will thaime not forbeir,
sum craft thay have, yit foolish are indeid,
with liyng quhyles esteiming best to speid.[1]

Brought up as he was under the misogynistic influence which led him to hold such views, and lacking any experience to counteract them, it was not surprising that the first object of James's love was a man. But it was probably decisive for the direction of his emotional development that the man in question had every reason to encourage his affections. The legendary charm of Esmé Stuart won James's heart at their first meeting, which took place on 15 September 1579 in the Great Hall of Stirling Castle.

On the evidence of his portraits, supported by contemporary references, Esmé Stuart was a strikingly handsome man, auburn-haired and red-bearded, colouring which contrasted unusually with brilliant dark eyes. He possessed the indefinable quality of glamour, which had been absent from the Scottish Court since the fall of Mary, Queen of Scots. Apart from the elderly Lord Robert Stuart, he was the King's nearest male relative, descended in the Lennox line from James II; through his French mother, Anne de la Queulle, he was descended from the Bourbons and from the Visconti of Milan.

The King, on whom he made so overwhelming an impression, had a curiously old look for his thirteen years; yet portraits of James VI in adolescence suggest that he had a certain sweetness of expression, which he was to lose in later life. His hair, light brown when he grew older, was still a pale red. He was by no means bad looking, and he had been fortunate in recovering unscarred from smallpox. Descriptions of his physical disabilities derive in the main from Sir Anthony Weldon's 'Character' or pen-portrait of him in late middle age, and it is therefore probably mistaken to imagine him as an ungainly youth. Sir Henry Killigrew, on his visit to Scotland in 1574, observed that the boy King danced 'with a very good grace', and in 1579 William Hudson, a musician at the Scottish Court, was employed as the King's 'balladine' or dancing-master.[2] Whatever the cause of his clumsy gait in later life, and his necessity to walk 'ever leaning on other men's shoulders', it had not shown itself when he passed from childhood into youth.

After the excitements of 1578, Stirling had begun to seem too small a world for James. Esmé Stuart entered his life just as he was ready to challenge the controls of childhood and to embrace anyone who could show him the means to do so. Esmé's arrival coincided with plans for the King's first excursion beyond the limits of his childhood world. Previously, he had never ridden farther from Stirling Castle than he could go in the course of a day or two's hunting; in the autumn of 1579 he was planning his first visit to Edinburgh. The King left Stirling on 29 September, taking his newly acquired kinsman with him : a few days had served to make him reluctant to allow Esmé Stuart to stray far from his side.

In spite of wild weather – 'ane great wynd quhilk threattin thair stay' – the King and his attendant Lords rode from Stirling, dined at Dunipace and stayed the night at Linlithgow Palace. Next day, accompanied by Esmé and his French entourage, by Morton and his nephew the Earl of Angus, by the Earls of Argyll, Mar and Montrose, numerous other lords and a cavalcade of two thousand horse, the King approached Edinburgh. He did not enter it, for the pageantry in preparation for his state entry was not yet ready. The guns of the castle fired a salute as his escort made a detour of the city and brought him to the Palace of Holyroodhouse.

Edinburgh, in Moray Maclaren's well-chosen phrase, is a 'precipitous city'. Time has extended its limits and altered its buildings, but nothing can change the craggy profile which

James VI saw as he rode to Holyrood. Fynes Moryson, the English traveller who visited Edinburgh in 1598, wrote a description of it, and his first impression was probably very like the one which James received in 1579:

The city is high seated, in a fruitful soil and wholesome air, and is adorned with many noblemen's towers lying about it, and aboundeth with many springs of sweet waters. At the end towards the east is the King's palace, joining to the monastery of the Holy Cross [Holyrood Abbey], which King David the First built, over which in a park of hares, conies and deer a high mountain hangs, called the chair of Arthur [Arthur's seat]. . . . From the King's palace at the east, the city still riseth higher and higher towards the west, and consists especially of one broad and very fair street [the Royal Mile]. . . . At the farthest end towards the west is a very strong castle which the Scots hold inexpugnable. . . . And from this castle towards the west is a most steep rock, pointed in the highest top, out of which this castle is cut. . . . The houses are built of unpolished stone, and in the fair street a good part of them is of freestone, which in that broad street would make a fair show, but that the outside of them are faced with wooden galleries built upon the second storey of the houses; yet these galleries give the owners a fair and pleasant prospect . . . when they sit or stand in the same.[3]

On 17 October those 'galleries' or forestairs were hung with tapestries and crowded with as many people as they would hold, and the broad street was strewn with autumnal flowers, to welcome the first King of Scots to be seen in Edinburgh for thirty-seven years. It was no wonder that he was 'ane great delyt to the beholderis'.[4]

After James had been 'receaved by the magistrates of the toun, under a pompous pale of purple velvet',[5] at the West Port, he was entertained by a play representing the Judgment of Solomon. This was the first of many such compliments to his growing reputation for wisdom and learning. He progressed towards the castle, his procession frequently stayed by pageants and addresses, including orations by 'four fair young maides' personifying Prudence, Temperance, Justice and Fortitude. 'Dame Religion' then required him to enter the High Kirk of St Giles, to listen to a sermon, from which he emerged to encounter the incongruous person of Bacchus at the Mercat Cross, sitting astride a great wine-cask and garlanded with flowers. 'He welcomed the King to his own toun, and dranke manie glasses, and cast them among the people. There were there runne three puncheons of wine.'[6]

'At the Salt Trone [salt market cross] was described the Genealogie of the Kings of Scotland: a number of trumpets sounded melodiouslie, and crying with a loude voice "Weele fare to the King." ' The primitive portraits of the five preceding Jameses, now in the Scottish National Portrait Gallery, may have been painted to decorate and illustrate this genealogy, as part of a series depicting the long line of ancestors and mythological predecessors of James VI.[7]

As the years passed, and the ceremonies of entry to one burgh or another became commonplace to the King, the limited range of complimentary pageant, panegyric and exhortation to virtue developed a certain capacity to bore him. Probably the illustrated genealogy never threatened his patience: the prestigious longevity of the Scottish monarchy served to enhance James's views of the exalted nature of kingship itself. No doubt it made a strong impression upon him when he received his first heady draught of adulation at the age of thirteen.

A good example of the type of adulation-with-exhortation which was offered to the young King is provided by the following extract from *The Navigation*, a poem by Alexander Montgomerie, who entered the King's circle at this time and was soon in high favour with him. The poem was written as a contribution to the festivities of October 1579:

> Haill bravest burgeon brekking to the rose,
> The deu of grace thy leivis mot inclose
> The stalk of treuth mot grant the [e] nurishing
> The air of faith support thy florishing. . . .
> They of thy bluid mot grou about thy bordour
> To hold thy hedge into ane perfyt ordour
> As fragrant flouris of ane helthsome smell
> All venomous beistis from the [e] to expell.
> Thy preachers treu mot ay thy gardners be
> To clense thy root from weeds of heresie.
> Thy garden wall mak the Neu Testament
> So sall thou grou without impediment;
> All lands about sall feir thy Excellence
> And come fra far to do thee reverence. . . .[8]

The following month Parliament met in Edinburgh and, among other business, formally conferred on Esmé Stuart the Abbey of Arbroath, one of the forfeited properties of the Hamiltons. This was the first of many gifts which he received from the King. The earldom of Lennox followed early in the next year. After the death of Lord Charles Stuart, it had been granted to his uncle and the King's, Lord Robert Stuart; but the latter was prevailed upon to resign it in Esmé's favour and to accept in recompense the earldom of March. Thereafter Esmé, Earl of Lennox, received a golden shower of honours: he became First Gentleman of the King's Bedchamber, Master of the Wardrobe, Governor of Dumbarton Castle, Privy Councillor and Lord Chamberlain of Scotland. It was not surprising that James, who was vulnerable to aspersions cast upon his paternity and who consequently valued his descent from the Lennox Stuarts, should have delighted to honour his closest kinsman in that line. But other aspects of their relationship did not pass unnoticed.

The chronicler David Moysie, who was clerk to the Privy Council, retailed the gossip of the Court when he wrote, 'At this time his Majestie having conceivit an invaird affection to the said Lord Obynnie [Aubigny] enterit in great familiareties and quyet purpoisses with him . . .',[9] the implication being that those purposes were amorous; and Bishop John Hacket, who was a late contemporary of the King and observed the public displays of affection in which he indulged with his later favourites, wrote, '. . . From the time that he was fourteen years old and no more, that is when the Lord d'Aubigny came into Scotland out of France to visit him, even then he began, and with that noble personage, to clasp someone gratioso in the embraces of his great love, above all others.'[10] For James began as he was to continue throughout his life, to conduct himself with a total disregard for public opinion once his love was engaged. At the height of his attachment to Esmé Stuart, in 1581, it was reported that James was 'in such love with him as in the open sight of the people, oftentimes he will clasp him about the neck with his arms and kiss him'.[11]

The precise nature of their relationship, however, retains its mystery. Whether the favourite received innocent ardours with kindness and accepted immense gifts as the dues of close kinship, or whether he was indeed the young King's lover, will probably never be known. What is obvious, from his surviving letters, is that he responded to the King's passionate devotion with a tender reverence; and how far this style of address would have endeared him to the King may easily be imagined if one contrasts it with the intimidation of Buchanan and the bluff authoritarianism of Morton.

In the extremely outspoken sermons of the ministers of Edinburgh there were many references to the King's being 'corrupted' and 'abused', and it is not always clear whether moral or religious corruption was implied. The religio-political implications of the King's attachment to his kinsman caused great alarm to the Kirk and its more radical supporters. The new Earl of Lennox was a Catholic, and wild rumours arose that he was a Counter-Reformation agent sent by the Pope, the King of France and the Duc de Guise to work for the restoration of Mary, Queen of Scots, the ruin of the reformed religion and even the abduction of the King to France. Against these dangers the ministers of Edinburgh 'like faithfull watchmen, made loude and tymous warning'.[12]

There were certain apparent justifications for these rumours: Lennox was a Gentleman of the Bedchamber to Henri III of France, he was a friend and distant connection of the Duc de Guise, and he had come to Scotland with a larger supply of European gold than his mortgaged estates could have provided.[13] But the Queen of Scots was strongly prejudiced against him. That he was the nephew of Matthew, Earl of Lennox, and the first cousin of Darnley was quite enough to make her think him thoroughly untrustworthy and potentially treacherous to her cause. Furthermore, once he was established as the King's favourite, and his position in the succession was secured by the Lennox title, it would have been contrary to his own interests, which he had come to Scotland to pursue, to have disturbed the *status quo*. He had no intention of spiriting the King to France; the reality was otherwise, for he brought France to the King.

James '. . . heard, in those tones of respect which Esmé Stuart knew well how to convey, of all the glory of the Court of France, the nobles immensely separated from the blood royal, the graded services.' This is Archbishop Mathew's view of the way in which their hours of privacy were spent. 'Paris itself would be brought before him, the hall of the Caryatides in the

Louvre, the Centaurs and Neptunes in its decoration, the ceiling of lime and walnut gilt and carved. Outside in the town was the new Fontaine des Innocents with the naiads placed between the pilasters. . . . In these conversations the King had painted for him the graded life of the great monarchies.'[14]

If Lennox possessed the visual sense to evoke the Paris of the last Valois for James VI, his descriptions summoned little response, for James's imagination was always verbal rather than visual. But James was intensely interested in the ceremonial surrounding monarchy, and the details of French Court life clearly made a profound appeal to him. In later years a man who possessed a veneer of French Court culture was always attractive to him, perhaps as a mirror of the unattainable world which Lennox had represented and described.

There was, however, a cultural exchange. Lennox was obliged to listen as well as to talk, and James offered him a lucid exposition of the truth of the reformed religion. Lennox frequently heard himself and his French companions in Scotland abused by the ministers as 'papists' and 'atheists'; their resulting unpopularity showed the power of rhetorical abuse, for it is hard to see how they could have been both. However, it was clear to Lennox that, if his future in Scotland were to be peaceful and prosperous, conversion was required of him. He also understood James's desire to convince him of the truth, and he yielded slowly to the King's earnest reasoning.

In July 1580 the fortieth General Assembly of the Kirk received a letter from him which began, 'It is not, I think, unknown to you how it hath pleased God, of his infinite goodness, to call me by his grace and mercy to the knowledge of my salvation, since my coming in this land. . . .'[15]

The Kirk was temporarily gratified by the acquisition of such a prestigious convert.

The establishment of Lennox as the King's favourite carried the implication that he would aspire to supreme power in Scotland; a man in his thirties would not expect to be the powerless minion of an adolescent boy. The removal of Morton was the main prerequisite in the realization of Lennox's ambition.

Morton was strangely supine throughout 1580. He could scarcely have prevented James from bestowing honours on his kinsman, yet, if he had indeed eliminated Mar and Atholl, he might not have scrupled to deal likewise with Lennox. Possibly the fatigue of age had caught up with him at last; possibly he did not realize the extent to which he was threatened until it was too late.

The destruction of Morton was an unsavoury business, in which Lennox concealed his own part as far as possible. The henchman he chose to play the leading part was Captain James Stewart of Bothwellmuir, who was apt for any mischief which might bring him advancement. On 31 December 1580 he interrupted a session of the Privy Council, fell on his knees before the King and dramatically accused Morton of having been 'art and part' in the murder of James's father. Lennox, who had not acquired more than half a dozen words of Scots (his letter to the General Assembly had presumably been written for him), was able to look on the ensuing uproar with well-simulated incomprehension.

Morton was arrested and imprisoned in Edinburgh Castle and later transferred to Dumbarton. During the next few months Elizabeth I employed strong diplomatic pressure to secure his release. She shared the darkest suspicions concerning Lennox's presence in Scotland as a papal or Guisard agent. In the course of 1580 the English ambassador, Robert Bowes, had been instructed to warn James against his favourite and had many times attempted to do so, with predictably poor results. After Morton's arrest, Thomas Randolph was despatched to Scotland to use what persuasions and threats might secure his release; but Elizabeth's notorious lack of generosity to her allies robbed the threats of most of their force, and the persuasions fell on deaf ears. Many of Morton's old enemies had formed a pro-Lennox party of sufficient strength to enable James to ignore Elizabeth's embassy.

On 2 June 1581 Morton was publicly executed in Edinburgh, having denied 'art and part' (planning and participation) in Darnley's death but having admitted foreknowledge and concealment. Two ministers who attended Morton before his execution demanded why he had not revealed his knowledge that Darnley was about to be murdered. His reply was, '... Whom to sould I have reveeled it? To the Queene? – she was the doer thereof. I was minded, indeid, to the King's father, but I durst not for my life; for I knew him to be suche a bairne, that there was nothing told him but he would reveele it to her againe.'[16]

Morton died with the courage that was to be expected of such a man; and James, who had been a party to his downfall, experienced an uneasy conscience on the score of his own foreknowledge. On the morning of the execution he refused to read a letter which his ex-Regent had written him 'but ranged up and doun the floor of his chamber, clanking with his finger and his thowme'.[17]

James recovered his composure, and the honours were shared out: Lennox received a dukedom, the only dukedom in Scotland at the time, which accorded him tacit recognition as heir presumptive; Captain James Stewart was created Earl of Arran, despite the fact that the lawful Earl was still alive and had two brothers; Lord Ruthven, the Lord Treasurer (the son of that Ruthven who had risen from his sickbed to murder Riccio, and himself a participant in that event), became Earl of Gowrie.

The rejoicing had scarcely had time to die down before the political weather changed. Lennox, as the inheritor of Morton's greatness, inevitably inherited the resentment, enmity and scheming to which Morton had long been subjected; and inevitably he lacked the network of alliances and the instinctive understanding of the tissue of feud and friendship which the maintenance of power in sixteenth-century Scotland required. Not only did he lack the experience to dominate the system, but his situation was very like that of Darnley a generation earlier. Whereas Darnley's only strong asset had been the Queen's love, that of Lennox was the King's love. Unlike Darnley, he did not throw that asset away, but it was not strong enough to sustain him in power. James was too young and powerless to formulate his own policy; he was, and for a time remained, a prey to extremists. Lennox, who was probably by instinct a *politique*, became the victim of the Catholic interest which he was believed to serve.

The fall and death of Morton were welcomed by Mary, Queen of Scots as preliminaries to what she called 'the re-establishment of my affairs'. Her plan, which had the support of the Duc de Guise, was known as 'the Association', and it proposed her restoration to the throne of Scotland as joint sovereign in association with her son. This scheme Mary endeavoured to bring to fruition between 1581 and 1584, both by direct negotiation with Elizabeth and by plotting for the assistance of Spanish arms. Mary did not forget that, if she had married Don Carlos in the 1560s, Spanish military power might have won her the English throne. Perhaps it was not too late : there was discussion of a marriage between her and the widowed Philip II of Spain in 1584.

Predictably the first rumours of the proposed 'Association' which reached Scotland caused a fresh wave of anti-Catholic hysteria, in which Lennox was the principal object of suspicion as a representative of the Catholic powers which had penetrated the defences of the northern citadel of Calvinism.

Lennox had endeavoured to destroy this image of himself by his conversion to Protestantism, and he attempted to obliterate it afresh by signing 'the Negative Confession', a Protestant confession of faith in which the signatories abjured in detail a wide range of Catholic doctrine and practice :

> ... We abhor and detest [they declared] ... all kind of papistry in general and particular heads even as they are now damned and confuted by the word of God and Kirk of Scotland; but in special we detest and refute the usurped authority of that Roman Antichrist. ... All his tyrannous laws made upon indifferent things against our Christian liberty ... his cruel judgment against infants departing without the sacrament, his absolute necessity of baptism, his blasphemous opinion of transsubstantiation ... his cruelty against the innocent divorced ... his profane sacrifice for the sins of the dead and the quick, his canonization of men, calling upon angels ... and multitude of advocates and mediators. ...[18]

The King was the first signatory, and Lennox the second; but extreme Protestants remained unconvinced, preferring to believe the contradictions.

The pro-Lennox party which formed the administration after the fall of Morton, contained previous supporters of Mary, Queen of Scots, including Lord Seton, Lord Maxwell (who after Morton's execution received his earldom), the Laird of Ferniherst (who had participated in the raid on Stirling in 1571, in which the King's grandfather had lost his life), John Maitland of Thirlstane, the younger brother of Maitland of Lethington, and Robert Melville of Murdocairney, the younger brother of Sir James Melville of Halhill, the memoirist.

A more dramatic cause for Protestant alarm than the advancement of erstwhile Marians was the arrival in Scotland during 1581 and 1582 of Spanish and Guisard agents involved in the scheme to bring about 'the Association' by a Spanish invasion. Despite Queen Mary's prejudice against Lennox, these agents cast him for a leading role in the proposed military operations. His personal attitude to 'the Association' remains undefined, but his tenure of power was too precarious to allow of his ignoring any international movement which on the one hand might threaten it or on the other might serve to buttress it. On balance, it seems inevitable that he would have preferred the *status quo* to the unknown contingencies which would arise if 'the Association' were realized. This was almost certainly James's attitude also, but 'the Association' had one advantage to offer him: it would confer unquestionable legality on his sovereignty, which could be impugned since his mother had abdicated under duress and had revoked her abdication while she was at liberty in 1568. During 1582 James wrote letters of courtesy to his mother, tactfully addressing her as Queen and signing himself 'James R'. Rumours of these flirtations, and sinister reports of disguised Jesuits visiting Lennox and the King, aroused the ministers of the Kirk to a fever of anti-popery and caused the rapid coalescence of an anti-Lennox party.

James, at the age of sixteen, was by no means out of his depth in these political intricacies. Under the tutelage of Lennox he began to participate in government and diplomacy, and he was an active participant in the attempt of his favourite's faction to secure a degree of control over the Kirk by a revival of the power of episcopacy. But the appointment of Robert Montgomerie, minister of Stirling, to the bishopric of Glasgow caused a further furore. The man himself lacked the strength of character to oppose Andrew Melvill and his adherents, and the appointment, which brought financial advantages to Lennox, only served to exacerbate Presbyterian opinion against him.

The anti-Lennox party included such notable Protestants as Lord Lindsay and the Earl of Glencairn, and two of Morton's kinsmen, the Earl of Angus and Douglas of Lochleven. The new Earl of Gowrie, who had supported Lennox against Morton, changed sides, reputedly under the influence of Drumwhasel, who had found Lennox's régime as unsatisfactory as he had previously found Morton's.[19] The young Earl of Mar gave his support to a projected *coup d'état*, as also did Francis Stewart, fifth Earl of Bothwell (the nephew of Queen Mary's Bothwell), who initiated a career of troublemaking by participating in the famous 'Raid of Ruthven'.

In August 1582 James and Lennox were for once apart. James went hunting in Atholl, while Lennox remained in Edinburgh to preside over a court of justice, in his judicial capacity as Lord Chamberlain. On the 22nd, as James, riding south again, approached Perth, he was met by Gowrie, who offered him hospitality at his nearby castle of Ruthven. Unsuspecting, James accepted, and the following morning when he prepared to leave, discovered the trap into which he had walked. The conspirators surrounded him and, without violence, quietly forbade his departure. Storms of rage, and ultimately of tears, availed nothing. He was a prisoner. 'And sa the King and the Duc war dissivered,' wrote James Melvill laconically, 'and never saw [each] uther againe.'[20]

A few days later, under cruel compulsion, James signed a proclamation declaring himself a free king and wrote to Lennox ordering him to leave the country. However, secret contact was soon established between them, and James wrote one stern order after another, covertly accompanied by messages of reassurance and anguished pleas for liberation. Lennox subsisted uncomfortably at Dumbarton throughout the autumn, plotting his own recovery of power and the King's rescue. The Earl of Arran more boldly rode alone to Ruthven Castle, apparently expecting Gowrie to free James on demand. He was detained and imprisoned. It was clear that Gowrie had seized power and intended to hold it.

Lennox capitulated to fate and left Scotland on 21 December. He had received James's last official communication unaccompanied by the usual reassurance, and possibly he genuinely feared that Gowrie and his associates had at last succeeded in poisoning the King's mind against him. James had apparently been forced to write accusing him of 'disloyalty and inconstancy' in not leaving Scotland in obedience to previous orders. In answer Lennox wrote James a farewell letter which must have made extremely painful reading. It is worth quoting as one of the few documents in which their relationship speaks for itself (the original French is here translated):

> Sire . . . Whatever may befall, I shall always be your very faithful servant; and though there may befall this misfortune, that you may wish to banish me from your good graces, yet in spite of all you will always be my true master, and he alone in this world whom my heart is resolved to serve. And would to God my body could be cut open, so that there should be seen what is written upon my heart; for I am sure there would not be seen there those words 'disloyalty and inconstancy' – but rather these, 'fidelity and obedience'. . . . I desire to die rather than to live, fearing that in your disdain you have found a cause for loving me no more. And should I thus fall from grace, then in truth it would be a greater punishment, and one mort cruel to endure, than death itself – which I long for, and shall long for, until I know that the proofs you have of my obedience have freed you from all the evil thoughts that you have had of me . . . And to end my letter I make you a very humble request – forgive me if I have offended you in anything, and remember always your poor servant, who prays Our Lord to have you, Sire, in His Holy Keeping. . . .[21]

There was little that James could do except obey Lennox's last injunction to remember him, for James was still Gowrie's prisoner when Lennox died in France on 26 May 1583. On his deathbed he refused the last rites from the Catholic priest who came to attend him and declared that he died in the religion to which he had been converted. He bequeathed the King his embalmed heart.

On the whole, Lennox's conversion has not received much more credence from historians than it received from the ministers of the Kirk. In all probability religion sat lightly upon him, but in common with most men of the time he would have felt the necessity of making a religious end. He had excellent reasons for choosing to die as a Protestant: to do so was the supreme compliment that he could pay to the young King who had converted him and the most certain means of securing the King's future favour to his family.

It was probably during the winter of 1583 that James, once more at liberty, occupied some sad hours of leisure in writing a long poem of lament for Lennox, which he called *Ane Metaphoricall Invention of a Tragedie called Phoenix*. In the opening verses James exalts his grief for the Phoenix above all ordinary sorrows:

> The dyvers falls, that Fortune gevis to men,
> By turning ouer her quheill to their annoy,
> When I do heare them grudge, although they ken
> That old blinde Dame delytes to let the joy
> Of all, suche is her use, which dois convoy
> Her quheill by gess: not looking to the right,
> Bot still turnis up that pairt quhilk is too light.

> Thus quhen I hard so many did complaine,
> Some for the loss of worldly wealth and geir,
> Some death of friends, quho can not come again;
> Some losse of health, which unto all is deir,
> Some losse of fame, which still with it dois beir
> Ane greif to them, who mereits it indeid:
> Yet for all thir appearis there some remeid.

> For as to geir, lyke chance as made you want it,
> Restore you may the same againe or mair
> For death of friends, althought the same (I grant it)
> Can noght returne, yet men are not so rair
> Bot ye may get the lyke. For seiknes sair
> Your health may come: or to ane better place
> Ye must. For fame, good deids will mend disgrace.

> Then, fra I saw (as I already told)
> How men complaind for things whilk might amend,
> How David Lyndsay did complaine of old
> His Papingo, her death and sudden end,[22]
> Ane common foule, whose kinde be all is kend.
> All these hes moved me presently to tell
> Ane Tragedie, in griefe thir to excell.

> For I complaine not of sic common cace,
> Which diversly by divers means dois fall:
> But I lament by Phoenix rare, whose race
> Whose kynde, whose kin, whose offspring, they be all
> In her alone, whome I the Phoenix call.
> That fowle which only one at onis did live,
> Not lives, alas! Though I her praise revive. . . .

Having characterized Lennox as the unique bird of mythology, James sustains the analogy successfully: as Lennox came from France, so the Phoenix flew to Scotland from Arabia; as Lennox was converted to Protestantism, so the Phoenix was tamed; as Lennox experienced the enmity of the ministers of the Kirk and of Gowrie and his associates, so the Phoenix was persecuted by birds of prey; and as Lennox was exiled and died in France, so the Phoenix flew away to Arabia and immolated itself on its own pyre.

Having related the story, James addresses the Phoenix in lamentation:

> And thou (O Phoenix) why was thow so moved
> Thou foule of light, be enemies to thee,
> For to forget thy heavenly hewes, whilkis loved
> Were baith by men and fowlis that did them see?
> And syne in hewe of ashe that they sould bee
> Converted all: and that thy goodly shape
> In Chaos sould, and noght the fyre escape?

But from the ruins of the pyre emerged a worm of ash, which by the influence of Apollo might be metamorphosed into a new-made Phoenix. James concludes his poem with an invocation to Apollo to approach and work this miracle:

> Draw farr from heir, mount heigh up through the air,
> To gar thy heat and beam be law and neir.
> That in this countrey, which is colde and bair,
> Thy glistring beames als ardent may appeir
> As they were oft in Arabie: so heir
> Let them be now, to make ane Phoenix new
> Even of this worne of Phoenix ashe which grew....

The unassuming offspring of the Phoenix represents Ludovic Stuart, the eldest son of Esmé, Duke of Lennox, who was brought to Scotland in November 1583, to be invested with his father's dukedom. The analogous reference to him at the end of the poem suggests this time as the probable date of its composition. It was published in 1584 in the King's first book of verses *The Essayes of a Prentise in the Divine Art of Poesie*.[23]

Esmé Stuart had been married to a cousin on his mother's side, Catherine de Balsac d'Entragues: she had borne him several children for whose welfare James made himself responsible. Catherine de Balsac was an austerely devout Catholic, who ignored her husband's conversion and buried his remains at Aubigny by Catholic rites. Understandably, the King of Scots

never showed the slightest desire to make her acquaintance;
nor did she to make his. But she was glad to take advantage of
the fact that his favour to her late husband extended to his
children. While the eldest son, Ludovic, became Duke of Lennox, the younger, Esmé, inherited the Aubigny title, and the
dukedom on his brother's death, in 1624. There were three
daughters: Henriette was married to the Earl of Huntly, Marie to
the Earl of Mar; Gabrielle, who was said to have been destined
for the Earl of Eglinton, chose to become a nun in France.[24]

Ane Metaphoricall Invention of a Tragedie called Phoenix
bears witness to the intense grief which James experienced in
1583; and his lifelong concern for the children of Lennox
testifies to his fidelity to Lennox's memory. Though he had
suffered a grievous loss, he was left with a great gift: the
memory of a relationship which death had made inviolable,
secure from the eroding influences of daily irritations, increasingly frequent quarrels and gradual disillusionment. These
mundane experiences James would encounter in the later
relationships through which he sought to recapture the brief
happiness of his youth.

CHAPTER FOUR

'How to Make Vertue of a Need'

Since thought is free, thinke what thow will,
  O troubled heart, to ease thy paine.
Thought unreveeled can doe no ill,
  But words past out turne not again.
    Be carefull, ay, for to invent
    The way to gett thyne owne intent. . . .

Since fool-haste is not greatest speed,
  I would thou shouldest learn to know
How to make vertue of a need,
  Since that necessitie hath no law.
With patience, then, see thow attend,
    And hope to vanquishe at the end.

James VI, *The King's verses when
he was fyfteene yeere old*

THE verses quoted, to which Calderwood gave the title *The King's verses, when he was fyfteene yeere old*, must, if correctly dated, have been written in 1581, in the troubled period which followed the execution of Morton. How much more apposite to the King's situation they would have seemed the following year, when he was the captive of Gowrie and his confederates after the Raid of Ruthven. Then indeed it behoved James to learn how to make virtue of a need and how to attend with patience, in the hope of vanquishing in the end.

The Raid of Ruthven had been a *coup d'état* achieved with a minimum of violence; but its effect upon James was as profound as if he had been subjected to gross brutality. The restraint upon his liberty at Ruthven had dealt a terrible blow to his youthful self-esteem and to his growing confidence in his own authority. The insult to his sovereignty, of which he had so keen an awareness, could scarcely be exaggerated, and his continuing captivity during the months that followed extended the insult without mitigation. Two objectives, escape and revenge, occupied his mind from the earliest days of his captivity.

The Earl of Gowrie and his confederates – to whom it will be convenient to refer by the euphemistic title which they gave themselves, 'the Lords Enterprisers' – though temporarily victorious, were in an unenviable position. James was sixteen in 1582: a little too mature to be safely subjected to compulsion. Moreover, the history of his ancestors was as familiar to him as his own memories, and he knew that the earlier Stewart kings had cast off the restraints of minority during their late teens.[1] No doubt their example was a forceful influence in resolving James VI to rid himself of the Lords Enterprisers at the earliest opportunity.

In the meantime the government of Scotland was in the hands of a group which represented a reaction against the ecclesiastical policy and the suspect foreign diplomacy of the Lennox régime, and which urgently required to secure its tenure of power. Naturally Gowrie could look for the support of the Kirk, which was officially expressed by the forty-sixth General Assembly, in which reference was made to the Raid of Ruthven as 'the late act of reformation' and to the purpose of the Lords Enterprisers as a 'good and godly cause'.[2] These words James did not readily forget or forgive.

Gowrie may have expected an equally warm response from Elizabeth, but her reaction to the Raid of Ruthven was characteristically equivocal. Her approval of any régime in Scotland was largely won by the extent to which it was amenable to English control. Gowrie's religious affiliations mattered less to her than this practical consideration. Therefore, while expressing general approval of the Gowrie administration, Elizabeth entered direct negotiations with Mary, Queen of Scots upon possible terms for her liberation and 'Association' with James in the sovereignty of Scotland: negotiations of which the principal purpose was 'to hold the threat of Mary's release over the Ruthven party in order to keep it subservient to her'.[3] As in the instance of Morton, the support which Elizabeth was prepared to extend to a more or less anglophile administration in Scotland lacked the substance to ensure its survival. From the viewpoint of James's personal wishes, Elizabeth's coolness towards his captors was fortunate.

His first opportunity to make any active effort to regain his liberty came as early as December 1582, with the arrival of a French ambassador, M. de la Mothe-Fénélon, who actually encountered the departing Duke of Lennox in Yorkshire, as the ambassador was riding north and Lennox south. La Mothe-Fénélon was able to assure Lennox that he would be working for the overthrow of his enemies and his return to Scotland and recovery of power. For this very purpose James greeted the ambassador with open arms and extended an equally warm welcome to a second Frenchman, the Marquis de Mainville, who arrived early in 1583. Upon the King's secret assurance that 'although he had two eyes, two ears, two hands, he had but one heart, and that was French',[4] the ambassadors, Mainville in particular since he remained in Scotland some weeks after La Mothe-Fénélon's departure, began to work towards establishing an anti-Gowrie party.

By the time that Mainville left Scotland in May, a group of noblemen, which included Huntly, Atholl, Montrose, Rothes, Eglinton, Bothwell, Seton and Maxwell,[5] was ready to support the King in a bid to escape from and overthrow the Gowrie faction.

James had taken to heart his own maxims on the necessity of patience. Exercising his growing powers of dissimulation to the full, he studied to convince the Lords Enterprisers that he was resigned to remaining in their hands. His bursts of ill temper, his defiant drinking of Lennox's health which none would pledge, both ceased. He even conceded on one occasion that Lennox was 'not wise'. His settled sullenness gave way to feigned good humour and in particular to a surprising graciousness towards the Earl of Gowrie.

The bitter blow of the news of Lennox's death fell at the beginning of June. The intensity of James's grief, however, did nothing to dilute his resolution to escape. Indeed, it probably strengthened his determination to do so, for in his mind the death of his beloved cousin was one more wrong demanding

69

future vengeance. Justly or unjustly James held Gowrie as much responsible for the death of Lennox as if he had had him murdered, for James believed that he had died as a result of his privations at Dumbarton in the autumn of 1582, followed by the rigours of the winter journey back to France, undertaken at Gowrie's insistence, from which his health had never recovered.[6]

In June 1583 James was staying at Falkland Place in Fife, where he was not heavily guarded. By this time he had successfully quenched any lingering suspicions in the minds of the Lords Enterprisers that he might make a bid to escape. With his penchant for classical allusions, he would perhaps have imagined himself as having lulled a hundred-eyed Argus to sleep.

He took Sir James Melville into his confidence and entreated him 'as a sworn gentleman of his chamber' to abet his escape. 'This commission was to me very unpleasant,' wrote Melville frankly; no doubt the prospect of the Lords Enterprisers' enmity made no small contribution to his reluctance. But James insisted that he was resolved 'to liberate himself fully or die in the attempt', so in the end Melville capitulated and agreed to help him.[7]

A plan was devised whereby James should summon the lords opposed to the Gowrie administration to meet him at St Andrews, while his great-uncle the Earl of March should invite him there beforehand 'by reason of his preparation of wild meat and other fresh fleshes that would spoil in case His Majesty came not to make good cheer with him some days before'.[8]

So James, thus innocently invited, rode out from Falkland on a clear summer morning, 27 June, attended by Melville, to be met by the Earl of March and the Provost of St Andrews at Dairsie; 'where meeting them, His Majesty thought himself at liberty, with great joy and exclamation, like a bird flown out of a cage, passing his time in hawking by the way after his meeting them, thinking himself sure enough, albeit I thought his estate far surer when he was in Falkland.'[9]

Melville remained as nervous as a mother hen until James was safely lodged in the castle of St Andrews, late in the evening. After ten months' captivity the young King was free at last, and when the expected pursuit came, the Lords Enterprisers were met by a proclamation forbidding them to approach the King's person. The counter-coup had taken place as easily and as non-violently as the Raid of Ruthven itself the previous year. The Earl of Gowrie alone of all the conspirators was admitted to the King's presence and on his knees 'in all humility asked pardon of the King's Majesty . . . and show[ed] himself penitent in particular in the offences that he had made and uttered against the umquhile [i.e. the late] Duke of Lennox'.[10] The King first reproached and then pardoned him; the reckoning was deferred until James's new authority was secure.

The King's need for strong support brought to the forefront of the political scene a man whose position had been steadily strengthening before the Raid of Ruthven, and whose imprisonment had been only a temporary setback in a meteoric career: Captain James Stewart, on whom the King had bestowed the Hamilton earldom of Arran.[11]

No portrait of James Stewart, Earl of Arran, has survived, but the impression created by his personality is clear enough. Sir Edward Hoby, who met him in 1584, wrote, '. . . He carrieth a princely presence and gait, goodly of personage, representing a brave countenance of a captain of middle age, very resolute, very wise and learned, and one of the best spoken men that ever I heard . . .'.[12] Arran's biographer, Sir James Fergusson, however, remarked that, 'At first meeting he impressed people very favourably; on better acquaintance they often changed their minds.'[13] Sir James Melville, whose knowledge of him was a great deal more intimate than Hoby's, declared, 'The Earl of Arran was a scorner of religion, presumptious, ambitious, greedy, careless of the commonwealth, a despiser of the nobility and of all honest men.'[14]

Undoubtedly the 'princely presence' was accompanied by an overweening ambition and an overbearing manner. He cared nothing for public opinion, and during the ascendancy of Lennox he had caused great scandal by seducing the young wife of the Earl of March and then marrying her after she had divorced her husband on the grounds of his impotence.[15] Arran enjoyed the incongruous distinction of having been the brother-in-law of John Knox: his sister Margaret Stewart of Ochiltree had, at the age of sixteen, become the elderly Knox's second wife.[16] This connection with the great reformer did nothing to win Arran any credit in the eyes of the Kirk.

The King, however, had long been amenable to his attraction, which was great when he chose to exert it; and while none could rival Lennox in the King's affections, even before the Raid of Ruthven had been recognized as a secondary favourite. After Lennox's death Arran inherited his place in the King's favour and his position of political pre-eminence.

The overthrow of the Lords Enterprisers was viewed with extreme alarm by the English government. The appointment to the King's Council of Huntly, Crawford, Argyll and Montrose, and the reinstatement of Maitland of Thirlestane and Melville of Murdocairney, led to the same kind of scare in England as had the establishment of the Lennox régime after the execution of Morton. Elizabeth decided to send no less a man than her Secretary of State, Sir Francis Walsingham, to investigate the situation.

Walsingham thoroughly disliked his mission. He was in poor health and was profoundly prejudiced against the régime he was sent to observe. On his arrival in Scotland he behaved in a singularly undiplomatic manner: he refused to hold any meetings with Arran, and he lectured James heavily on his irresponsible conduct in changing his councillors without having ascertained Elizabeth's views. James showed spirit and, as Walsingham reported to Elizabeth, 'with a kind of jollity said that he was an absolute King, and therefore prayed Your Majesty that he might take such order with his subjects as should best like himself, and that your Highness would be no more curious to examine the affection of his Councillors than he is of yours'.[17] Walsingham's reply was to give James an acid reminder of his inexperience and to tell him that he ought to be thankful for Elizabeth's friendship and her interest in his affairs.

Walsingham returned to England confirmed in his prejudice against Arran and deeply disapproving of James's favour towards him. The result of the mission was English encouragement of the displaced Lords Enterprisers in a plot to reassert themselves. The Earl of Mar and the Master of Glamis, supported by Angus and the long-exiled Lords John and Claud

Hamilton, succeeded in occupying Stirling Castle in April 1584, as a preliminary to the intended *coup*; but James and Arran retaliated swiftly. A force of twelve thousand men which was rapidly mustered advanced on Stirling with the King and the Earl at its head. The castle surrendered at the first summons, and the captain of the garrison was hanged. The rebel lords, who had fled precipitately on the King's advance, sought refuge in England. This small incident, reminiscent of his mother's triumph in 'the Chaseabout Raid', deserves to be remembered as an uncharacteristic but not completely isolated incident in James's principally pacific career.

The Earl of Gowrie, who had been a party to the conspiracy though he had not joined the rebels at Stirling, had been arrested before the surrender of the castle. He was executed on 3 May 1584, ostensibly for his new treason, though it was generally believed that he went to his death for his insult to James's sovereignty at the Raid of Ruthven and for James's belief in his culpability for the death of Lennox. There was an unpleasant story that Arran tricked Gowrie into making a full confession of his second plot by a promise to obtain him the King's clemency,[18] which, if true, was a shabby return for the mercy that Gowrie had shown the captured Arran after the Raid of Ruthven.

These sharp reverses inflicted upon Scottish opposition and English plots gave James the clearest authority in his kingdom that he had yet enjoyed, and at this juncture he was fortunate in having the political ability of Arran upon which to rely. Archbishop Mathew has characterized Arran, who became Chancellor in 1584, as a 'pseudo-regent',[19] but this perhaps is to underestimate James's political maturity. The King had rapidly developing views on the policies he wished to pursue, but while his youth would have lent insufficient weight to his wishes, the support of Arran as a powerful minister enabled him to carry them out.

His initial resolve was the subjection of the Kirk to the royal authority, and in May 1584 'the Black Acts' (so labelled by their Presbyterian opponents) declared the King head of both Kirk and State, asserted the authority of bishops within the Kirk and condemned that of 'pretended presbyteries'. Shortly before the promulgation of the Acts, Andrew Melvill, summoned before the Privy Council for preaching a seditious sermon, had first refused to acknowledge the Council's jurisdiction and then taken prudent refuge in England. He was followed by those of his brethren whose consciences found 'the Black Acts' indigestible.[20]

James's approach to foreign relations was understandably less assertive, for his choice of paths through the jungle of European politics is more clearly discernible from the standpoint of posterity than it would have appeared to him in 1584. He was approaching a final parting of the ways between the traditional alliance of Scotland with France, and the post-Reformation link with England. In one direction lay alliance with the foreign friends of his mother and probable commitment to attempting to bring about 'the Association' with foreign arms; in the other lay a firm alliance with England, bearing the risk of English domination, yet perhaps also bringing some assurance concerning the English succession. During the next year James made an exact assessment of the direction in which his personal advantage lay, and followed it.

In August 1584 James was visited by a French envoy, M. de Fontenay, whose purpose was to ascertain James's attitude to 'the Association' and to discover what action he was prepared to take in his mother's interests.

Fontenay wrote the Queen of Scots a long, rambling report of his mission, in which he attempted to offer assurance of her son's goodwill towards her. Very much more informative was the letter which Fontenay addressed to his brother-in-law, Claud Nau, who was Mary's secretary. It bore the superscription, 'My brother, the letter which follows will remain secret between you and me.'

This letter contained the observation, '... He [James] has never asked anything about the Queen, neither of her health, nor of the way she is treated, nor of her servants, nor of what she eats or drinks, nor of her recreation, nor any similar matter, and yet, notwithstanding this, I know that he loves and honours her much in his heart.' One is left with the impression that

Fontenay had added the final observation in case Nau failed to honour his confidence and showed the letter to the Queen.

Fontenay's ensuing description of the young King of Scots provides an exceptionally illuminating appraisal of his character:

To tell you frankly what I have learned about him, he is for his age the premier Prince who has ever lived. He has three qualities of soul in perfection. He apprehends and understands everything. He judges reasonably. He carries much in his memory and for a long time. In his questions he is lively and perceptive, and sound in his answers. In any matter which is being debated, be it Religion or any other thing, he believes and always maintains what seems to him to be true and just. He is learned in many tongues, sciences and affairs of state, more so, I dare say, than any others of his realm. In brief he has a marvellous mind, filled with virtuous grandeur and a good opinion of himself.

Having given due credit to a rather impressive young sovereign of eighteen years, Fontenay turned his attention to the debit column:

He hates the dance and music in general, like all fopperies of the Court, be they amorous talk or curiosities of dress. . . . His manners . . . are aggressive and very uncivil, both in speaking, eating, clothes, games and conversation in the company of women. He never stays still in one place, taking a singular pleasure in walking up and down, but his carriage is ungainly, his steps erratic and vagabond, even in his own chamber. He loves the chase above all the pleasures of this world, living in the saddle for six hours on end. . . . He has a feeble body even if he is not delicate. In sum, to put it in a word, he is an old young man. . . .

In this passage Fontenay makes the earliest reference to James's lack of physical grace. To say that he hated music and dance was obviously an exaggeration, for he must have spent hundreds of hours in the course of his life as a spectator and listener to Court dance and music, which he need not have done unless he had taken pleasure in both. Possibly by 1584 he had experienced a revulsion against dancing in person, and it appears that he did not play any musical instrument. Previously it has been suggested that his ungainly walk was caused by his having suffered from rickets in childhood; but in view of the kind of hardy if unimpressive physique which Fontenay described, possibly the explanation is that he had developed the bandy gait of a horseman.

After his general criticisms of the King's manners, Fontenay struck a more sombre note:

I have noted in him only three defects which may possibly be harmful to the conservation of his estate and government. The first is his ignorance and failure to appreciate his poverty and lack of strength, overrating himself and despising other princes. The second is that he loves indiscreetly and obstinately despite the disapprobation of his subjects. The third is that he is too idle and too little concerned about business, too addicted to his pleasure, principally that of the chase, leaving the conduct of business to the Earl of Arran, Montrose [the Treasurer] and the Secretary [Maitland of Thirlestane]. . . .[21]

The first point scarcely requires explanation, for James had experienced sovereignty only in his own person, since he had neither known his mother nor met any foreign prince. The second point refers to public disapproval of his indiscreet love for Lennox, his attachment to the generally unpopular Arran and his attraction to a rising favourite, Patrick, Master of Gray. The third point, his neglect of the practicalities of government, was a criticism levelled against James during most of his life. As the earlier passages of Fontenay's description suggest, it was James's intellectual ability, not his attention to administration, which made him remarkable as a king.

At this period the proportion of his leisure which was not spent in the hunting field James enjoyed in the company of Alexander Montgomerie and a group of lesser poets nicknamed 'the Castalian Band' or 'the brethir to the sister nine' (i.e. the brethren of the Muses).

The first period of literary activity at the Court of James VI had coincided with the ascendancy of Lennox, in whose service Alexander Montgomerie had been.[22] Besides Montgomerie, the poets active at this period were Sir Patrick Hume of Polwarth; Alexander Scott, who had written 'Welcome, illustrat Lady and our Queen' and who was now 'old Scott'; the brothers

Robert and Thomas Hudson, who came of a family of Court musicians; John Stewart of Baldynneis, who had a distant kinship with the King; and, surprisingly, a poetess, Christian Lindsay.

Helena Mennie Shire, in her study of *Song, Dance and Poetry of the Court of Scotland under King James VI*, has observed, 'Poetry of the Renaissance Court with its centripetal gaze coined significant metaphor for the monarch, and, in terms of that metaphor a coherent "little world" was made.'[23] In the 'little world' created by this coterie James was 'King Cupid'; at his male-oriented Court a King Cupid who reigned in the absence of Venus. The leading poet, Montgomerie, besides presenting poetic tributes to the King, was able 'by example and flattery to draw him into the pleasant discovery that he too was a poet'.[24]

All this came to an abrupt end with the Raid of Ruthven. During the King's captivity, Montgomerie, as a result of his association with Lennox, was *persona non grata* to the Lords Enterprisers, and the others probably shared the same contagion.

When the King regained his liberty, his coterie of poets gathered around him again, and a new 'little world' was created in which the maturer James, by now a seasoned verse-maker himself, became the 'royal Apollo', with the brethren of the Muses as his devotees.

James delighted both to set poetic tasks and to perform them. It is possible that each of the 'brethren' was set a task appropriate to the character of the Muse who was his 'sister', though this has not been established in detail. James elected kinship with Urania, the Muse of astronomy, who had become by association of ideas the 'heavenly Muse' presiding over sacred verse: he made it his task to translate the *Uranie* of du Bartas. Possibly Stewart of Baldynneis who translated *Orlando furioso* (which he called *Roland Furious*) and Thomas Hudson who translated du Bartas' *Judith* were brothers of Clio, the Muse of history and epic; both Scott and Montgomerie could have qualified as the brothers of Erato, the Muse of love poetry; Robert Hudson and another Court musician James Lauder may have been characterized as the brothers of Terpsichore, the Muse of choral dance and song,[25] while a newcomer to the group, William

Fowler, who translated the *Triumphs* of Petrarch, may have personified the brother of Euterpe.*

The brethren wrote zealously, in a glow of mutual admiration, and both Thomas Hudson's *Judith* and the King's *Essayes of a Prentise in the Divine Art of Poesie* were published in 1584. James's book contained his translation of the *Uranie*, other miscellaneous short translations, *Ane Metaphoricall Invention of a Tragedie called Phoenix* and a sonnet sequence invoking the blessings of the Olympian gods and goddesses upon his work. The sonnet form James used is that known as 'Spenserian', though his first use of it antedates Spenser's first publication of it by six years.[26] Here, as an example, is his invocation to the god with whom the Court poets frequently identified him, Phoebus-Apollo:

> And first, O Phoebus, when I do descrive
> The Springtime sproutar of the herbes and flowris
> Whomewith in rank none of the foure do strive
> But nearest thee do stande all tymes and howris,
> Grant readers may esteme they sie the showris
> Whose halesome dropps so softlie dois distell
> Which watrie cloudds in measure such downe powris
> As makis the herbis and verie earth to smell
> With savours sweit, fra time that onis thy sell [thyself].
> The vapouris softlie sowkis with smyling cheare,
> Whilks syne in cloudds are keiped close and well
> Whill vehement winter come in tyme of yeare.
>   Graunt, when I lyke the Springtyme to displaye
>   That readers think they sie the Spring alway.

Besides the King's poems, *Essayes of a Prentise* included *Ane Schort Treatise, Conteining some Rewlis and Cautelis to be observit and eschewit in Scottis Poesie.* Once dismissed as a schoolroom essay in criticism included to give bulk to a slim volume, this treatise has been recognized by Dr Shire as 'the manifesto of the new poetry of Renaissance Scotland'.

'It was', she writes, 'the work of a schoolboy, perhaps . . . but

*The word 'triumph' derives from the Greek 'thriambos', the Dionysiac hymn; Euterpe was the Muse of Dionysiac music.

also of Buchanan's gifted pupil and the King of Scotland. It is dogmatic in tone and concerned above all with techniques of verse composition. . . . The national complexion that the treatise shows throughout is worthy of emphasis.'[27]

It is evident that James, with his developing concept of his own authority, took seriously his role of 'royal Apollo': to inspire and to command the activities of his national poets.

While the King exercised his rule in literary matters, his foreign policy was directed to preliminary exploration of the possibility of an alliance with England. In the same month as Fontenay visited James himself, Arran was sent to meet a representative of the English government, Elizabeth's cousin Lord Hunsdon, at Fauldon Kirk, near Berwick.

Elizabeth's choice is significant of her changed attitude since the previous year. She was no longer condescending to confer the favour of England's friendship upon James but was seeking his alliance. Her worsening relations with Spain had led to the expulsion from England of the Spanish ambassador, Don Bernardino de Mendoza, in January 1584. The increasing threat of war with Spain made the friendship of Scotland essential to secure the northern frontier in the event of invasion.

Lord Hunsdon, the son of Elizabeth's aunt Mary Boleyn, was a soldier and an aristocrat: he was exactly the right man to treat with Arran. They appreciated each other, and though their meeting did not bear immediate fruit, after that meeting the seeds of amity began to grow.[28]

The next move was to send a Scottish ambassador to England, and Arran took the opportunity of presenting to Hunsdon the ambassador of James's choice, Patrick, Master of Gray. As with Arran, so with Gray, it seems that no portrait exists; but his appearance is remembered as having been 'pre-eminently beautiful, though too feminine to please some tastes'.[29] He was a highly intelligent young man, wholly dedicated to self-advancement, and a compulsive traitor. However, his personal charm had its diplomatic applications, and in October 1584 he was sent to ingratiate himself, and thereby his sovereign, with Elizabeth. He was successful in suggesting James's preference for an alliance with England to 'the Association' with his mother, and he had brought the formulation of the Anglo-Scottish alliance a step nearer when he returned to Scotland at the end of January 1585.

Gray had ingratiated himself personally with the English government by giving away the information he possessed concerning the foreign intrigues of Mary, Queen of Scots, in whose service he had once been. After his return to Scotland, Gray worked covertly to undermine Arran's influence and to take his place in the King's counsels and affections. His plan to destroy Arran's power involved intriguing for the return to Scotland of Arran's most intransigent enemies, the exiled Lords Enterprisers and the Lords John and Claud Hamilton; that their return was contrary to his sovereign's wishes did not unduly trouble the Master of Gray.

In the spring of 1585 Sir Edward Wotton, who was inimical to Arran, arrived in Scotland to act as Gray's opposite number and to ingratiate himself and his Queen with the King of Scots. He offered James on Elizabeth's behalf £4,000 and a yearly pension of the same sum thereafter. Thus wooed, James committed himself to the English alliance and declared that he would no longer contemplate 'the Association' with his mother. The rights and wrongs of his decision have been much discussed, but the Queen of Scots naturally regarded herself as having been betrayed. The crisis in the relations between mother and son was not reached, however, until the following year, after the Anglo-Scottish treaty had been concluded.

While the preliminary diplomacy proceeded, Gray continued to rise in the King's favour and to enjoy the approval of the English government, while Arran was steadily losing ground with both. The already long list of his enemies daily lengthened as his arrogance and covetousness, in which he was equalled by his wife, increasingly alienated influential Scotsmen, including Maitland of Thirlestane, who had initially supported him.[30]

The incident which led directly to his ruin occurred on 27 July, a 'day of truce' on which Scots and English representatives met for the settlement of Border disputes. A quarrel broke out, and Sir Thomas Ker of Ferniherst, the Scottish Warden of the Middle March, shot and killed Lord Francis Russell, son of the Earl of Bedford. As Ferniherst owed his appointment to Arran, it was easy for Arran's enemies to accuse him of having instigated the killing as an international incident intended to prevent the conclusion of the treaty. There is no evidence that Arran, who had initiated the Anglo-Scottish discussions at his meeting with Lord Hunsdon, had any such wish, but this was a fact which his enemies conveniently ignored. Sir Edward Wotton, on his own admission 'aggravated the matter not more than it deserved but as much as he could'.[31]

James protested his desire for the treaty even to the point of shedding tears of impassioned eloquence and showed his good faith by ordering Arran's imprisonment in St Andrews Castle. Arran, who had not altogether forfeited the King's favour, was let out again a week later, but his prestige had been irreparably damaged, and, as the autumn drew on, his enemies plotted the *coup* which brought about his fall. In October, at Gray's recommendation, Elizabeth sent the exiled Lords back to Scotland: they raced north like a pack of hounds with Arran as their quarry.

Arran and the King, who was still supporting him, were outmanœuvred. The Lords were in Scotland before the end of the month. There was no time for a muster, and no time to provision Stirling Castle, where James was in residence. On 2 November Mar, Glamis, Angus and the two Hamiltons, joined by sympathizers from within Scotland, appeared before Stirling with sufficient forces to compel the King's surrender.

Inside the castle there were violent scenes of recrimination, in which Arran denounced Gray as the author of the exiles' return. Gray managed to persuade James of his innocence, and in the morning Arran's nerve broke, and he decided to save himself by flight. His political career was at an end. James conceded that he should forfeit his earldom and the chancellorship, but, remembering with gratitude Arran's gallant attempt to rescue him after the Raid of Ruthven, he refused to allow his enemies to pursue him further. The erstwhile Earl, once again Captain James Stewart, lived the rest of his life in obscurity. He was murdered in 1596 by a nephew of the Regent Morton, a Douglas with a patient sense of duty to a vendetta.

On 3 November 1585 James was once again obliged to 'make virtue of a need' and receive the returned exiles in the Great Hall of Stirling Castle. They fell on their knees and protested their loyalty, and James answered with the best grace that he could muster. He showed his rapidly developing adroitness by the speed with which he turned the situation to his advantage: by accepting the overthrow of Arran and reinstating the exiles in Scotland, James freed himself from further compulsion.

Significant of the fact that recent policy had been the King's, not Arran's, was the continuance of that policy after Arran's fall.

'The Black Acts' were modified in application but not rescinded, and when the exiled ministers returned in the wake of the lords, Andrew Melvill was ordered to the north of Scotland to look for Jesuits and 'travail, so far as in him lies, to reduce them to the true and Christian religion'[32] – an efficacious method of keeping him quiet, and one to which he could make no valid objection!

The negotiation of the Anglo-Scottish treaty was pressed forward, its conclusion made the more imperative from the English viewpoint by the arrival in Scotland in January 1586 of a French resident ambassador, M. de Courcelles, whose possible influence in favour of a reversion to Scotland's traditional alliance was much feared. The following month Thomas Randolph, a veteran in Anglo-Scottish diplomacy, arrived in Scotland empowered to conclude the treaty.

James was as eager as Elizabeth to conclude it, for the Raid of Ruthven and the *coup* of the previous autumn were forcible reminders of the baneful influence of English interference in Scottish politics: by becoming Elizabeth's ally he would destroy the inspiration for such interference in the future. However, his power to negotiate advantageous terms was reduced by his avid desire for official recognition as heir to the English throne, and the nearest that Elizabeth would come to recognition was a 'firm promise in the word of a queen that she would never directly or indirectly do or suffer to be done anything that she could withstand to the diminution or derogation of any right or title that might be due to him in any time present or future, unless by manifest ingratitude she should be justly moved and provoked to the contrary'.[33] It was a form of words designed to give her the maximum control over James's future policy.

There was, however, more to Elizabeth's reluctance than her wish to keep James committed to alliance with her: she could not give James more than the vaguest of assurances while Mary, Queen of Scots lived, without also committing herself to recognition of Mary's position in the succession, which she had always steadfastly resisted. Nonetheless, the first step towards James's eventual inheritance of the throne of England was taken when the treaty of alliance between Scotland and England was formally concluded on 5 July 1586.

CHAPTER FIVE

'We Deal for a Dead Lady'

'[We are] in a despair to do any good in the errand we came for, all things dishearting us on every side, and every hour giving us new advertisement that we deal for a dead lady. . . .'

> George Young, reporting on the mission of James VI's ambassadors sent to England to plead for the life of Mary, Queen of Scots, 10 January 1587.

A PORTRAIT of King James VI, painted in the mid-1580s, captures his appearance at his transition from adolescence to early manhood. It is an undistinguished picture, but its interest is enhanced by Carlyle's observation that even an 'indifferent if sincere' portrait is an illuminating adjunct to biography.

King James's likeness at this period shows a slender young man, richly dressed, his head framed by the immense cartwheel ruff which was the height of fashion in the 1580s. His expression suggests the wariness and disillusionment which were the fruits of his experience during the past few years. His face is pale and thin, the roundness of childhood suddenly fallen away. The arched brows, heavy eyelids and slightly curving mouth are strikingly reminiscent of portraits of his mother in her youth; his resemblance was closest to her when their relationship embroiled him in the greatest diplomatic embarrassment of his reign.

The King of Scots had just passed his twentieth birthday when the Anglo-Scottish treaty was concluded. Unknown to him, during the last stages of its negotiation, Sir Francis Walsingham, who played the double role of Secretary of State and head of the English secret service, had been intent on securing evidence of Mary, Queen of Scots' complicity in the Babington conspiracy to dethrone and assassinate Elizabeth, and to establish Mary as a Catholic sovereign on the throne of England.

Anthony Babington, a young Catholic landowner of Dethick in Derbyshire, and at one time a page in the household of the Earl of Shrewsbury (who had been Mary's gaoler from 1569 to 1585), was a member of the first generation of Counter-Reformation Catholics, to whom Mary, Queen of Scots was already a legendary sufferer for their embattled religion. The rights and wrongs of her personal conduct during her reign in Scotland, and the political machinations which had led to her imprisonment in England, were irrelevant to Anthony Babington and his chivalrous co-religionists. To them, Mary, Queen of Scots was simultaneously an imprisoned lady – a genuine *princesse lointaine* – and a persecuted Catholic; sentiments both of *amour courtois* and of militant Catholicism inspired them to espouse her cause.

It was a pathetically amateurish plot which brought about the downfall of so practised an intriguer as the Queen of Scots. The ranks of the conspirators were penetrated by *agents provocateurs*; the plot was encouraged; the secret correspondence established with the captive Queen was intercepted, deciphered, copied, re-sealed and sent on its way by Walsingham's agents without the least of suspicions being aroused. About a fortnight after the conclusion of the Anglo-Scottish treaty, Mary, who at first had hesitated to commit herself, finally expressed her approval of the plot. Walsingham was satisfied. During the early days of August the conspirators were easily rounded up and arrested. On the 11th the Queen of Scots was seized while she was enjoying the rare privilege of a staghunt and placed in closer confinement than she had previously endured.

James was in so unenviable a position that only slowly could he bring himself to acknowledge its implications. Recently he must have recognized that his mother's life precluded Elizabeth's official recognition of him as heir presumptive to the English throne. By formulating the alliance with England, he had chosen to gamble on the likelihood of his peaceful succession to the southern kingdom in preference to the greater risk of attempting to secure it by 'Association' with his mother and the assistance of foreign arms. He must have known that his mother was in poor health, and he cannot have failed to hope that by natural causes she would predecease Elizabeth.

When the Babington conspiracy was unmasked, James's own flirtations with Catholic plots had not sunk so far into oblivion that he could afford to ignore the contagion of suspicion. Evidently his first thought was to exculpate himself. He expressed his pleasure that a plot which threatened the life of Elizabeth had been brought to light. At the beginning of September he despatched a messenger to congratulate the English Queen on the discovery of the conspiracy. His remarks on the subject of his mother's plight, as reported by the French Ambassador in Scotland, M. de Courcelles, sound sufficiently callous to indicate that he was extremely angry at the embarrassment which her intrigues had caused him. Mary 'might well drink the ale and beer which she herself had brewed', he said, adding that it would be appropriate for her to be placed in stricter confinement because 'it was meet for her to meddle with nothing but prayer and serving of God.'[1]

Later in the month he was informed that Mary would be put on trial for her part in the conspiracy. James initially persuaded himself that such a trial could only be a matter of form. The Master of Gray reported that James was 'content the law go forward, her life being safe, and would gladly wish that all foreign princes should know how evil she had used herself towards the Q. Majesty there [Elizabeth], and that she receives favour through her clemency'.[2]

James was still primarily thinking of dissociating himself from his mother's intrigues; but the unpleasing realization gradually entered his mind that the trial might not be a matter of form. If she were found guilty, then her life might indeed be in danger. And what effect would a judgment against his mother have upon his own expectations of the English succession? In 1584, when England was swept by rumours of Catholic plots, while Mary was postulating her own scheme for 'Association' with James, many of Elizabeth's subjects formed a 'Bond of Association' of their own, pledging themselves to 'prosecute to death' any person on whose behalf a plot to assassinate Elizabeth should be initiated. The principal provisions of 'the Bond of Association' were enacted by the English Parliament and entered the Statute Book as '27 Eliz. I c.1'. It was clearly framed with reference to plots on behalf of Mary, Queen of Scots, and if she

Henrie Stewart Duke of
Albanye and Marie
Quem of Scotland
1566

1 The parents of James VI: Mary, Queen of Scots, and her second husband
Henry Stuart, Lord Darnley, here designated by one of the titles she bestowed
on him, Duke of Albany

2 (*Above left*) Henry Stuart, Lord Darnley (detail)

3 (*Above right*) A coin of Mary, Queen of Scots, dated 1555; this delicate profile suggests the Queen's beauty more successfully than do her portraits

4 (*Above*) The earliest representation of the child King James VI. He is shown praying for vengeance beside the murdered body of his father

5 James VI as a boy,
by Arnold Bronckorst

6 A miniature of James VI, kept by Mary, Queen of Scots, during her
imprisonment

7 The palace building, Stirling Castle, in which King James spent many hours of his childhood

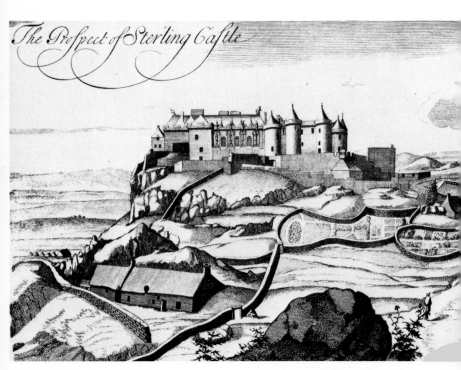

The Prospect of Sterling Castle

8 A view of Stirling Castle from John Slezer's *Theatrum Scotiae* (1693). The palace and gatehouse are clearly visible, unchanged since James VI's day

9 Portrait of the Regent Mar, by an unknown artist

10 A drawing of the Regent Morton, probably related to the portrait of him by Arnold Bronckorst

11 Drawing of Esmé Stuart d'Aubigny as a young man in France, before he grew the distinctive red beard mentioned in contemporary descriptions

12 Portrait of Esmé Stuart after his creation as Duke of Lennox, by an unknown artist. (Lennox died in 1583; the date 1590 is probably the year in which the picture reproduced was copied from an existing likeness)

13 (*Above*) A view of Edinburgh

14 (*Below*) A view of Falkland
Both from Slezer's *Theatrum Scotiae*

15 Portrait of Mary, Queen of Scots and James VI in 1583. Though mother and son never met, this portrait, painted from existing likenesses, shows them together. It was probably painted to encourage interest in the scheme for their 'Association' or joint sovereignty in Scotland

16 Portrait of James VI as a youth, by an unknown artist

17 Portrait of James VI, as a young man, by an unknown artist. This portrait has probably been cut down in size, as the fingertips of the King's right hand and the jewel of his hat are missing from the edges of the picture

18/19 Miniatures of King James VI and his Queen, Anne of Denmark, both dated 1595, by an unknown artist

20 Enlargement of a miniature of Queen Elizabeth I in the late 1580s by
Nicholas Hilliard

21 Portrait of King James VI, dated 1595, by an unknown artist. This picture, like the portrait of the King as a youth, appears to have been cut

were 'prosecuted to death' in accordance with it, James's claim to the English succession might be nullified by her attainder. This possibility became a matter of almost obsessive anxiety to him.

James had no personal feelings for his mother. Throughout his childhood his mind had been systematically poisoned against her, and though there is some evidence that he had attempted to resist Buchanan's view that she was a lewd and criminal woman, he had never had an opportunity to formulate an impression of her for himself. Nevertheless, if she were found guilty, whatever the effect upon his own future, every consideration of honour and decency would oblige James to attempt to save her life.

Mary's chances of survival were severely reduced by the conflicting ambitions and behaviour of everyone involved in the attempt to save her.

James's representative in London was Archibald Douglas, a kinsman of the late Regent Morton. Douglas was believed to have been implicated in the murder of Darnley, and the accusation which had brought Morton to execution had also included the name of Archibald Douglas. The latter had saved himself by flight to England in 1581, and he had been employed by the English secret service until the spring of 1586, when he had been repatriated to stand trial and had been found innocent. The chronicler David Moysie considered his acquittal 'the filthiest iniquity that was heard of in Scotland'.[3] James, however, had already shown that he took a cynical view of accusations relating to the murder of his father. He decided to make use of Douglas's English connections and sent him back to London with semi-official status. Douglas probably intended to serve the King's best interests, after he had taken care of his own; he was in the habit of exchanging information with the Master of Gray, whose priorities were similar.

Douglas accepted Walsingham's quiet suggestion that James would do more harm than good if he interceded for his mother's life, because such intercession might carry the implication that James had approved her intrigues. Douglas passed on this advice to his sovereign, who rejected it.

The Master of Gray, who had already told Douglas that James

D

was 'very instant for his mother', expected instructions to go to the English Court to intercede for her, which he was anxious to avoid if he could. He had betrayed Mary's secrets, and he would have been easier in his mind if she were dead than alive. It is an often-repeated story that on his previous embassy to England he had said to Elizabeth with reference to Mary, Queen of Scots, '*Mortui non mordent*' – 'The dead do not bite'.

Two of those who were to be involved in James's attempt to save his mother were less than lukewarm in her cause. But opinion in Scotland was pressing James very strongly to make a vehement effort on Mary's behalf. There was some truth in Gray's slightly later observation: 'They that hated most her prosperity regret her adversity.' James resolved to send a special ambassador to plead for her, and it was perhaps unfortunate for Mary that Maitland of Thirlestane resisted the commission, for he would have possessed the necessary prestige to make strong representations at the English Court. In Professor Robert S. Rait's opinion, he 'honestly wished to save Mary's life, but did not wish to be involved in the disgrace of a failure to achieve the object of his embassy'.[4] It was a pusillanimous if understandable viewpoint.

James accepted the reluctance of Gray and Maitland, and his choice lighted upon a young member of his household, William Keith of Delnies, who seems to have fulfilled his commission honestly, though he lacked the weight of reputation to carry it out with great effect. However, he was the bearer of a minatory letter from James to Archibald Douglas, in which the King of Scots made it clear that he expected no more counsels of discretion from Douglas:

Reserve up yourself no longer in the earnest dealing for my mother for ye have done it too long and think not that any dealing will do good if her life be lost, for then adieu with my dealing with that estate [England]; and therefore if ye look for the continuance of my favour spare no pains nor plainness in this case . . . and in this request let me reap the fruits of your great credit there either now or never. Farewell. James R.[5]

This letter was written on 20 October, by which time James probably knew that his mother was on trial for her life. By implication James's letter threatened the only action which might have saved her: the severing of diplomatic relations with England.

On 21 September Mary, Queen of Scots was escorted from Chartley Hall in Staffordshire, where she had recently resided in close confinement under the grimly unsympathetic guardianship of Sir Amyas Paulet. A four days' journey brought her to Fotheringhay Castle in Northamptonshire, a massive fourteenth-century fortress now level with the ground, in which she was to stand her trial.

Mary was now almost forty-four, and she was no longer the lithe and untiring dancer and horsewoman who had reigned in Scotland. With years of imprisonment and ill-health she had grown stout and lame, but nothing could rob her of her innate regality or of her powerful charm, which seldom failed to be effective when she chose to exert it.

On 6 October Elizabeth wrote to Mary informing her that a commission had been appointed for her trial, and on the 11th the commissioners began to arrive at Fotheringhay. They included Elizabeth's principal adviser, William Cecil, Lord Burghley; Sir Francis Walsingham; Sir Christopher Hatton; Ambrose Dudley, Earl of Warwick, the brother of Elizabeth's favourite the Earl of Leicester; and Mary's erstwhile gaoler the Earl of Shrewsbury, who came with sorrow and reluctance, for he had always felt sympathy, and perhaps even some tenderness, for his royal captive.

Mary's first reaction was to deny the competence of the commission to try her. Justice demanded that she should be tried by her peers, and who were her peers but the sovereigns of Europe? She was accused of treason against Elizabeth, but how could one sovereign be guilty of treason to another, since treason was a crime of a subject against a sovereign?

'As an absolute Queen,' said Mary, 'I cannot submit to orders, nor can I submit to the laws of the land without injury to myself, the King my son and all other sovereign princes.'[6] The final words were especially pertinent. But Mary ceased to advance her powerful arguments when she was curtly told that the trial would take place and the verdict would be delivered whether or not she chose to recognize the competence of the commission and appear before it. Mary, so long hidden from the public gaze by prison walls, was not to be denied the opportunity of appearing in what she herself described as 'the theatre of the world'.

On 15 October, dramatically clad in the costume of uncompromising *grisaille* – black dress, black mantle and white gauze veil – which she had worn throughout her imprisonment, Mary confronted her judges.

'Ah,' she said, as she paused to survey the commissioners grouped before her, 'here are many counsellors, but not one for me.'[7]

Her defence was perhaps more courageous than convincing. She denied corresponding with Babington or possessing any knowledge of his conspiracy. She demanded to know how she could be held responsible for 'the criminal projects of a few desperate men', which had been planned without her cognizance. For answer, she was read the confessions of Babington and his fellow-plotters, and the confessions of her two secretaries, who, arrested and faced with the threat of torture, had not hesitated to implicate her. Adroitly, she desired to be shown her correspondence with the plotters in her own handwriting, which of course was impossible, since she had dictated the letters, which had then been put into cipher. She resolutely denied that she had been a party to any plot to assassinate Elizabeth, but she readily admitted that she had done her utmost to secure her own liberation and to support the Catholic cause in England. Before the end of the trial she had skilfully shifted the emphasis: the commisssioners had come to try the Queen for political intrigue, but she had presented herself in the theatre of the world as a sufferer for the Catholic religion. 'My Lords and Gentlemen,' she said at the conclusion of her trial, 'I place my cause in the hands of God.'

It is a familiar statement that a sixteenth-century treason trial was held not to establish the guilt or innocence of the person tried but to display the process which led to the verdict of 'guilty'. So it was with the trial of Mary, Queen of Scots. The verdict was not delivered in Mary's presence at Fotheringhay. The commissioners left the castle on 16 October and re-assembled on the 25th in the Star Chamber at Westminster, where they declared the Queen of Scots guilty of 'compassing and imagining since June 1st matters tending to the death and destruction of the Queen of England'. On 12 November the English Parliament petitioned Elizabeth to order the Queen of Scots' execution. Elizabeth was face to face with the conclusion to which recent events had tended and the necessity which her deepest instinct was to avoid, the making of an irrevocable decision. She answered her Parliament: 'I pray God to illuminate my understanding, and, for that I know delay is dangerous, you shall have with all conveniency our resolution. . . .'[8]

There, for the present, the matter rested. In the long pause of Elizabeth's indecision James had his last chance to save his mother's life.

William Keith of Delnies had reached London on 5 November and requested an immediate audience with the English Queen.

Elizabeth received Keith and Archibald Douglas together five days later, listened to their petitions and promised them an answer in a few days' time. It was two days later that Parliament received Elizabeth's evasive reply to the opposing request for Mary's death. But on 16 November Elizabeth despatched Lord Buckhurst and Robert Beale, the Clerk of the Council, to Fotheringhay, to inform Mary of the verdict of her trial and to warn her to prepare for death.

When Douglas wrote to the Master of Gray on 22 November, it was to inform him that Mary was 'in extreme danger of her life'.[9] This letter crossed with one from Gray, reporting on reactions in Scotland to the news which had already arrived there of Mary's condemnation:

The King nor no man ever believed the matter would have gone so far. . . . The King has commanded me to set down to you and his other ambassador [Keith] both his intent, deeply touching his mother, as also the opinion of all his people. And first for himself, he thinketh the matter so far toucheth his honour that he cannot but deal more earnestly . . . and if her life be touched or her blood meddled with, he can no longer remain on good terms with the Queen or estate of that realm. He will find it hard to keep peace with the realm if her life be touched. . . . I never saw all the people so willing to concur in anything as in this same. . . .[10]

On 27 November James himself wrote to William Keith, a strongly worded letter which was intended for Elizabeth's eyes:

I perceive by your last letter the Queen my mother still continueth in that miserable strait that the pretended condemnation of that Parliament has put her in. A strange example indeed, and so very rare, as for my part I never read nor heard of the like practice in such a case. I am sorry that beyond my expectation, the Queen [Elizabeth] hath suffered this to proceed to my dishonour, and so contrary to her good fame, as by subjects' mouth to condemn a sovereign prince descended of all hands of the best blood in Europe. King Henry the Eighth's reputation was never prejudged in anything but in the beheading of his bedfellow, but yet that tragedy was far inferior to this, if it should proceed as seemeth to be intended; which I can never believe, since I know it the nature of noble princes at that time chiefly to spare when it is most concluded in all men's minds that they will strike. . . . Fail not but let her [Elizabeth] see all this letter: and would God she might see the inward parts of my heart where she should see a great jewel of honesty towards her, locked up in a coffer of perplexity, she only having the key which by her good behaviour in this case may open the same. Guess ye in what strait my honour will be in, this 'unhappe' [i.e. unhappy event] being perfected; since, before God, I already dare scarce go abroad [outside] for crying out of the whole people; and what is spoken by them of the Queen of England, it grieves me to hear, and yet dare not find fault with it except I would dethrone myself, so is whole Scotland incensed with this matter. . . .[11]

King James's letter dealt Elizabeth a shrewd blow since it drew a parallel between her father's beheading of his 'bedfellow' – her mother Anne Boleyn – and her own projected execution of Mary, Queen of Scots, and stressed that the beheading of a presumably delinquent consort was a tragedy 'far inferior' to the beheading of a 'sovereign prince'. He also implied that it might be beyond his power to control the violence of Scottish sentiment if the Queen of Scots lost her head.

The letter reached William Keith on 3 December, and Elizabeth read it when she received both Keith and Douglas on the 6th. According to Douglas, she 'conceived such passion as it was a great deal of work to us all . . . to appease her'. The execution of her mother was an unmentionable subject to her, and almost as unwelcome was any criticism of her father. James, the relations of whose parents had been equally tragic, had known how to inflict a wound where she was most vulnerable; but the pleasure which he doubtless derived from so doing may have been purchased at material cost to his cause.

Elizabeth recouped the effects of the hysterical rage with which she had reacted to James's letter by sending a message to Keith informing him that if he 'had not delivered unto Her Majesty so strange and unseasonable a message as did directly touch her noble father and herself', she would have delayed proceedings against the Queen of Scots until two noblemen of Scotland should have arrived to plead for her (as Keith, on James's behalf, had requested); as it was, she could not promise to delay the execution if any emergency should arise. She refused, in any event, to receive a new embassy of two noblemen, but agreed that she would receive two commoners. She thus ensured that the last embassy which came to plead for the Queen of Scots should lack the prestige of nobility to lend it influence.

The embassy which James despatched in compliance with Elizabeth's strictures comprised the reluctant Master of Gray, who, though not a nobleman, was excluded from the peerage of Scotland only by the continued survival of his father, and Sir Robert Melville of Murdocairney, of whom previous mention has been made as a steadfast partisan of Queen Mary, and who had enjoyed the King's favour during the Lennox régime. Gray and Melville were accompanied by George Young, a member of the King's Household, and Sir Alexander Stewart, whose father was a friend of Archibald Douglas. Stewart, like Douglas, played a dubious part in the events which followed.

On 3 December, before Elizabeth had read James's letter to William Keith, Archibald Douglas had informed the Earl of Leicester that James would not sever diplomatic relations with England if his mother were executed. Douglas's statement may have been no more than an expression of personal opinion, yet it received sufficient attention to reduce the effect of the representations later made by Gray and Melville.

The instructions addressed to Gray as principal ambassador constituted James's most forceful and cogent plea for his mother's life. They included several constructive suggestions for assuring the Queen of Scots' future abstinence from political intrigue and insuring Elizabeth's security from conspiracies, and concluded:

> If neither of the overtures aforesaid be thought sufficient, ye shall with all instance press our dearest sister to set down by advice of her wisest and best affected counsellors such form of security as she and they shall think sufficient, or possibly or conveniently may be craved, whereunto we will not only yield for ourselves but also do our best endeavour to obtain the performance thereof of all others with whom she will capitulate in this behalf, protesting before God the life of our dearest sister is no less dear unto us in all respects than the life of our dearest mother or our own.[12]

(For the full text in modern English see Appendix.)

The embassy journeyed south over the Christmas season, to fulfil the King's instructions. In the meantime, on 15 December, James had written to the Earl of Leicester, specifically to counteract any impression that his intercession for his mother implied approval of her schemes and probably to reassure the English government that he had no lingering interest in 'the Association'.

> ... I am honest [he wrote], no changer of course, altogether in all things as I profess to be, and whosoever will affirm that I had intelligence with my mother since the Master of Gray's being in England [i.e. before the conclusion of the treaty], or ever thought to prefer her to myself in the title ... they lie falsely and unhonestly of me. But specially how fond and inconstant I were if I should prefer my mother to the title, let all men judge. My religion ever moved me to hate her course although my honour constrains me to insist for her life.[13]

It was unfortunate for James that the word 'prefer' subsequently underwent a change of meaning which placed a different interpretation upon his letter. He intended to stress upon Leicester that intercession for his mother implied no approval of her policies: so much was clear in the statement 'my religion ever moved me to hate her course.' The words 'how fond and inconstant I were if I should prefer my mother to the title' mean, translated into modern English, 'how deluded and inconsistent I would be if I were to press my mother's claim to the succession.' James, as a Protestant claimant, was dissociating himself from the suggestion that he was connected in forwarding the claims of a Catholic claimant. He was, as he had been from the beginning of the crisis, intensely anxious not to jeopardize his own position; but he was not expressing the callous indifference to his mother's plight which his letter, at first reading, appears to imply.

The embassy of Gray and Melville was received by Elizabeth on 6 January 1587, the feast of Epiphany. There was dancing at Court, and in the midst of the festivities the ambassadors had little chance for serious conversation with the Queen. However, she left them perturbed by the untruthful statement that she did not know whether the Queen of Scots were living or dead.

Probably ever since the despatch of Buckhurst and Beale to Fotheringhay to warn Queen Mary to prepare for death, the official decision of the English government had been that she was to die. The efforts of the Scottish ambassadors were therefore predestined to failure unless the decision could be reversed. Two strong influences weighed against this possibility: the first was the opinion expressed by Douglas that James would not sever the alliance if his mother were executed; the second was the absolute determination of Elizabeth's chief ministers, Burghley and Walsingham in particular, that the execution should take place. In a sense they had risked their lives in passing sentence upon Mary, for if she were spared and then predeceased by Elizabeth, their own expectations of survival were slight indeed.

Elizabeth had a great and not groundless fear of assassination. In the second half of the sixteenth century political murders took place in Scotland, in the Netherlands and in France, and *avant-garde* political theorists, both Catholic and Protestant, argued the justifiability of tyrannicide. In this climate of opinion, and in the actuality of the danger, Elizabeth accepted the expediency of executing the rival on whose behalf an attempt on her own life might be made. She was probably permitted by Walsingham to believe that the danger of the Babington plot had been greater than in truth it had; to that extent Elizabeth was the victim of her own servant's zeal in her defence. But though she accepted the expediency of executing Mary, Elizabeth shrank from taking responsibility for the deed. Her final part in it would be to sign the death warrant, authorizing the execution. Throughout the month of January she listened to the pleas of the Scottish ambassadors, answered them with lies and half-truths and avoided the decision which her increasingly desperate ministers were resolved to force upon her.

'King Henry the Eighth's reputation was never prejudged in anything but in the beheading of his bedfellow ...': James's words must have brought home to her how much her own reputation would be 'prejudged' by the beheading of a 'sovereign prince'. She shrank from it, yet slowly the sense of expediency and the pressure exerted upon her by her counsellors defeated her reluctance.

When George Young wrote the eloquent words 'we deal for a dead lady', he was reporting the first information which the Scots ambassadors received, that the Queen of England had 'directed out the warrant long ago and wished not to be made privy to the day of execution. Since then all our intelligence assures us she is gone. . . .'[14] Though the next few days revealed that the Queen of Scots had not yet 'gone', the ambassadors might have concluded that, if they did not deal for a 'dead lady', they dealt for one who was as good as dead.

This impression was doubtless enhanced by the rumour of a new plot against Elizabeth, involving the French resident ambassador Châteauneuf, who was arrested for questioning, while his secretary was sent to the Tower. Later the alarm was admitted to have been a mistake, and Châteauneuf received an official apology. At the time, the manœuvre served to nullify the efforts of the special ambassador, Pomponne de Bellièvre, sent by Henri III of France to plead for Mary's life, and further to convince Gray and Melville that their mission was a pre-ordained failure.

The Master of Gray, by his own account, made a strenuous effort to obey James's instructions, and, according to a letter which he wrote to James on 12 January, he advanced every argument contained in his instructions to persuade Elizabeth to spare Mary's life. He quoted the words with which Elizabeth concluded the audience, giving her own view of the role which her imprisonment of Mary had played in Scottish politics:

'Tell your King what good I have done for him in holding the crown on his head since he was born; and that I mind to keep the league that stands now between us, and if he break, it shall be a double fault.'

Gray requested that Mary's life be spared for another fifteen days, and upon Elizabeth's refusal Melville asked for a reprieve of eight days.

'Not for an hour!' was Elizabeth's answer.

The Master of Gray was probably more worried for himself than for anyone else: the survival of the Queen of Scots threatened him; the failure of his mission might cost him the favour of the King. He wrote in anxiety: 'Your Majesty sees we have delivered all we had for offers. But all is for nothing, for she and her Council has laid a determination that they mind to follow forth. . . . So I pray Your Majesty consider my upright dealing in your service, and not the effect. . . .'[15]

Gray's conviction that the embassy had failed was undoubtedly justified, especially after Alexander Stewart announced that he had secret information that James would 'digest' the fact of his mother's execution for the sake of securing the succession. James repudiated the imputation, when the information reached him, and according to Courcelles he fell into a 'marvellous choler' and said that when Alexander Stewart returned to Scotland he would 'hang him before he put off his boots'.[16] In the event, he took no action against Stewart, possibly because he accepted Gray's view that the English government's decision had already been made.

However, in spite of Elizabeth's refusal to reprieve the Queen of Scots even for an hour, the rest of January wore away before Elizabeth could bring herself to sign the death warrant. She signed it on 1 February and gave it to William Davison, the Secretary to the Council, who took it upon himself to see it despatched to Fotheringhay and thus became the scapegoat for her subsequent wrath.

The date of the Scottish ambassadors' return to Scotland is uncertain. According to a French source, a ruse was employed against them similar to that used against Châteauneuf: they were accused of plotting against the life of Elizabeth on the frail evidence that Gray had sent a brace of pistols to a friend.[17]

They were back in Scotland early in February, and on the 8th they received the official thanks of the King's Council for their services.

On that very morning the Queen of Scots entered the great hall of Fotheringhay Castle, to die with a consummate courage which not even the most venomous of her enemies could impugn. She knew how to die not only with courage but with effect. She approached the block shaking off the unwanted ministrations of the Protestant Dean of Peterborough with the words: 'I am settled in the ancient Catholic Roman religion and mind to spend my blood in defence of it.' Stripped of her black dress and white veil, she knelt at the block in a crimson petticoat. With loud repetition she cried out, *'In manus tuas, Domine, confido spiritum meum'* – 'Into thy hands, O Lord, I commend my spirit' – until the axe fell. Though she had been convicted as a political intriguer, she had contrived to die as a Catholic martyr.

Between 1 and 7 February Elizabeth had sought to persuade Mary's gaoler, Sir Amyas Paulet, to accept the responsibility of arranging for her death by some secret means. Paulet, who had never offered Mary the slightest gesture of sympathy or kindness, answered his own sovereign with well-known words: 'God forbid that I should make so foul a shipwreck of my conscience or leave so great a blot to my poor posterity to shed blood without law or warrant.'[18] So the axe fell publicly, and Elizabeth was obliged to assume responsibility for the trial, condemnation and execution of a fellow-sovereign, in the knowledge that the axe which severed Mary's neck struck a blow at the prestige of monarchy itself. Elizabeth strove to escape her responsibility by blaming Burghley and Walsingham, sending Davison to the Tower, protesting that she had never intended that Mary should die.

On 14 February she wrote James her incredible explanation of his mother's death:

My dear brother, I would you knew, though not felt, the extreme dolour that overwhelmeth my mind for that miserable accident which far contrary to my meaning hath been befallen. . . . I beseech you that as God and so many more knows how innocent I am in this case, so you will believe me that if I had bidden do it I would have abiden by it. I am not so base minded that fear of any living creature or prince should make me afraid to do that were in just [sic], or done, to deny the same. I am not of so base a lineage nor carry so vile a mind; but as not to disguise fits most a king, so I will never dissemble my actions, but cause them show even as I mean them. . . . The circumstances it may please you to hear of this bearer. And for your part, think you have not in the world a more loving kinswoman nor more dear friend, nor any that will watch more carefully to preserve you and your state, and whosoever should otherwise persuade you, judge them more partial to others than you. And thus in haste I leave to trouble you, beseeching God to send you a long reign. Your most assured loving sister and cousin.[19]

The bearer of the letter was Robert Carey, the son of Elizabeth's cousin Lord Hunsdon. He took back James's answer, which was coldly sceptical:

Madam and dearest sister, whereas by your letter and bearer Robert Carey your servant and ambassador, ye purge yourself of yon unhappy fact [i.e. the execution]. As on the one part, considering your rank and sex, consanguinity and long professed goodwill to the defunct, together with your many and solemn attestations of your innocency, I dare not wrong you so far as not to judge honourably of your unspotted part therein, so, on the other side, I wish that your honourable behaviour in all times hereafter may fully persuade the whole world of the same. And, as for my part, I look that ye will give me at this time such full satisfaction in all respects, as shall be a mean to strengthen and unite this isle, establish and maintain the true religion, and oblige me to be, as before I was, your most loving.[20]

There was no point in severing the alliance after the Queen of Scots was dead. James had considered that honour constrained him to 'insist' for his mother's life, and he had 'insisted' more vehemently than perhaps has been recognized. Reason had persuaded him not to make the ultimate gesture on her behalf of breaking the treaty with England, thus jeopardizing his chances of the succession. Love for her had not existed to urge him to act against the dictates of reason.

James's reception of the news of his mother's execution was variously reported. Calderwood, who was a child at the time of Mary's death and not a witness of James's reaction, wrote: 'When the King heard of the execution he could not conceal his inward joy, howbeit outwardly he seemed to be sorrow-ful. . . . He said that night to some few that were beside him, "I am now sole King." '[21] He could have made that observation, which was true, without vulgar jubilation. A contemporary, writing to Archibald Douglas, remarked that, 'The King moved never his countenance at the rehearsal [report] of his mother's execution, nor leaves not his pastime and hunting more than of before.'[22]

If James had expressed extravagant grief for his mother, he would have been accused, with justification, of hypocrisy. He obeyed the usages of decency by wearing a 'dule weid' (mourn-ing costume) of dark purple and was told by the young Earl of Bothwell that the proper mourning would be a suit of armour. He had difficulty in controlling the hotheads who wanted to make war with England; but he contained a dangerous situation and kept the alliance with England intact. Neither he nor Eliza-beth wished to see the Anglo-Scottish treaty broken by quixotic reactions to the death of Mary, Queen of Scots.

Mary was buried with royal honours in Peterborough Cathedral, exactly as though she had died of natural causes, an honoured guest in England. Her death inspired a spate of elegies, varying in quality from the exquisite lament of the Jesuit poet and saint Robert Southwell:

> Rue not my death, rejoice at my repose,
> It was not death to me but to my woe;
> The bud was opened to let out the rose,
> The chain was loosed to let the captive go.

to the savage quatrain addressed to Elizabeth by an anonymous Scots versifier with the gift of a rope noose:

> To Jesabell that English heure [whore]
>   receyve this Scottish cheyne,
> As presagies of her gret malhoeur
>   for murthering of our Quene.

But Queen Mary's son, who was frequently moved to lament or to celebrate political and personal events in verse, was silent.

CHAPTER SIX

'The Great Fleet Invincible'

The nations banded 'gainst the Lord of might
Prepar'd a force, and set them on the way :
Mars drest himself in such an awfull plight,
The like whereof was never seene they say :
They forward came in monstrous array,
Both sea and land beset us everywhere
Bragges threatened us a ruinous decay.
What came of that the issue did declare.
The windes began to tosse them here and there,
The seas begun in foming waves to swell :
The number that escap'd, it fell them faire :
The rest were swallowed up in gulfes of hell :
But how were all these things miraculous done?
God laught at them out of his heavenly throne.

> Sonnet by James VI on the defeat of the
> Spanish Armada, 1588

'I LOOK that ye will give me at this time such full satisfaction in all respects, as shall be a mean to strengthen and unite this isle,' James had written to Elizabeth, shortly after his mother's death. In other words, he demanded that Elizabeth should grant him the recognition as her heir presumptive which would guarantee the union of their kingdoms in the future.

Elizabeth had a new reason for disappointing James's expectations, in her fear of the militant Counter-Reformation, manifested not by the futile zeal of Babington and his kind but by the great enterprise which was slowly maturing in the mind of Philip II of Spain. To continue to dangle before James, and to withhold from him, the object of his desires, seemed to Elizabeth the best means of holding him true to the alliance in the face of the Spanish threat, for he was under considerable pressure to go to war with England to avenge his mother's execution.

The King of Spain's plan had been maturing, and changing, since 1585. At the outset the avowed aim of the Spanish crusade had been to vindicate the rights of Mary, Queen of Scots, the lawful Catholic ruler of England, to rescue the English Catholics from the tyranny of their heretical Queen and to reconvert England to Catholicism. While Mary lived, Philip's purpose remained officially unchanged, but during the last months of her life, as he received reports from England and learned of the increasing likelihood of her execution, Philip's thoughts turned to his own tenuous claim to the English throne and to the possibility of employing the Spanish crusade as the means of Spanish conquest.

Philip II was descended from Edward III's son John of Gaunt, Duke of Lancaster, two daughters of whom had married into the royal Houses of Portugal and Castile, thus linking Philip to the Plantagenet dynasty through both his maternal and paternal ancestry. And if that were not good enough to establish his claim, Philip declared that Mary, Queen of Scots had willed her own claim to the English throne to him, Philip, should James remain an obstinate heretic at the time of her death.[1]

Since the Papacy had been persuaded to make a heavy financial contribution to the Spanish crusade against England, Philip felt it important to convince Pope Sixtus V that a Spanish conquest would be a perfectly justified result. He wrote an illuminating letter on the subject to the Count of Olivares, his ambassador at the papal Court:

> You will cautiously approach his Holiness and ... obtain from him a secret brief that, failing the Queen of Scotland, the right to the English crown falls to me. My claim, as you are aware, rests upon my descent from the House of Lancaster, and upon the Will made by the Queen of Scotland. ... You will impress upon His Holiness that I cannot undertake a war in England for the purpose merely of placing upon that throne a young heretic like the King of Scotland, who, indeed, is by his heresy incapacitated to succeed. His Holiness must, however, be assured that I have no intention of adding England to my own domains, but to settle the crown upon my daughter, the Infanta.[2]

The phrase 'failing the Queen of Scotland' gives away the fact that Philip was assuming that she would be executed, or judging that if she were still alive when the Spaniards landed in England, she would be done to death at once. He wrote the letter on 11 February 1587, ignorant of the fact that Mary had been dead for four days. When he learned of her death he saw the path to the English throne as already clear for his daughter, since he denied the rights of Elizabeth to occupy it and chose to regard as invalid the claims of that 'young heretic' James VI.

Throughout 1587 Anglo-Scottish relations remained uneasy. James continued to press for recognition as Elizabeth's heir, and he added new demands: an English dukedom and the right to be consulted about the marriage of his first cousin, Arbella Stuart. Arbella, the daughter of James's uncle Lord Charles Stuart, had been born and brought up in England; her claim to the English throne was inferior to that of James, except that she enjoyed the advantage of not having been 'alien born'. James's best method of disposing of her claim would have been to absorb it by marrying her himself; but such an alliance would have been less prestigious and less profitable than marriage to a foreign princess, besides which, the precedent of Mary's marriage to Darnley for similar reasons was not especially encouraging. However, the problem of Arbella added a further element of stress to the relations of James and Elizabeth; and in all matters Elizabeth steadfastly refused James the satisfaction he required.

As the threat of Spanish invasion grew closer, the English were somewhat reassured of James's intention to stand by the alliance when, in April 1587, he banished Lord Maxwell, the leading Catholic magnate in the south-west of Scotland. But the assurance evaporated with equal suddenness the following month, when the Master of Gray was banished in his turn, and the Abbey of Dunfermline, which had belonged to him, was granted to the Earl of Huntly, the most powerful Scottish Catholic nobleman of all.

James made Gray the scapegoat for having failed to save the Queen of Scots' life, just as Elizabeth had made Davison the scapegoat for having caused her death. Neither was justly treated by his sovereign, but the difference was that Elizabeth dispensed with a loyal servant, James with a dangerous troublemaker. It was a piquant end to Gray's diplomatic career that on his last assignment he appears to have behaved honestly. The following year he was replaced in the King's affections by a very much more ordinary young man, Alexander Lindsay, the younger brother of the Earl of Crawford, who was ennobled as Lord Spynie in 1590. He was described as 'the King's only minion and conceit . . . his nightly bedfellow',[3] an unambiguous comment on the nature of their relationship.

The King's relations with Huntly, who increasingly enjoyed his favour, were extraordinarily complex. George Gordon, sixth Earl of Huntly, was a kinsman of the King through the marriages of two of his forebears with members of the royal House.[4] James was attracted to him and, with characteristic lack of inhibition, was sometimes seen to kiss him publicly 'to the amazement of many'.[5] But Huntly was not a favourite in the same sense as Alexander Lindsay. According to Archbishop Mathew's shrewd observation, 'Together with the Earl of Mar, who had been the companion of the royal childhood . . . he formed the tiny group of the King's most intimate and faithful friends. This was a friendship which, as far as Huntly was concerned, was truly exacerbating to the Kirk and was the more remarkable in that the Earl was so frequently in at least apparent opposition to the sovereign's wishes.'[6]

'Apparent' is the key word in that passage, for Huntly ceaselessly indulged in international Catholic intrigues, yet James forgave him his 'apparent' treasons; and when the situation arose in which James was obliged to take up arms against him, his ready surrender and nominal punishment almost hinted at collusion.

The initial explanation was that James, in the event of Elizabeth's failure to resist the power of Spain, wished to keep open a channel of communication between Scotland and Spain, so that, should the might of militant Catholicism be revealed arrayed upon his threshold, his own sympathy for his Catholic subjects might make his régime appear worthy of permission to survive. Long after the crisis of imminent invasion had passed, James continued to pursue the same policy in order to encourage the hopes of the English Catholics, who, as the century drew to its close, increasingly expected to become his subjects, and to retain the sympathy of their co-religionists throughout Europe.

While James may have delighted in his own deviousness, his personal commitment to the reformed religion was never in doubt.

In June 1587 he received the French Huguenot poet Guillaume de Salluste du Bartas, whose *Uranie* he had translated and published in *Essayes of a Prentise in the Divine Art of Poesie*. Du Bartas came as an unofficial envoy from Henri of Navarre, to make preliminary enquiries into the possibility of a marriage between King James and Henri's sister, Catherine of Navarre. James kept the option open and entertained the devout poet by taking him to a theology lecture by Andrew Melvill at the University of St Andrews.

The following month James appointed Maitland of Thirlestane Chancellor of Scotland. In the frequently quoted words of Andrew Melvill's nephew James Melvill, Maitland 'held the King upon two grounds sure, neither to cast out with the Kirk nor with England'.[7] James Melvill wrote as one who witnessed James VI's inexplicable leniency to Catholic delinquents; he was unaware that the King had already digested the lesson which he imputed to Maitland's teaching.

During the autumn and winter of 1587–8, James cultivated the golden opinions of the Kirk 'in commenting of the Apocalypse and in setting out of sermons thereupon against the Papists and Spaniards'.[8] A short meditation, suitable to the occasion, was published early in 1588, and an expanded *Paraphrase upon the Revelation of the Apostle S. John* was published in 1616. James also displayed his orthodoxy in the new year by challenging Father James Gordon, a Jesuit and uncle of the Earl of Huntly, to a public debate. It was conducted with the utmost courtesy on both sides, and the Jesuit admitted that no one could 'use his arguments better nor quote the Scriptures and other authorities more effectively' than the King.[9]

The year 1588 was ushered in with a fanfare of prophecies. 'Excellent astronomers', observed Calderwood, 'foretold it to be fatal to all estates; and if the world did not perish, yet there should be great alterations in kingdoms and empires, so that thereafter it should be called the year of wonders. . . . Yet did this, and other like prophecies, resolve only upon the invasion of this isle. But the Lord disappointed the enterprisers and fought for us.'[10]

In Spain the year was declared to be 'pregnant with misfortune',[11] but perhaps such prognostications were not surprising, for the previous year had brought its own unnerving crop of disasters, when the daring exploits of Sir Francis Drake had destroyed a vast tonnage of Spanish shipping and delayed the departure of the Armada until 1588. The damage was repaired as speedily as possible, and by the new year the reputedly invincible fleet was ready to put to sea. King Philip was eager that it should set sail at once, but he was dissuaded from sending it forth without awaiting fair weather by his experienced admiral Santa Cruz, who, having delivered his restraining advice, died in February, leaving his master the problem of finding another commander for the fleet. Spanish protocol demanded that such an expedition should be led by a nobleman of the highest rank, for in the Spanish service rank commanded greater respect than experience. The only man of the required standing was the Duke of Medina Sidonia, a pessimistic grandee who, when appointed, informed King Philip: 'I possess neither aptitude, ability, health nor fortune for the expedition.'[12] Nonetheless, he obediently accepted the commission.

The King's plan was that the Armada should escort to England the Spanish army commanded by the Prince of Parma, which should be ferried across from the Netherlands, and that the decisive battle, resulting in the Spanish conquest, should be fought on English soil, when Parma's troops had been successfully landed. Thus the role of the Armada itself was essentially conceived as that of escorting and supporting the invading army.

The resolute preparations of the English to repel the Spaniards were accompanied by James's Janus-like arrangements north of the Border. In April 1588 Lord Maxwell, who had been banished the previous year, returned on his own initiative, to be denounced as a rebel and greeted by a muster of the lieges. James undertook one of his few military adventures, marched against Maxwell and summoned his castles to surrender. Langholm, Caerlaverock and Threave all yielded upon the summons, but Lochmaben was defended by one David Maxwell until 9 June.

The castle was reduced with the assistance of English guns borrowed from Carlisle, and the captain and five members of the garrison were hanged. Lord Maxwell himself was brought back to Edinburgh as a prisoner.

The English were naturally disposed to see this act of Anglo-Scottish co-operation, and the imprisonment of a prominent Catholic, as assurances that James would stand by the alliance in the impending crisis. But once again James followed an encouraging act with a hint of unpredictability. The following month the Earl of Huntly was admitted to the closest circle of the royal kindred by his marriage to Lady Henriette Stuart, the eldest daughter of Esmé, Duke of Lennox. The fact that both bride and bridegroom were obliged to profess the reformed religion for the occasion did nothing to disguise the fact that the King had chosen to form a close tie with the leading Catholic magnate of Scotland. Huntly maintained his Catholic affiliations, and Henriette throughout her life displayed the unyielding Catholicism which had characterized her mother.

Archibald Douglas, who had been adroit enough to retain his semi-official appointment in England, despite the unwelcome advice he had given to James before the execution of Queen Mary, and despite even his untimely words to Leicester, was told to inform the English government that James would 'take the best course for his own surety and state of his country that he may'.[13]

James undoubtedly hoped that Elizabeth would be induced to grant all that he required of her, in order to be sure of him when the crisis came. If she did not do so, there remained the possibility that his careful duality might secure his survival as king in the event of a Spanish victory; though, in the light of Philip II's letter to Olivares, it seems that James was more realistic when he remarked that, if the worst came to the worst, he would receive from Philip 'the same which Polyphemus promised to Ulysses, to devour him after his fellows'.[14]

The Spanish Armada sailed out of Corunna on 12 July 1588, and on the 19th it came in sight of the Lizard. The English were un-aware that the terrible appearance of the enemy concealed the crippling pessimism of Medina Sidonia, besides a great deal of disorganization which had resulted in rotting food supplies and consequently in widespread sickness among the Spaniards. The English fleet, commanded by Lord Howard of Effingham, a patriotic Catholic nobleman who might fairly be described as Medina Sidonia's English counterpart, emerged from Plymouth, and on the 21st the two fleets joined in battle. From 21 to 30 July an almost continuous sea fight took place, and the Spanish Armada was never able to effect a junction with the Prince of Parma. On the night of the 28th the English use of fireships wreaked havoc in the Spanish fleet, and the following day the naval battle of Gravelines decided the issue in favour of the English. Medina Sidonia was bluntly told by his more experienced subordinates that 'only the mercy of God could save him from destruction.'[15] Wild summer storms blew the damaged Spanish ships remorselessly northwards, and Medina Sidonia accepted the necessity of obeying the winds and the waves and returning to Spain by a northward circumnavigation of the British Isles.

News of the warfare at sea was slow in reaching the rulers of England and Scotland. While the sea battle was being fought out, a new English ambassador to Scotland, William Ashby, promised James much of what he had demanded, in return for a firm assurance of support for England. James was to receive an English dukedom with its revenues, together with a pension of £5,000 *per annum*; in addition he was to be paid the salaries of a royal guard of fifty men-at-arms and their commanding officers, and the money to pay a force of a hundred men to police the Borders. These offers were made on 31 July, the very day after Medina Sidonia, all unknown to Ashby, had acknowledged the failure of his expedition. James made haste to clinch his agreement with Ashby's offers and wrote to Elizabeth 'hereby to offer unto you my forces, my person and all that I may command to be employed against your strangers . . . as may best serve for the defence of your country. Wherein I promise to behave myself not as a stranger and foreign prince but as your natural son and compatriot of your country in all respects. . . .'[16]

Both Scotland and England waited in suspense while the elements took further responsibility from the defenders of their coasts and completed the ruin of the ambitions of Spain. During the next few weeks the Armada was blown helplessly before the wind, and the great ships were scattered and wrecked on the rocks of the Scottish mainland, the Northern and Western Isles and the shores of Ireland.

Late in September Medina Sidonia, with approximately half of his battered fleet, limped into Santander, leaving thirty-five ships unaccounted for, two sunk and two captured by the enemy, five lost off France and Holland and nineteen wrecked in the course of the circumnavigation of Scotland.[17]

In the meantime, before the news of the Spanish disaster had reached either England or Scotland, William Ashby had reported to Walsingham the promises by which he had secured James's certain support. But on 12 August, when the defeat of the Spaniards had been conclusively recognized, Ashby wrote a grovelling apology for having exceeded his instructions and offered the Scottish King far more than the circumstances had warranted or his own commission had permitted.[18] He was heavily reproved, but, unlike the unfortunate Davison, he remained unpunished; his *felix culpa* had served the purpose of holding James loyal to the alliance with England while the Armada crisis was at its height.

Towards the end of the year the exiled Master of Gray, who seems to have borne the King of Scots no ill-will for the reversal of his fortunes, wrote to Archibald Douglas: 'I am sorry to know from Scotland that the King our master has, of all the golden mountains offered, received a fiddler's wages.'[19] Elizabeth, in fact, presented James with £3,000, 'a fiddler's wages' indeed by comparison with Ashby's promises, but a princely gift in the view of so reluctant a giver.

The Armada episode served to illustrate to James that Elizabeth, in all likelihood, would make no commitment on the subject of the succession: 'If she would not make it when the Spanish fleet was approaching her shores, she would not make it at all.'[20] Therefore he eased if not ceased his pressure for recognition as Elizabeth's heir, and he continued to cultivate the good opinion of Scottish, English and European Catholics. In the words of a distinguished modern scholar: 'This policy was much safer and more attractive than it had been before, since the defeat of the Armada made it impossible for Spain to harm him, for the time being at least. Since the Scottish Catholic leaders were in touch with Continental informants, friendliness to those leaders had the additional advantage of keeping the King partly informed as to Spanish activities and intentions.'[21]

The King's policy was perhaps the background to the humane treatment which the majority of the shipwrecked Spaniards received in Scotland during the autumn of 1588.

On 28 October the Provost of Edinburgh issued a pass (or passport) to forty-six Spaniards, entitling them to make their homeward journey on board Scottish ships:

Forasmickle as there came lately into this our city to the number of forty-six persons, strangers, naked and bare and in a most miserable state, whom we understood to be of the Spanish navy ... we were moved to pity their state and of Christian charity ... not only to clothe their nakedness and a certain space to sustain and feed their hungry bellies, but also by occasion of certain Scottish ships passing in their merchandise towards the ports of France, to ... disperse them among the said ships to be transported to the said ports where it shall be found most expedient to set them on land, that they may safely pass to their native countries. . . .[22]

In November William Ashby reported the wreck of a Spanish ship on Fair Isle, where five hundred seamen struggled to land: 'But it is thought they will be famished [starved to death] it is so little and barren.'[23] However, towards the end of the month two hundred survivors reached Anstruther in Fife, intending to hire a ship to take them back to Spain; they were among the fortunate who had contrived to save their ship's treasure and reach a port 'unspoiled'.[24]

December witnessed the ultimate act of Scottish courtesy, when the nephew of the Duke of Medina Sidonia, together with other Spanish noblemen, reached Edinburgh. They were received honourably by James and given all the help they required to return to Spain. A total of four hundred Spaniards received Scottish assistance to make their way home. Calderwood tartly observed: 'They found greater clemency and charity nor [than] they either deserved or expected,'[25] and James himself, in his sonnet celebrating the Spanish defeat, correctly declared: 'The number that escap'd it fell them faire.'

He was also truthful concerning his own role when he imputed the defeat of the inappropriately styled 'Invincible Armada' to the mockery of God and not to any heroic efforts on his own part or that of his nation.

CHAPTER SEVEN

Hero and Leander

What mortall man may live but hart*
As I doe now, suche is my cace,
For now the whole is from the part
Devided eache in divers place.
   The seas are now the barr
   Which make us distance farr
   That we may soone winn narr†
    God graunte us grace. . . .

          James VI to Anne of Denmark, in
          anticipation of their marriage, 1589

THE sailing of the Spanish Armada had resulted in one of the greatest anticlimaxes of English history. When Medina Sidonia had excused his own incapacity to his King, he had summed up the character of the whole enterprise. In Scotland the aftermath of the Armada crisis was far more dramatic than the event itself.

Early in 1589 letters signed by the Earls of Huntly, Errol and Crawford and Lords Maxwell and Claud Hamilton were intercepted in England. In these letters the Catholic lords expressed their regret at the failure of the Armada and promised their assistance to the King of Spain if he should choose to attempt another invasion of England. Elizabeth sent the letters to William Ashby, who presented them to James with an accompanying letter from Elizabeth in which she wrote: 'Good Lord! Methink I do but dream. No King a week would bear this!'[1] ('No King would bear this for a week').

The scandal obliged James to dismiss Huntly from the captaincy of the royal guard, to which the Earl had only recently been appointed. Huntly imputed his fall from grace to the influ-

*without love
†near

ence of the Chancellor Maitland and gathered a force prepara-
tory to marching on Edinburgh and recovering his position by
force. James retaliated in a manner which Huntly had not foreseen. He mustered an army from the south of Scotland and
marched as far as the Brig of Dee. Huntly's forces were not
prepared to resist the King; they deserted, obliging Huntly and
Crawford to surrender when James entered Aberdeen. The
Catholic Earls were placed in informal confinement, and Maitland's position remained unimpaired.

James wrote Huntly a reproachful letter, reminding him that
his marriage had been accompanied by a profession of the
reformed faith and suggesting that a proper acknowledgment
of his fault, like that of the Prodigal Son, would be appropriate:
'Peccavi in Coelum et contra te'[2] ('I have sinned against Heaven
and against you'). It was a mild enough rebuke after all the
trouble he had caused.

In the midst of that trouble an informant of the English
government had written: 'The King hath a strange, extraordinary affection to Huntly, such as is yet unremoveable. . . .
The Chancellor is beloved of the King in another sort, for he
manages the whole affairs of this country. . . . The King hath
had a special care to make and keep these, his two well-beloved
servants, friends, but it never lasted forty days without some
suspicion or jar.'[3]

However, though the King's desire to maintain the balance of
power between these conflicting interests was upset by the
interception of the Catholic lords' letters in England, the truth
was that the face-saving exchanges of Huntly and his partisans
with the King of Spain had less interest for James than the
dying sparks of a display of fireworks. Inevitably the Queen of
England overestimated their potential importance to James,
because for her the threat of Spain had been more immediate
than it had for him.

To the King of Scots, 1589 was memorable for a happier matter
than the drama with which it had opened. It was the year of
his marriage.

With varying degrees of seriousness, James's marriage had
been under discussion since 1582. The eligibility of several
Catholic and Protestant princesses had been canvassed, accord-

ing to the religio-political bias of the régime which held power in Scotland. By 1589 there was a short-list of two: the Calvinist Catherine of Navarre and the Lutheran Anne of Denmark.

It is important to stress that in the late sixteenth century mere anti-Catholicism did not imply community of religion. Calvinist and Calvinist were co-religionists; Calvinist and Lutheran were not. Those who regarded community of religion as essential to the maintenance of a united front against the Counter-Reformation supported the marriage of James VI with Catherine of Navarre; those who were anti-Catholic, yet principally concerned with preserving a commercial and friendly alliance between Scotland and Denmark, naturally hoped to see the fruition of the Danish match.

A marriage between James VI and a princess of Denmark had been one of the earliest to be suggested, and the project had been intermittently discussed since 1585. During the spring and summer of 1587 an embassy, headed by the King's erstwhile tutor, Peter Young, and Sir Patrick Vaus of Barnbarroch, had been empowered to negotiate the Danish marriage, but problems connected with the dowry had resulted in the breakdown of negotiations. Then the visit of du Bartas to Scotland had led James to experience some interest in marriage with the Princess of Navarre, and in September 1587 James had sent William Melville of Tongland, brother of the Melvilles of Halhill and Murdocairney, to report on the charms and qualities of the Calvinist Princess.

'My brother', wrote Sir James Melville, '... became well acquainted with the said Princess and was well treated and rewarded by the King her brother, now King of France [Henri IV], and brought with him the picture of the Princess, with a good report of her rare qualities.'[4]

However, personal considerations could not fail to influence the King of Scots. Catherine of Navarre was eight years older than James VI, and Anne of Denmark was eight years younger. Had James been wholly indifferent to the appearance of his future wife, he might at least have reflected that a woman eight years older than himself could present a disciplinary problem, whereas a girl eight years younger would be likely to prove more biddable; but once he had accepted the necessity of matrimony, he found his interest increasingly aroused, and it began to appear

to him a more attractive prospect to acquire a young and pretty
wife than a plain one who was past her first youth. His current
favourite, Alexander Lindsay, was a young man to whom he
felt no serious emotional commitment; for the first time in his
life he was prepared to entertain the possibility of falling in love
with a woman. Nonetheless, his account of how he came to
decide between the two available women was, according to
Sir James Melville, pious and unromantic:

His Majesty determined first to seek counsel of God by earnest
prayer, to direct him where it would be meetest for the weal of
himself and his country. So that after fifteen days' advertisement and
devout prayer, as said is, he called his Council together in his cabinet
and told them how he had been advising and praying to God the
space of fifteen days to move his heart the way that was meetest,
and that he was resolved to marry in Denmark.[5]

His preference for a princess who possessed youth and reputed
beauty thus received the encouragement of Heaven, which
opposed the choice of one who, in a less chivalrous estimate
than that of Melville of Tongland, was 'old, cracked and something worse if all were known'.[6] The burgesses of Edinburgh,
who preferred the profitable trade with Denmark to religious
scruples or nice considerations of ladies' charms, rioted against
the Navarre match in May 1589, in the belief that Maitland was
pressing the King to conclude it. James reassured his subjects
that his mind was already made up, and his preference was
for the King of Denmark's daughter.

The choice of the Princess was followed by the choice of the
ambassador who would celebrate the marriage as the King's
proxy and escort the new Queen to Scotland. The King chose
George Keith, the Earl Marischal, because he combined aristocracy and dependability of character with sufficient personal
wealth to enable him to bear part of the cost of the expedition.
To make good the difference he was given part of the money
with which Elizabeth had rewarded James's support against the
Armada. Elizabeth, who had done what she could to discourage
James's marriage diplomacy, was displeased by the application
of her gift.

Marischal sailed in mid-June, and, after certain unresolved
points concerning Anne's dowry had been settled, he acted as

James's proxy at the marriage, which took place on 28 August 1589. James received a dowry of 75,000 thalers. When negotiations had been opened, he had also hoped to receive Danish acknowledgment of Scottish sovereignty of Orkney, where an uneasy situation had pertained ever since the marriage of James III of Scotland and Margaret of Denmark in 1469. Since Christian I, the father of Margaret, had been unable to pay the agreed dowry in full, he had pledged his estates in Orkney to the Scottish Crown in lieu of the remainder. Scottish interests found the resultant possession of Orkney preferable to the proffered payment, and James VI sought the present opportunity to settle the matter. Anne of Denmark's father, who had resisted James's desires on this point, had died in 1588, and since his successor, Anne's younger brother Christian IV, was a boy ten years old, it was agreed that a decision should await his coming of age. James regally remarked that he 'would not be a merchant for his bride' and thus assured the continuance of the *status quo*, which was to Scotland's advantage so long as the matter remained unsettled either way.

Anne set sail on 1 September, and throughout the month James awaited with rising impatience the arrival of the unknown girl who was officially his Queen.

'This young Prince', William Ashby informed one of his correspondents, 'chaste and continent as Hypolites, spending the time in Diana's exercise, is now far in love with the Princess of Denmark, hearing of her beauty and virtue and her affection towards him.'[7] He was assured that her emotions echoed his own when he was told that she had been learning French in order to be able to converse with him. It is interesting that she chose to learn French in preference to Scots, but numerous letters survive to testify that she picked up her husband's native tongue and rapidly anglicized it after his accession to the English throne. It was, however, in Scots that James wrote several poems to his Queen, some of them before he had met her, while he was still in love with his imagined bride.

His anxiety increased as the month of September passed, and Ashby reported: 'The King, as a true lover, wholly passionate and half out of patience with the wind and weather, is troubled that he hath been so long without intelligence of the fleet and thinketh every day a year till he see his joy and love approach.'[8]

On 8 October he wrote her a letter in which his anxiety is expressed in a tone which appropriately mingles formality and tenderness. The original French is here translated:

Only to one who knows me as well as his own reflection in a glass could I express, my dearest love, the fears which I have experienced because of the contrary winds and the violent storms since you embarked, the more especially since the arrival here of some ships which put to sea after your own and came without word of you. My resultant anguish, and the fear which ceaselessly pierces my heart, has driven me to despatch a messenger to seek for you, both to bring me news of you and to give you the same of me. . . . I pray you therefore to give credence to all that he will tell you. And so I end by praying the Creator, my only love, to grant you a safe, swift and happy arrival upon these shores, so that you may receive proof of the entire devotion of him who has vowed to you his whole-hearted love. James R.[9]

Two days later news reached Scotland that the storms had forced the Danish fleet to seek the refuge of the Norwegian coast. At the height of the storm the young Queen herself had narrowly escaped death or injury when three cannon had broken loose from their positions and been flung to and fro across the deck as the helpless ship was battered by the waves. In this desperate situation two clergymen who had sailed with the Queen, Drs Knibbe and Krage, had been urged to pray for calm and safety, and when their prayers had had no noticeable effect on the elements, the Danish Admiral Peter Munk had reached the unfortunate conclusion that the storms must have been the work of witches. His courage had failed him when he remembered that he had quarrelled with a citizen of Copenhagen whose wife was a reputed witch. The conclusion that seamanship was no match for the black arts had led him to seek the shelter of a fjord.[10]

James was horrified to learn how well-justified his fears had been. He ordered the Earl of Bothwell, who was Lord Admiral of Scotland, to take a fleet of six ships to sea to bring the Queen home. But when Bothwell told the King his estimate of the cost of the expedition, James realized that he could not raise the money to meet it. So Maitland, to whom some of the opprobrium of having opposed the popular Danish match still clung, immediately offered to equip a vessel at his own expense and to sail in person to bring back the Queen. James thankfully accepted, and then, in a fever of impatience to end the long weeks of waiting and see his Queen all the sooner, he suddenly resolved that he would undertake the voyage himself. It was a familiar story to him that his grandfather James v had sailed to France and brought home his first Queen, Madeleine de Valois. the daughter of François I. It would be a regal gesture to emulate the earlier James's voyage, and a chivalrous one to rescue his bride from the dangers of the sea.

For fear of meeting concerted resistance to his plan, James kept his projected departure secret from his Council. He composed a proclamation to his subjects, explaining his reasons for sailing. Personally written, in a direct and unofficial style, it is a remarkably self-revealing document and therefore well worth quoting at some length :

In respect I know that the motion of my voyage at this time will be diversely scanned upon, the misinterpretation whereof may tend as well to my great dishonour as to the wrongous blame of innocents, I have thereupon been moved to set down this present declaration with my own hand, hereby to resolve all good subjects, first of the causes briefly that moved me to take this purpose in head, and next in what fashion I resolved myself thereof.

As to the causes, I doubt not it is manifestly known to all, how far I was generally found fault with by all men for the delaying so long of my marriage. The reasons were that I was alone, without father or mother, brother or sister, King of this realm and heir apparent of England.

This my nakedness made me to be weak and my enemies strong; one man was as no man, and the want of the hope of succession breeds disdain; yea, my delay bred in the breasts of many a great jealousy of inability as if I were a barren stock.

These reasons, and immeasurable others hourly objected, moved me to hasten the treaty of my marriage; for as to my own nature, God is my witness how I could have abstained longer nor [than] the weal of my patrie [native land] could have permitted. . . .

This treaty then being perfected, and the Queen my bedfellow coming on her journey, how the contrarious winds stayed her and where she was driven it is more than notorious to all men. . . . The word then coming to me that she was stayed from coming through the notorious tempests of winds, and that her ships were not able to perfect her voyage this year, through the great hurt they had received. . . . I, upon the instant, yea, very moment, resolved to make possible on my part that which was impossible on hers.

The place where I resolved this was Craigmillar, not one of the whole Council being present there. And as I take this resolution only of myself, as I am a true Prince, so advised with myself only what way to follow forth the same.[11]

James went on to exculpate the unpopular Maitland from either having influenced him in his decision to put to sea or even having been let into the secret of his resolution to do so. From the former, Maitland can be exculpated without hesitation, for he would certainly have restrained rather than encouraged James; but almost certainly he must have been admitted to the secret, for James would have required his co-operation, however reluctantly conceded.

The King concluded his proclamation with a firm exhortation to his subjects:

It is my pleasure, then, that no man grudge or murmur at these my proceedings, but let every man lead a peaceable and quiet life without offending of any. . . . Let all men assure themselves that whosoever contraries my directions in my absence I will think it a sufficient proof that he bears no love towards me in his heart; and by the contrary, these will I only have respect to at my return that reverences my commandment and will in my absence. Farewell. James *Rex*.[12]

James did his best to ensure that his actions guaranteed the efficacy of his words. He distributed responsibilities in such a way that all interests were represented in the government of Scotland during his absence. The young Ludovic, Duke of Lennox, the official 'Second Person' or heir presumptive, was appointed President of the Council, with the Earl of Bothwell next in dignity. Melville of Murdocairney was deputed to carry out the routine duties of the Chancellor, in the absence of Maitland who was to accompany the King. Lord John Hamilton was made responsible for the affairs of the Border. Robert Bruce, a minister of the Kirk whom the King liked and respected, was given a watching brief, in the knowledge that he 'could be relied on to protest loudly against any sort of governmental misbehaviour'.[13]

The King was wise to take Maitland with him, for thereby

E

he protected his Chancellor from the enmity of Huntly and the pro-Catholic contingent and from that of Bothwell, who had been involved in Huntly's rebellion earlier in the year and who during the next few years was to play the part of a dangerous joker among the Scottish Court cards. Maitland's safety and the King's were both secured, except insofar as the elements threatened them.

On 22 October 1589 the King committed his person to the dangers of the North Sea, in a ship of 130 tons; well provisioned with food, wine and livestock, it was the largest of a flotilla of five vessels.[14] James has never enjoyed a reputation for bravery, but though he had an unconcealable terror of the immediate threat of naked steel, he was not devoid of the courage to face the challenge of dangerous circumstances.

Inevitably the secret of his intended departure leaked out before he sailed, and William Ashby wrote: 'The King's impatience for his love and lady hath so transported him in mind and body that he is about to commit himself, Leander-like, to the waves of the ocean....'[15] The same classical parallel had naturally suggested itself to James's mythology-stocked mind. He wrote a song, in similar stanza form to the song previously quoted, in which the plight of the royal lovers is equated with that of Hero and Leander:

> When as the skilfull archer false
> Inflam'd and pearc'd by craftie arte
> Leander's hart and Hero's als [also]
> By his so firie golden darte
>   Fra Cupide blinde assailde
>   With bows and shaft
>   His will they never failde
>   Such was his craft....[16]

When James, obeying the dictates of 'Cupide blinde', put to sea in the tempestuous autumn of 1589, the prevailing winds favoured him as much as they had opposed his bride. He reached the Flekkefjord in Norway on 28 October. During the ensuing days, in bitter winter weather, James made his way to Oslo, where his bride awaited him.

He entered her presence with the pseudo-informality which the ritual of renaissance royal wooing required: booted and spurred, unannounced and with every appearance of a dramatic haste which brushed aside conventions. In the spirit in which Shakespeare represented the wooing of Henry v and Katherine of France – 'O Kate, nice customs curtsy to great kings' – James impetuously made to kiss Anne of Denmark; and Anne, like Katherine, demurred with well-schooled modesty, protesting that the ladies of Denmark did not kiss before they were married. In the end, having displayed her virtuous reticence, she acquiesced. The ritual accomplished, James withdrew and visited his bride in state the following day, preceded by six heralds clad in suits of red velvet, over which they wore cloaks lined with sable. The King himself, who was now a grave-looking, bearded young man of twenty-three, was dressed in a suit of blue velvet. At their second meeting Anne received him with a willing kiss.

Anne of Denmark, still almost a month short of her fifteenth birthday, which fell on 12 December, was a slender girl with a fair complexion and hair of a radiant pale gold. Her looks were greatly admired as she grew from delicate girlhood to the statuesque beauty of maturity. Her intelligence is usually the subject of slighting comment, yet, as previously observed, she was evidently a facile linguist, and she became a discerning patron of the arts. If she was not politically minded, it is likely that her husband, with his disinclination to respect the female mind, would have regarded her lack of interest in affairs of state as an asset rather than a liability. Her intrigues were initiated for reasons which possessed a personal validity – for example, the upbringing of the royal children – and the cumulative wisdom of experience gradually led her to a decreasing inclination to intrigue. She became, with the passage of years, a shrewd judge of character and a discreet influence on the affairs of the Court.

At first acquaintance James was delighted with his wife. Her immediate attractions fulfilled his romantic hopes. Her ability to speak French and her rapid acquisition of Scots facilitated a swift development of familiarity between them, and for so long as political stresses did not strain their relationship it remained idyllic.

Though a proxy marriage had already taken place, James and Anne were married in person at St Halvard's Church, Oslo, by

David Lindsay, the minister of Leith, who had been brought from Scotland to officiate at the ceremony, conducted in French. The marriage was solemnized yet again, by Lutheran rites, in the presence of the Danish royal family in the castle of Kronborg, on 21 January 1590.

The King of Scots enjoyed his winter's entertainment at the Danish Court, which was characterized by festive evenings of heavy drinking. Probably he enjoyed even more the scholarly contacts which he made in Denmark, which enabled him simultaneously to display his own scholarship and to extend the scope of his learning. He visited Roskilde to discuss the Calvinist doctrine of Predestination with the learned Dr Niels Hemmingsen, and he addressed the theological faculty of Copenhagen University with a three hours' oration in Latin and received a silver cup in honour of the occasion.[17] The most famous and perhaps the most interesting of his intellectual encounters in Denmark was that with the great astronomer Tycho Brahe, who had built a castle and observatory named Uranienborg, in honour of the Muse Urania, on the island of Hveen. There Brahe had his own printing-press, on which part of his book *Astronomiae Instauratae Progymnasmata* was being printed.

Tycho Brahe, who was an intensely arrogant and difficult man, entertained with the greatest affability the young King who was probably the only living royalty capable of understanding what he was talking about. James, deeply impressed, honoured him with a sonnet:

> That onlie essence who made all of noght
> Our great and mightie Lord the life of all
> When he in ordour everie thing hade broght
> At the creating of this earthlie ball
> Then made he man at last. 'Thy raigne it shall
> Extend (quod Jehova) in everie cace
> Over all these breathing beasts that flatlie fall
> For humble hommage here before thy face.'
> He also pitched each planete in his place
> And made them rulers of the ruling lord*
> As heavenlie impes to governe bodies basse
> Be [by] subtle and celestiall sweet accord.
> Then great is Ticho who by this his booke
> Commandement doth over these commanders brooke.[18]

*i.e. rulers over Man himself.

James and Anne remained in Denmark until Easter, to be present at the wedding of Anne's elder sister, Elizabeth, to the Duke of Brunswick. This marriage had been arranged before the conclusion of the negotiations preceding James's marriage, which explained why the elder Danish Princess was married to a duke while the younger made the greater match, with a king. The impression of the greater glory of a royal marriage strongly influenced Queen Anne, and her resultant pride was to have a disproportionately baneful influence on the history of Europe.

The King of Scots and his Queen sailed from Denmark on 21 April 1590, and on 1 May they landed at Leith, where they lodged in 'the King's Wark', a building which did double duty as a customs house and a royal or ambassadorial lodging, while preparations were made for the Queen's state entry into Edinburgh. Anne had brought with her from Denmark a coach of silver which was drawn by eight white horses. On 6 May she entered Edinburgh in this fairy-tale equipage, with the King, the Duke of Lennox, the Earl of Bothwell and Lord John Hamilton riding beside her. During the King's absence his kingdom had remained more or less at peace, and James could ride through his capital in satisfaction with those accompanying lords who throughout the winter had acted with commendable restraint.

The minsters of the Kirk behaved in a manner less seemly than the magnates when the preparations for the Queen's coronation were discussed. James, who had been anointed by Bishop Bothwell of Orkney and firmly held the view that anointing conferred the sacred character of kingship, was resolved that his consort should be anointed queen. His method of achieving his desire was characteristically adroit. He chose Robert Bruce to perform the ceremony, and when more radical kirkmen objected to one of their brethren participating in a 'popish' ceremony, James reminded them firstly that anointing had been instituted in Old Testament times and secondly that, if they objected to Bruce's performing it, a bishop could always be called upon to do so. If the Presbyterian purists hated anointing, they hated bishops more, and Robert Bruce was grudgingly permitted to do the King's will.

On 17 May a resplendent procession entered the Abbey Church of Holyrood, where the ensuing ceremony lasted seven hours. After sermons and orations in Latin, French and Scots, the disputed anointing was performed. The Countess of Mar opened the Queen's gown, and Robert Bruce poured on her breast and shoulder 'a bonny quantity of oil'.[19] The King took the crown in his own hands and honoured Maitland of Thirlestane by giving it to him to place on the Queen's head. Lord John Hamilton offered her the sceptre, and the Earl of Angus the sword of state. She pronounced the following oath :

I, Queen of Scotland, profess and before God and his angels wholly promise that during the whole course of my life, as far as I can, I shall sincerely worship the same eternal God according to his will revealed in the Holy Scriptures; that I withstand and despise all papistical superstitions and ceremonies and rites contrary to the word of God, and I will procure peace to the Kirk of God within this kingdom. So God, the father of all mercies, have mercy upon me.[20]

No doubt under the influence of the awesome solemnity of the occasion, the young Lutheran Queen swore sincerely to defend the Calvinist Kirk; in time other influences would bring her to yield to the 'papistical superstitions' which she had sworn to withstand and despise.

In the meantime, the King had seen his will obeyed, and he was united with a Queen whom he loved. His life offered him ingredients of delight which he had seldom experienced. The tender aspect of a rather brief period of conjugal bliss is captured in one of the sonnets which he wrote to his Queen :

As on the wings of your enchanting fame
I was transported ou'r the stormie seas
Who could not quenche that restless burning flame
Which onlie ye by sympathie did mease [allay],
So can I troubled be with no disease
Bot ye my onlie Medicinar remaines
And easilie whenever that ye please
May salve my sores and mitigatt my paines.
Your smiling is an antidote againes
The melancholie that oppresseth me
And when a raging wrathe into me raignes
Your loving lookes may make me calme to be.
How oft you see me have an heavie hart
Remember then sweet Doctour on your art.[21]

Dynastically the marriage of James VI and Anne of Denmark

was successful. Anne bore her husband seven children: Henry Frederick, a somewhat long-awaited heir, was born in 1594, and two daughters followed, Elizabeth in 1596 and Margaret in 1598; the future Charles I was born in 1600, Robert in 1601, Mary in 1605 and Sophia in 1607. Only Henry, Elizabeth and Charles survived childhood, and the promising and greatly loved Henry died on the threshold of manhood at the age of eighteen.

Domestic discord, resulting chiefly from disputes about the upbringing of their children, marred the conjugal happiness of James and his Queen during their procreative years. Yet perfect credence has always been accorded to Bishop Goodman's statement that James was 'never taxed nor tainted with the love of any other lady'.[22] However, there is some evidence that during the 1590s the King had a mistress, Anne Murray of Tullibardine, who was married to Patrick Lyon, Lord Glamis, later first Earl of Kinghorn. There is a reference in a letter written by Sir John Carey to Lord Burghley on 10 May 1595 to 'fair mistress Anne Murray, the King's mistress', and on 3 June the same correspondent reported that 'shortly the great marriage shall be solemnized at "Lythquo" [Linlithgow] between young Lord Glamis and the King's mistress.'[23]

James addressed to Anne Murray a poem entitled *A Dreame on his Mistress my Ladie Glammes*. In the narrative of the poem the King dreams that the god Morpheus brings his mistress to him as he lies sleeping, and that she presents him with an amethyst and a gold writing-tablet. While he seeks to interpret the symbolism of these gifts, he reflects that the traditional property of the amethyst is to grant its wearer courage, and that no woman ever loves a timorous man. Upon this thought he forms a resolution:

> And therefore, for my part I vowe
>   If as the rumours be
> Of jarrs and broyles, I happen in
>   Effect the same to see,
> I shall not from the enemies' sight
>   To anie part remove
> Unkithing* once in honour of
>   My Mistress and my love:

*without displaying valour

> Bot onlie mot I conquered be
> And onlie will I yeelde
> To Cupid's shot, whose firie darts
> Resist could never sheelde. . . .[24]

This poem, written at a period when James was several times involved in 'jarrs and broyles', provides an unexpected sidelight on his character. For a brief period of his life James played the gallant, even if it was a part which he lacked the conviction to sustain.

His affair with Lady Glamis, so faintly adumbrated in contemporary references, though celebrated in his own verses, had evidently been consigned to oblivion by the time that he became King of England and Bishop Goodman praised his marital fidelity. After the birth and death of his last child it is apparent and strongly arguable that the homosexual preference of his youth reasserted itself.

Queen Anne, of whose conduct likewise there were echoes of scandal during the 1590s, with the onset of middle age accepted the role of a virtuous wife to an inattentive husband, a role which she was perhaps aided to play by the undemanding nature of her own sexuality. Hunting and dancing, her pleasure in the arts, and some agreeable friendships, in the end came to fill her days; but this plateau of tranquility was far in the future when she was crowned Queen of Scotland, still a stranger in her husband's kingdom.

CHAPTER EIGHT

'Debellare Superbos'

'Parcere subiectis et debellare superbos'
'To spare the conquered and to subjugate the proud' –
motto on a twenty-pound piece by James VI

KING JAMES VI's horizons were broadened by his Danish marriage and its concomitant diplomacy. It inspired him to envisage a League of Protestant Princes against the power of Spain, and his negotiations to construct such a league represent his first attempt to act as an arbiter in European affairs. His ambitions came to nothing, partly as a result of the apathy of other intended participants, partly because more pressing matters came to absorb his attention after his return to Scotland in May 1590.

The King's marriage was accompanied by some of the manifestations of general goodwill which characterize such occasions; but once this mood had evaporated, he found that he was face to face with a multitude of troubles. This situation, in which he had been born and bred, held only rare terrors for him.

The troubles which James encountered on his return from Denmark were of three kinds: the first, recent in origin and brief in duration; the second, endemic though not inerradicable; the third, sufficiently vigorous to survive his reign and to trouble his successors. The troubles of the first type were the dramas which followed the revelation that witchcraft had been employed in an attempt to prevent the arrival of Anne of Denmark in Scotland; the troubles of the second variety, which were highlighted by the first, could be described as problems of aristocratic delinquency; the troubles of the third and most serious kind were caused by Presbyterian extremists within the Kirk, the enforcement of whose views would have placed severe limitations on the royal authority.

The Scottish witch-hunt of 1590 may have originated in the belief of the Danish admiral Peter Munk that the storms which forced the Danish fleet to seek the refuge of a Norwegian fjord had been raised by witchcraft.

James would undoubtedly have heard this opinion when he arrived to rescue his bride, and naturally he would have been outraged by the thought that such evil had been practised against her. Furthermore, their homeward voyage in the spring was also extremely stormy, which probably implanted in James's mind the idea that he too was the subject of destructive efforts which sought to harness malevolent powers. It was not surprising that he determined to investigate the evil doings and, if they proved to have substance, to put an end to them.

King James has been much criticized for believing in witches and witchcraft, as though neither had any existence except in the delusions of persecutors. But there were – and indeed still are – people known as witches and rituals known as witchcraft. The efficacy of the rituals to bring about the intended results is now generally denied credence, but during King James's lifetime few people doubted the efficacy of witchcraft, and James was not among them. His credulity was shared by many learned men and was not, in the mental climate of the period, naïve.

It has been stated by most of James's biographers that he had a lifelong obsession with witchcraft, developed during his early years.[1] But recently Dr Christina Larner has convincingly argued that his interest in the subject was non-existent before 1590 and at its height after his return from Denmark, during the period of the witch-trials, that it continued until he wrote his book on the subject, *Daemonologie*, published in 1597, and that it declined thereafter, and during his later years manifested itself chiefly as an interest in exposing frauds.[2]

The same author has suggested that it was in Denmark that James first heard of the interesting theory of the 'demonic pact' – that is, 'the witch became a witch by virtue of a personal arrangement with the devil who appeared to his potential recruit in some physical form. At this meeting, in return for renunciation of baptism, services on earth and the soul of the witch at death, the devil promised material advantages and magical powers.'[3] The concept of the demonic pact remains familiar through the musical and dramatic versions of the story of Faust, and it is therefore not difficult to imagine how forcefully the idea would have affected James, when he heard of it for the first time.

Much has been written concerning the trials of the North Berwick witches in 1590–91, and the burden of the evidence is that there had been demonic pacts in plenty. Unfortunately, the confessions of witches cannot be accorded much credence because they were elicited under torture, and therefore it is likely that they contain the matter which the interrogators desired to hear, for few people in any age possess the strength to resist giving obliging answers to win a temporary cessation of pain.

Conversely, it would not have been surprising if worship of the devil had taken place in post-Reformation Scotland. The Calvinist doctrine of Predestination declared that some, 'the elect', were predestined to eternal salvation, while others, 'the reprobate', were equally predestined to be damned. The elect had a comforting 'assurance' of their own salvation; but to those who accepted the doctrine without experiencing assurance, it offered only despair. As Archbishop Mathew has observed, some of the witches 'appear to have possessed a long-established conviction of their own reprobation'.[4] The worship of the devil might be described as almost the natural outcome of this appalling state of mind. Thereafter, the vivid belief in the personal character of the devil which his worshippers possessed could readily lead to the performing of a demonic pact with some person believed to be the devil's emissary or representative.

Sir James Melville reported in his memoirs that the witches met by night in the kirk of North Berwick, 'where the devil, clad in a black gown, with a black hat upon his head, preached unto a great number of them out of the pulpit, having like light candles round about him. . . . Then divers among them entered in reasoning, marvelling that all their devilry could do no harm to the King, as it had done to divers others. The devil answered, *"Il est un homme de Dieu"*. ["He is a man of God"].'[5]

Doubtless the man who impersonated the devil was baffled and impressed by the fact that the disagreeable rituals of the witches to whom he was preaching had failed to do the King harm, a failure for which he could think of only one explanation, James's religiosity, which, for all his faults, was genuine.

The desire of the captured witches to gain a respite from their torture may perhaps account for the description of the devil which Melville recorded: 'His face was terrible; his nose like the beak of an eagle, great burning eyes; his hands and legs were hairy, with claws upon his hands and feet like a griffin; he spoke with a hollow voice.'[6]

This is the traditional description of the devil, and no doubt representations of him in such a form still existed in some church murals which had escaped the attentions of Reformation iconoclasts. At any rate, the idea of such an appearance would have survived to inform the imaginations of the witches who tried to oblige their tormentors with a description. Nor is it impossible that the Devil's representative did his best to assume an appropriate disguise.

Unhappily, the story of the devil's corporeal presence and the witches' worship was believed, and a number of witches suffered execution, among them Geillis Duncan, a maidservant, Barbara Napier, a *bourgeoise* of Edinburgh, Euphemia Macalzean, the daughter of a judge, Lord Cliftonhall, and Agnes Samson (whom Melville calls Annie Sampsoun), 'a renowned midwife'.[7] The last mentioned

affirmed that she, in company with nine other witches, being convened in the night beside Prestonpans, the devil their master being present, standing in the midst of them, a body of wax, shapen and made by the said Annie Sampsoun, wrapped within a linen cloth, was first delivered to the devil; who, after he had pronounced his verdict, delivered the said picture to Annie Sampsoun, and she to her next neighbour, and so everyone round about, saying, 'This is King James VI, ordained to be consumed at the instance of a nobleman, Francis, Earl Bothwell.[8]

As was natural enough in a period when confessions extracted by torture were assumed to be true, James accepted the substance of the witches' confessions. At some time he read an admirably scholarly work entitled *The Discoverie of Witchcraft* by Reginald Scot, published in England in 1584. Scot was brave enough to express scepticism at the efficacy of witchcraft – brave in that a refusal of outright condemnation was frequently assumed to imply approval of witchcraft and therefore possibly adeptship. James, who probably felt that he knew more about witchcraft at first hand, since he had almost lost his bride through storms which he believed that witches had raised and had himself been threatened by their rituals, was deeply shocked by Scot's book. When he came to write *Daemonologie*, he declared that he was eager to refute the 'damnable opinion' of Scot, who was 'not ashamed in public print to deny that there can be such a thing as witchcraft. . . .'[9]

Daemonologie now appears to be a very quaint example of James's learning, and Scot's *Discoverie of Witchcraft* gains more respect for its scepticism from twentieth-century sceptics. But James, though he was, from the viewpoint of posterity, absurdly credulous in his belief that witches could fly through the air to attend such meetings as had taken place in North Berwick Kirk, was at least deeply concerned to protect his subjects from the snares and temptations of adoring the devil, a proper and creditable desire in a religious king.

James's book, which is in the form of a dialogue between the uninformed and questioning Philomanthes and the didactic Epistemon, concludes with his own explanation (given by Epistemon, who speaks for him throughout) of the apparently sudden contemporary upsurge of witchcraft: 'The consummation of the world, and our deliverance drawing near, make Satan to rage the more in his instruments, knowing his kingdom to be so near an end.'[10]

Despite James's firm faith and his belief in the imminence of the devil's defeat, he could not fail to be deeply perturbed that the Earl of Bothwell had been the inspiration of the attempts to compass his destruction by witchcraft.

Francis Stewart, fifth Earl of Bothwell, was a close though illegitimate kinsman of the King. His father was Lord John Stewart, one of the numerous bastards of James v, and his mother was Jean Hepburn, the sister of Mary, Queen of Scots' Earl of Bothwell. He had been born in 1563 and was the godson of Queen Mary, who had named him after her first husband. Thus, he was very closely connected with the King, though it was an increasingly uncomfortable closeness. He possessed the veneer of French Court culture which attracted James, but he developed a terrifying unpredictability of behaviour which so alienated the King that Bothwell became the object of his deepest hatred.

The revelation of Bothwell's involvement with the North Berwick witches was made in April 1591, and if the accusation was not a frivolous one, it was a forewarning of his dangerous instability. Thereafter his behaviour could be fairly described as 'the natural fruit of an unstable mind'.[11] But, unfortunately for James, Bothwell's behaviour was as dangerous as that of a responsible traitor, because his high position, his personal power and his reputation as an unhesitating killer, caused other men to take him more seriously than his actual mental processes deserved.

The implication of the accusation that Bothwell had sought to compass the King's death by witchcraft was that he hoped to reign in his place; this in itself was an indication that he lived in a world of fantasy, for the Lennox-Stuart and Hamilton families had legitimate claims to the succession, both superior to whatever tenuous claim might be fabricated from Bothwell's illegitimate proximity to it. The birth of Prince Henry in 1594 removed him even further from the hope of a throne upon which no bastard had ever sat.

Upon the accusation of witchcraft, Bothwell was imprisoned, but he escaped in June 1591. He was pursued to the Borders, but he eluded arrest in the wilds of his own Liddesdale and was declared an outlaw. He then initiated a career of terrorism which seemed to be inspired by an insensate desire to overawe the King into restoring him to favour.

On the night of 27 December 1591 Bothwell carried out a surprise attack on Holyroodhouse. He caused scenes of wild disorder, and temporarily he badly frightened the King; but when order was restored, he escaped before he could be arrested. On this occasion the King's Master Stabler, John Shaw, was killed in defence of the royal person. James wrote an epitaph for him, which casts an agreeable light on his gratitude for faithful service:

> Thy kindness kithed* in loosing life for me
> My kindnesse on thy friends I utter shall;
> My perrill kindled courage into the [e],

*showed

Mine shall revenge thy saikles* famous fall.
Thy constant service ever shall remaine
As freshe with me as if thou lived againe.[12]

The following summer, in June 1592, Bothwell made an attack
on Falkland Palace, where the King was in residence, but again
he was beaten off and again he evaded capture. The next year,
in July 1593, he forced his way into Holyroodhouse and entered
the King's bedchamber, carrying a naked sword which, kneel-
ing, he laid at the King's feet. He may have been attempting to
convey by a symbolic gesture that he could force the King to
show him favour – as long ago the Earl of Gowrie and the
'Lords Enterprisers' had been able to do – but, although James
blanched at the sight of Bothwell's sword, he was no longer
amenable to compulsion. He temporized skilfully, and Bothwell
withdrew. The wild Earl's last escapade took place in the spring
of 1594, and when he failed to compel the King's favour by a
raid on Leith, he fled to the north and took refuge with Huntly.

Bothwell had the claim of kinship upon Huntly, for Lady Jean
Gordon, to whom the fourth Earl of Bothwell had been married
before his marriage to the Queen of Scots, was Huntly's aunt.
This complicated connection was sufficient to oblige Huntly to
shield Bothwell from the King's wrath. Huntly, trapped in an
embarrassing situation, did his best.

Huntly himself had, in the meantime, traversed some hazardous
ground. His political usefulness to the King, and his personal
favour with him, had been strained by his involvement in two
dramatic scandals.

The Earls of Huntly had long been at feud with the Earls of
Moray, because Mary, Queen of Scots had created her half-
brother Lord James Stewart, the later Regent, Earl of Moray,
thereby disappointing the hopes of the fourth Earl of Huntly to
acquire that earldom. James Stewart of Doune, who had married
the elder daughter of the Regent and inherited the title of Earl
of Moray in right of his wife, was resolved to extend his influence in the north-east of Scotland at the expense of Huntly's
family the Gordons, thus continuing the policy which Queen
Mary's half-brother had followed.

*innocent

James VI resolved to settle this feud and commanded Moray to come south and together with Huntly submit to his arbitration. Moray obediently came to his house of Donibristle, on the north side of the Forth, early in 1592. However, on the night of 7 February Huntly crossed the Forth, fired Donibristle and murdered, or instigated the murder of, Moray as he fled from the inferno of the ruins. It is a well-known embellishment of the story that Moray ran towards the shore with his hair and helmet-plume in flames, and that Huntly followed and despatched him among the rocks with a dagger-thrust in the face. Moray, who was renowned for his good looks, died with the words, 'You have spoilt a better face than your own.'

Since the King's affection for Huntly was well known, there was no lack of accusation that James had ordered Moray's death and not the ending of the feud. Popular gossip suggested his motive: the ballad of 'the Bonnie Earl of Moray' called the Earl 'the Queen's love'. But contradictorily this very ballad exculpated the King from responsibility for the murder, in the verse which imputed to him the words

> Now wae be to you, Huntly!
> And wherefore did ye sae?
> I bade you bring him wi' you
> But forbade you him to slay.

The uproar died away, but the King's favour for Huntly was strained again by the affair of 'the Spanish Blanks' in the autumn of 1592.

As in 1589, Huntly was inculpated in a matter of intercepted correspondence with Spain, but in this instance the interception was of blank pieces of paper, hence the name of 'the Spanish Blanks'. However, the blanks bore the signatures of Huntly, Errol and the tenth Earl of Angus, who was a convert to Catholicism. The bearer, George Kerr, confessed under torture that there was a new Spanish invasion plot afoot, the details of which were to be outlined on the blanks in due course.

Again, as in 1589, James's lenity towards the favoured Huntly caused serious alarm to the Kirk; and, as on the previous occasion, James made the gesture of advancing against Huntly in force. But when the Earl and his allies retreated into Caithness, the King did not pursue them. In the summer of 1593 the Parliament, which was expected to pass an act of forfeiture against Huntly and his confederates, did not do so; and the ensuing Parliament, which was held in November, passed an act of oblivion for their misdeeds, on the condition that they made a formal submission to the Kirk.

Bothwell, who apparently had thought to harness the devil to his ambitions, having escaped punishment for his involvement with the witches, went to the opposite extreme of allying himself with the Kirk. The ministers found him an embarrassing ally, but he had his uses as a counterpoise against the Catholic interest. The Kirk justified its support of him by deciding that he was a 'sanctified plague' whose purpose it was to cause the King to 'turn to God' – i.e. to desist from favouring Huntly and other 'papists'.[13]

It was a double embarrassment when Bothwell, having realized that his policy of terrorism was yielding diminishing returns, decided to throw in his lot with Huntly. As a result, in the spring of 1594, James and the Kirk were fortuitously disposed in opposition to their own erstwhile allies, who were temporarily leagued in equally unlikely coalition.

The coalition of King and Kirk could not have occurred at this juncture if James had hitherto ruled in constant and overt enmity to the Kirk.

Such overt enmity as he had shown had been displayed by 'the Black Acts' of 1584, to which previous reference has been made.[14] James had gone a very long way to nullify the ill-effect of 'the Black Acts' – which, anyway, fortunately for him, had been largely blamed on the Earl of Arran – by the conciliatory 'Golden Act' of 1592. By this act the Kirk had been permitted to develop its Presbyterian ecclesiastical polity: its Kirk Sessions, Presbyteries, Synods and General Assembly. 'The Golden Act' recognized a *fait accompli*, since these institutions were already unofficially in existence, and it neither granted the Kirk new material benefits nor abolished the tenuously existing but detested episcopacy, for which the King probably already had future plans. However, 'the Golden Act' created sufficient prejudice in his favour for James to be able to rely on the Kirk's support when Huntly and Bothwell, apparently a pair of aristocratic delinquents whom King and Kirk had separately and misapprehendingly favoured, made common cause.

In the autumn of 1594 James made his fourth military expedition to the north-east. He marched into Aberdeenshire, accompanied by Andrew Melvill, whose presence served to display to Huntly that this latest expedition was no ritual. The advance guard of the royal army was commanded by the young Earl of Argyll. Huntly displayed the extent of his power by defeating Argyll in a skirmish dignified by the name of 'the battle of Glenlivet'; but he offered no resistance to the King himself, though when required to surrender Bothwell, he demurred long enough to allow Bothwell to make his escape, thus honouring the obligations of kinship.

Bothwell fled into Caithness, and thence abroad. Huntly, in temporary disgrace, followed in the spring of 1595. Bothwell's later career curiously mirrored that of his uncle the fourth Earl: he fled by way of the extreme north and lived out his life in exile. The difference was that the unacceptable husband of the Queen of Scots fell into the hands of Scandinavian enemies and died imprisoned and insane, whereas the deranged young man who had plagued the life of James VI retained his freedom. He graduated southwards, to end his life in Naples in 1624, the year before the death of James himself. Since he had been forfeited of his Scottish estates, it is legitimate to pursue Archbishop Mathew's curiosity: 'One wonders how he lived, perhaps at times he practised astrology?'[15]

Huntly, despite his own personal brand of troublesomeness, was not an aristocratic delinquent of the same order as Bothwell. James's patience with him has to be seen in the context of his desire to use him to balance the power of the Kirk and as part of a diplomatic game of solitaire which the King was playing. Huntly's disgrace for his familial support of Bothwell was brief. He returned to Scotland in 1596 and was officially received into the Kirk in 1597.

It was illustrative of James's differing attitudes towards them that, while Bothwell was never permitted to return, Huntly very soon came back to Scotland to enjoy the same power and favour as had been his before. For his submission to the King's wishes concerning his religion he was rewarded with a marquisate; James VI 'appreciated an obedient friendship'.[16] However, in 1636 Huntly chose to die as a Catholic. He had always despised the Kirk, though in James's lifetime he had recognized the necessity to temporize.

Neither Bothwell nor Huntly had represented a serious threat to the authority of the Crown in Scotland, and certainly their basically divergent ambitions cannot possibly be seen in the context of a power struggle between the Crown and the nobility. The problem of troublesome individuals was endemic, but it did not constitute the problem of an entire troublesome class. The old theory that the history of the Stewart/Stuart dynasty in its relations with the Scottish nobility should be interpreted in terms of such a conflict is simply disproved by the fact of the dynasty's survival through a series of royal minorities (those of James II, James III, James V, Mary, Queen of Scots and James VI) during which it would have been possible for a series of 'overmighty subjects' to have usurped the crown, had not a sense of loyalty to it, and to the wearers of it, been deeply ingrained.

The serious challenge to the authority of James VI came not from the nobility but from the Kirk, and principally from the extremist Presbyterian party led by Andrew Melvill. It is important to stress that James himself remained a convinced Calvinist, albeit a 'regal Calvinist'. To all except the extreme Presbyterians of the Genevan persuasion, who regarded the perfect form of government as an ecclesiastically interpreted theocracy, he might have appeared to be the ideal ruler.[17] He had been educated within the structure of the Kirk; he respected it and accepted its doctrinal tenets. It was unfortunate for both the monarchy and the Kirk that Andrew Melvill should have opposed the King's reasonable and basically favourable views.

The clash between them is usually, and probably correctly, summed up by quoting James Melvill's report of the interview which took place between them at Falkland in September 1596. Andrew Melvill addressed the King with the following words: 'Sir, I must tell you, there are two Kings and two kingdoms in Scotland. There is Christ Jesus the King, and His Kingdom the Kirk; whose subject King James the Sixth is, and of whose kingdom not a king, nor a lord, nor a head, but a member.'[18]

It was upon the same occasion that Melvill informed James

that he was 'God's sillie vassal', by which he meant 'God's simple servant'. It has often been supposed that Melvill possessed sufficient power to insult his King with impunity, but this is to misinterpret his words, for which, if James had felt sufficiently insulted, he could have exiled Melvill (as he had before) or imprisoned him (as he was to do later). In fact, James thought of himself as being in very truth 'God's sillie vassal'; but it was the role of a king to be God's vassal in the sense of being his lieutenant. He had no intention of being Melvill's 'sillie vassal' in the sense of being a mere member of the Kirk, to which Melvill took it upon himself to interpret the will of God.

James had had his views on the authority of kings, and their responsibility to God, tempered by his resistance to the doctrines of Buchanan. He was convinced that while kings were subordinate to God, both Kirk and State should be subordinate to kings as God's lieutenants. His own instrument for the subordination of the Kirk was, he decided, to be found in the episcopate. He later summed up his views in words even more succinct than Melvill's own: 'No Bishop, no King.'

Undoubtedly James must have been highly exasperated when Queen Elizabeth I wrote to inform him of a problem of which he had been aware since his adolescence: 'There is risen both in your realm and mine, a sect of perilous consequence, such as would have no kings but a presbytery.'[19] However, her words probably led him increasingly to equate English Puritanism with Scottish Presbyterianism, an equation which was by no means justified, and to equate the Anglican episcopate, which was subject to the Crown and authoritative within the Church, with the kind of episcopacy which he desired to revive in Scotland, where again the situation was not to be equated.

In this context James bitterly regretted his 'Act of Annexation' of 1587, which had appropriated episcopal temporalities to the Crown and had thus contributed to the decline of the Scottish episcopacy, the more so by removing the material stimulus which had previously added its own encouragement to the ambitions of any aspirant to a bishopric.

James's capacity to rebuild the power of Scottish episcopacy depended upon his ability to gain control of the General Assembly of the Kirk, which was currently dominated by Andrew Melvill and his supporters and was therefore strongly anti-episcopal in temper. 'The Golden Act' of 1592, which had appeared to be 'the Magna Carta of presbytery',[20] was by no means so golden from the Melvillian viewpoint, in that it reserved for the King certain powers over the General Assembly, which, though apparently slight in themselves, proved in James's adroit hands to be eminently exploitable.

While the Assembly was to meet yearly, the King retained the power of deciding where it should meet. Melvill's stronghold was in St Andrews, and he could also be confident of finding in Edinburgh an Assembly solidly packed with his own supporters. But if the King chose to summon the Assembly to meet in Perth, Montrose or Aberdeen, then it was easier of access to ministers from the northern areas, where Melvill's ideology commanded less support. James exploited to the full his power of summoning the Assembly to meet where he desired, and he also employed his prerogative of deciding the date of its meeting in accordance with the dictates of his own policy.

On 17 December 1596 a riot occurred in Edinburgh, stimulated by an inflammatory sermon against the King. James turned this incident to good use by briefly imprisoning the ministers of Edinburgh and by levying a fine of twenty thousand marks on the city, as a punishment for disorder. He used the riot as an excuse for insisting that no ministers should be appointed in Edinburgh, or other leading towns, without his consent.

The General Assembly of 1597 was meek enough to appoint a commission to advise the King on ecclesiastical affairs, a situation very different from the dictatorially theocratic position which Melvill had aspired to assume. Predictably, the commission proved to be more amenable to the King's influence than he to that of the commission. By the end of the year the commission was eating out of the King's hand; it recommended what he fervently desired, the representation of the Kirk in Parliament. Such representation appeared desirable to the Kirk since the enactments of the General Assembly did not possess the force of law; therefore, parliamentary representation could secure beneficial legislation for the Kirk in a more dignified manner than that of ministers gaining the attention of Parliament by 'standing at the door giving in papers'.[21]

The clerical estate in Parliament had once consisted of the bishops and other great prelates, but since the Reformation it had come to consist of the commendators – laymen of noble families who had acquired ecclesiastical titles, and it had therefore become coterminous with the estate of the nobility. (In fact, in many instances the two estates merged, for certain 'commendams' were converted into temporal lordships, whose holders were referred to by the curious description of 'Lords of Erection').

James was able in 1597 to win the Kirk's approval that the original character of the clerical estate would be restored by his appointing ministers to vacant bishoprics, and that those appointees should sit in Parliament.

Looking back on this confidence trick, Calderwood reflected that the gradual rehabilitation of the episcopacy was 'nothing better than that which the Grecians used for the overthrow of the ancient city and town of Troy: busking up a brave horse and ... persuading them ... to receive that in their honour and welfare which served for their utter wreck and destruction'. He recalled that an old minister had said prophetically: 'Busk, busk, busk him as bonnily as ye can, and bring him in as fairly as ye will, we see him well enough: we see the horns of his mitre.'[22]

The first three 'parliamentary bishops', those of Ross, Aberdeen and Caithness, took their seats in 1600. James worked patiently, for while the Kirk had gained a voice in Parliament, the parliamentary bishops did not gain authority within the Kirk, where their status remained that of ministers.

But gradually the rebuilding of the stature of the Scottish episcopacy continued, the later stages after James had inherited the throne of England. In July 1606 the Scottish Parliament passed an 'Act for the restitution of the estate of bishops', which nullified the 'Act of Annexation' of 1587. While it improved the temporal condition of the bishops, the new act did nothing to raise their status within the structure of the Kirk. This further step James achieved by considerable chicanery, in December 1606, by securing the agreement of a carefully nominated assembly of ministers that the bishops should become 'constant [i.e. permanent] Moderators' of presbyteries and synods. By these means James achieved 'the extinction of ultra-Protestantism as a political danger',[23] though only for the term of his own lifetime. The later Stuart monarchs were all obliged to struggle with a resurgent power which James VI had most skilfully subjugated.

Before the end of his reign in Scotland, James had 'subjugated the proud' within his kingdom with no weapon except that of his own adroitness. Probably no ruler's ambition to extend his power or to exercise it in the way that he wishes is ever fully achieved; but by the end of the 1590s James felt sufficiently satisfied with his progress to write a handbook on the art of ruling for the future benefit of his young son, Prince Henry. He called it *Basilikon Doron – The Kingly Gift.*

CHAPTER NINE

The King's Books

... it only rests to pray thee (charitable reader) to interpret favourably this birth of mine, according to the integrity of the author and not looking for perfection in the work itself. ...

> James VI 'To the Reader', second preface to *Basilikon Doron*, 1599

To JAMES VI his kingship was the central fact of his life: the obedience which was owed to it, and the obligations which it imposed on him, were his deepest concerns.

During the later years of his reign in Scotland he wrote two books about kingship, a short tract entitled *The Trew Law of Free Monarchies*, which was published anonymously in 1598, and the aforementioned *Basilikon Doron*, which was intended to distil the essence of his experience as a ruler. The first was concerned chiefly with the theory which governed the institution of monarchy according to James's views; the second, though it had plenty to say about the theory, was principally concerned with the practice of monarchical government.

Though *The Trew Law of Free Monarchies* was published anonymously, its authorship could scarcely be in doubt; from the beginning it had an assured regality of tone, underlying the direct and informal style which characterized its author:

Accept, I pray you (my dear countrymen) [it began], as thankfully this pamphlet that I offer unto you, as lovingly as it is written for your weal [well-being]. . . . The profit I would wish you to make of it, is . . . so to frame all your actions according to these grounds, as may confirm you in the course of honest and obedient subjects to your King in all times coming. . . . So shall ye, by reaping profit unto yourselves, turn my pain into pleasure. But lest the whole pamphlet run out at the gaping mouth of this preface if it were any more enlarged, I end with committing you to God, and me to your charitable censures.[1]

James went on to inform his subjects: 'Kings are called gods by the prophetical King David, because they sit upon God his throne in the earth, and have the [ac]count of their administration to give unto Him.'[2] James elaborated this statement with examples from the Old Testament, stressing that passive obedience was the duty of subjects even of tyrannical kings. He then applied his argument to Scotland:

> ...as our chronicles bear witness, this Isle, and especially our part of it, being scantily inhabited ... there comes our first King Fergus, with a great number with him, out of Ireland ... and making himself master of the country, by his own friendship and force ... made himself King and Lord. ...[3]
>
> The Kings therefore in Scotland were before any estates or ranks of men within the same, before any Parliaments were holden, or laws made. ... And so it follows of necessity, that the Kings were the authors and makers of the laws, and not the laws of the Kings. ...
>
> ... A good King will frame all his actions to be according to the law; yet he is not bound thereto but of his good will, and for good example-giving to his subjects: for as in the law of abstaining from eating flesh in the Lenton [season of Lent], the King will, for example's sake, make his own house to observe the law; yet no man will think he needs to take a licence to eat flesh. ...[4]

James concluded his tract with the prayer and the hope

> that ye (my dear countrymen and charitable readers) may press by all means to procure the prosperity and welfare of your King; that as he must on the one part think of all his earthly felicity and happiness grounded upon your weal, caring more for himself for your sake than for his own, thinking himself only ordained for your weal; such holy and happy emulation may arise betwixt him and you, as his care for your quietness, and your care for his honour and preservation, may in your actions daily strive together, that the [inhabitants of the] land may think themselves blessed with such a King, and the King may think himself most happy in ruling over so loving and obedient subjects.[5]

It is deeply interesting to compare this final paragraph of *The Trew Law of Free Monarchies* with Buchanan's thumbnail sketch of his ideal king, written in verse to Thomas Randolph;[6] while James had repudiated Buchanan's contractual theory, he had retained the implicit foundation of the responsible nature of monarchy.

When he came to write *Basilikon Doron*, which was first published in an almost furtively limited edition of seven copies, James began by setting out his theory of kingship in one of the best of his sonnets, of which it had been truly observed that he was 'most nearly inspired'[7] by the theory which he held most dear:

> God gives not Kings the stile of Gods in vaine,
> For on his throne his Scepter doe they swey:
> And as their subjects ought them to obey,
> So Kings should feare and serve their God againe:
> If then ye would enjoy a happie raigne,
> Observe the Statutes of your heavenly King,
> And from his Law, make all your Lawes to spring:
> Since his Lieutenant here ye should remaine
> Reward the just, be stedfast, true and plaine,
> Represse the proud, maintayning aye the right,
> Walk alwayes so, as ever in his sight,
> Who guardes the godly, plaguing the prophane:
> And so ye shall in Princely vertues shine,
> Resembling right your mightie King Divine.[8]

In the prefatory address 'To Henry my dearest son and natural successor', James wrote:

I have ... divided this treatise in three parts. The first teacheth you your duty towards God as a Christian: the next, your duty in your office as a King: and the third informeth you how to behave yourself in indifferent things. . . . Receive and welcome this book ... keep it ever with you, as carefully as Alexander did the *Iliads* of Homer. . . . I take the great God to record, that this book shall one day be a witness betwixt me and you. . . . For I protest before that great God, I had rather not be a father, and childless, than be a father of wicked children. But hoping ... that God who in his great blessing sent you unto me, shall in the same blessing ... work effectually into you, the fruits of that blessing, which here from my heart I bestow up you.

Your loving father, I.R.[9]

In this address there was a curiously close echo of Buchanan's dedication of his verse drama *Baptistes* to the young James VI, in which Buchanan had written: 'I wish my book to be a standing witness with posterity that not with your teachers but yourself rested the fault, if impelled by evil counsellors, or your own undue desire for power, you should ever depart from the lessons you have received.'[10] Buchanan, if he had lived so long, might have permitted himself a dour smile at the thought of the pupil whom he seems to have imagined as a future tyrant, addressing his own son in similarly minatory and self-exculpating words.

In the first part of *Basilikon Doron*, concerning 'A King's Christian Duty Towards God', James wrote: '... First of all things learn to know and love that God, whom-to ye have a double obligation; first, for that he made you a man; and next, for that he made you a little god to sit on his throne, and rule over other men.'[11]

In the second part of the book he stressed the responsibility which this exalted concept of kingship imposed: 'A good king thinketh his highest honour to consist in the due discharge of his calling ... to procure and maintain the welfare and peace of his people; and as their natural father and kindly master, thinketh his greatest contentment standeth in their prosperity, and his greatest surety in having their hearts ... where by the contrary, an usurping tyrant ... thinketh never himself sure, but by ... building his surety upon his people's misery. . . .'[12]

Some of James's comments on his own kingdom are well known but, nonetheless, too important to be omitted. His remarks on the Scottish Reformation are extremely illuminating:

... The reformation of religion in Scotland, being extraordinarily wrought by God, wherein many things were inordinately done by a popular tumult and rebellion, of such as blindly were doing the work of God ... as well appeared by the destruction of our policy, and not proceeding from the Prince's order, as it did in our neighbour country of England, as likewise in Denmark, and sundry parts of Germany; some fiery-spirited men of the ministry got such a guiding of the people at that time of confusion, as finding the gust [taste] of government sweet, they begouth [began] to fantasy to themselves a democratic form of government ... and after usurping the liberty of the time in my long minority, settled themselves so fast upon that imagined democracy as they fed themselves with the hope to become *Tribuni plebis*: and so in a popular government by leading the people by the nose, to bear the sway of all the rule.[13]

James advised his son, with a certain dry humour, not to tolerate the pretensions of these 'fanatic spirits ... except ye would keep them for trying your patience, as Socrates did an evil wife'[14] – the proverbial shrew and scold Xanthippe.

James's observations on the Scottish nobility were not without humour either: 'The natural sickness that I have perceived this estate subject to in my time,' he wrote, 'hath been a feckless arrogant conceit of their own greatness and power ... [they] bang it out bravely, he and all his kin, against him and all his. ...' But not too much weight need be attached to these famous words, for James also urged his son to 'consider that virtue followeth oftest noble blood ... honour them therefore that are obedient to the law among them, as peers and fathers of your land: the more frequently that your Court can be garnished with them, think it the more your honour, acquainting and employing them in all your greatest affairs.'[15]

James did not hesitate to make some trenchant and humorous comments about other classes of Scottish society. Of the merchants, he wrote: 'They transport from us things necessary, bringing back sometimes unnecessary things, and at other times nothing at all,'[16] and of the craftsmen: '[They] think we should be content with their work, how bad and dear soever it be: and if they in anything be controlled, up goeth the Blue Blanket*.'[17]

The King recommended his son to gain his subjects' obedience in the first place by the severity of his justice and thereafter to win their hearts to a 'loving and willing obedience' by tempering justice with mercy. But, he added, there were certain crimes which a king was 'bound in conscience never to forgive':[18] witchcraft, wilful murder, incest, sodomy, poisoning and false coin. Few of James's biographers have failed to express surprise that, considering his own homosexual inclinations, he classified sodomy as unforgiveable. James, however, had a very precise mind. Probably he accepted the biblical prohibition of sodomy and regarded other homosexual acts as pardonable forms of physical pleasure. Furthermore, at this period of his life he was without a serious attachment to a male favourite, which would have enabled him to condemn sodomy in a spirit of detachment.

Basilikon Doron was written during the most intimate period of King James's married life: his children were being begotten

---

*The Blue Blanket was the banner of the Craft Guilds of Edinburgh, which was habitually carried on protest marches.

with regularity, and there was no foreshadowing of the gradual attenuation of his relationship with Anne of Denmark. His remarks concerning marriage were characteristic of a man of the sixteenth century: '. . . For your behaviour to your wife . . . treat her as your own flesh, command her as her lord, cherish her as your helper, rule her as your pupil, and please her in all things reasonable.'[19] All the same, he revealed his experience of domestic quarrels: '. . . Be never angry both at once, but when ye see her in a passion ye should with reason danton [subdue] yours: for when both ye are settled, ye are meeter to judge of her errors; and when she is come to herself, she may be best made to apprehend her offence. . . .'[20] Apparently it did not cross James's mind that on some occasions his wife might not be in the wrong! Yet, however much Anne might exasperate her husband, he never forgot that respect was due to her as his Queen; and therefore he admonished Henry, '. . . If it fall out that my wife shall out-live me, as ever ye think to purchase my blessing, honour your mother.'[21]

Perhaps the most surprising, because the least familiar, passages of *Basilikon Doron* concern warfare. The image of James as a pacific king and an uncourageous man is so firmly established that the fact that his hand 'in an extremity could reach for a sword'[22] is too easily forgotten. Yet when he wrote *Basilikon Doron*, his own expeditions against Huntly belonged to the recent past, and his advice on making war was not that of a man whose theories derived only from the theories of others. His remarks were conventional but sound: 'Choose old experimented [experienced] captains and young able soldiers. Be extremely strait and severe in martial discipline, as well for keeping of order, which is as requisite as hardiness in the wars, and punishing of sloth, which at a time put the whole army in hazard.'[23] He went on to praise the renowned discipline of the Spaniards: the reference was to Parma's infantry, not to the hapless navy which had been broken on the rocks of his own kingdom.

The ensuing passage has something more personal than theoretical about it: 'Be in your own person "walkrife" [wakeful], diligent and painful [painstaking]; using the advice of such as are skilful in the craft, as ye must do in all other. Be homely with your soldiers as your companions, for winning their hearts;

and extremely liberal, for then is no time of sparing.'[24] James, in the earlier part of his life, was not devoid of the common touch, and throughout his lifetime he was 'extremely liberal', to a fault.

Later in his book, in writing of suitable reading matter for the Prince, James urged him to study Caesar's *Commentaries*: 'For I have ever been of that opinion, that of all . . . great captains that ever were, he hath farthest excelled, both in his practice and in his precepts in martial affairs.'[25] With this judgment, both then and later, many military experts would have agreed.

The third part of *Basilikon Doron* was entitled 'Of a King's Behaviour in Indifferent Things', by which James meant matters other than religion, government or morality.

He was concerned with the importance of a king's public image: 'It is a true old saying, that a king is as one set on a stage, whose smallest actions and gestures, all the people gazeingly do behold. . . . Be careful, then, my son, so to frame all your indifferent actions and behaviour, as they may serve for the furtherance and forthsetting of your inward, virtuous disposition.'[26]

Though James appreciated the elegant manners of men who had resided at the Court of France, he evidently did not consider it desirable or appropriate for the heir to the Scottish throne to emulate them. The customs of his own Court were relatively simple, and it seems that he felt they should remain so.

. . . As kings use oft to eat publicly, it is meet and honourable that ye also do so. Let your table be honourably served; but serve your appetite with few dishes . . . which both is wholesomest, and freest from the vice of delicacy, which is a degree of gluttony. And use most to eat of reasonably gross and common meats, as well for making your body strong and durable for travel at all occasions, either in peace or in war, as that ye may be the heartlier [more heartily] received by your mean subjects in their houses, when their cheer may suffice you. . . .[27]

A King ought not to forget himself, even in private: 'Let not your chamber be throng and common in the time of your rest, as well for comeliness as for eschewing of carrying reports out of the same . . . for a king will have need to use secrecy in many things; but yet behave yourself so in your greatest secrets, as ye need not be ashamed, suppose they were all proclaimed at the Mercat Cross.'[28]

Recommendations concerning dress and conversational style followed:

... In your clothes keep a proportion, as well with the seasons of the year, as of your age: in the fashions of them being careless, using them according to the common form of the time, sometimes richlier, sometimes meanlier clothed, as occasion serveth. ...

Be not over-sparing in your courtesies, for that will be imputed to incivility and arrogance ... look gravely and with a majesty when you sit in judgment, or give audience to ambassadors; homely, when ye are in private with your own servants; merrily, when ye are at any passtime or merry discourse. ...[29]

Towards the end of his book James recommended suitable recreations to Prince Henry:

... The exercises that I would have you use (although but moderately, not making a craft of them) are running, leaping, wrestling, fencing, dancing and playing at the catch or tennis, archery, palle maillé, and suchlike other fair and pleasant field-games. And the honourablest and most commendable games that ye can use, are on horseback: for it becometh a prince, best of any man, to be a fair and good horseman.[30]

James concluded by urging upon his son the wisdom of

being content to let other excel in other things, let it be your chiefest earthy glory, to excel in your own craft ...

> *Tu regere imperio populos, Romane, memento*
> *(Hae tibi erunt artes) pacisque imponere morem,*
> *Parcere subiectis, et debellare superbos.*[31]
> [Remember, Roman, these be thy arts, to rule over
> the nations and impose the laws of peace, to spare
> the conquered, and to subjugate the proud.]

It was fitting that the last words of *Basilikon Doron* should be the Virgilian line which James had chosen as a motto upon his coinage.

A modern Scottish historian, Jennifer M. Brown, has shrewdly observed that, '... When writing about the practical business of running his kingdom, James ... was indeed saying exactly what his predecessors would have done had they written books on the subject.'[32] In other words, he was recommending no revolutionary courses to his son, and, within the context of the Scottish past and of contemporary conditions, he was offering him an excellent *vade mecum*. An English king's experience and advice would have been different, and for that reason – although James made references to Henry's hypothetical future as a king of England – *Basilikon Doron* should always be read with the Scottish setting of its composition in the reader's mind.

In 1601 the English diplomat and poet Sir Henry Wotton visited the Court of Scotland. He wrote a description of the King and Court which is vivid in itself and which is made all the more illuminating by some acquaintance with *Basilikon Doron*.

This King [Wotton wrote] though born in 1566, does not appear to be more than twenty-eight years old. He is of medium stature, and of robust constitution; his shoulders are broad but the rest of his person from the shoulders downward is rather slender. In his eyes and in his outward appearance there is a natural kindliness bordering on modesty. He is fond of literary discourse, especially of theology, and is a great lover of witty conceits. His speech is learned and even eloquent. In imitation of his grandfather, James v, he wears his hair cut short. About food and clothing he is quite indifferent. He is patient in the work of government, makes no decision without obtaining good counsel and is said to be one of the most secret princes of the world. On occasion he has shown bitter hatred, especially against the Earl of Gowrie,[33] and he reduced to obedience the ferocious spirit of Bothwell whom he banished. Yet by his lavish creations of marquises, earls and barons, he does not appear jealous of the great lords. Such creations, far more numerous than in England, he uses to bind his followers to him since he lacks the means to reward them in other ways. An admirable quality is his chastity which he has preserved without blemish, unlike to his predecessors who disturbed the kingdom by leaving many bastards.

His Court is governed more in the French than in the English fashion. Anyone may enter the King's presence while he is at dinner, and as he eats he converses with those about him. The domestics who wait upon him wear caps on their heads. Dinner finished, he remains at table for a time before he retires, listening to banter and to merry jests in which he takes great delight. With his domestics and with the gentlemen of his chamber he is extremely familiar, but with the great lords he is grave. He has no guard, either because he cannot afford one or because he relies upon the love of his people which he calls the true guardian of princes. Though the kingdom is small, his Court is composed of a large number of gentlemen, who, either from curiosity, or from zeal to protect their Prince, accost newcomers at once and ask them what they want.[34]

The historian previously quoted observes that this agreeable description 'shows why James could regard himself as a successful king'.[35] In it the author of *Basilikon Doron* and the small world of his Court are brought to life, and the abiding impression is that the reality and the King's aspirations, as revealed in his book, were not profoundly divergent.

F

CHAPTER TEN

'One of the Most Secret Princes of the World'

'... A king will have need to use secrecy in many things. ...'

James VI, *Basilikon Doron*, 1599

KING JAMES VI did not create the impression that he was a secretive man. As a talker he was fluent to the point of garrulity. His proclamation to his subjects on the occasion of his setting sail to bring home his bride was remarkably frank. Before 1600 he had published seven books: *The Essayes of a Prentise in the Divine Art of Poesie* (1584); *Ane Fruitfull Meditatioun* – on the seventh, eighth, ninth and tenth verses of Chapter xx of Revelation – (1588); *Ane Meditatioun upon the First Buke of the Chronicles of Kings* (1589); *His Majesties Poeticall Exercises* (1591); *Daemonologie* (1597); *The Trew Law of Free Monarchies* (1598); and *Basilikon Doron* (1599). These writings involved a considerable amount of self-revelation. Though *The Trew Law of Free Monarchies* was published anonymously, and *Basilikon Doron* in a very limited edition, neither the authorship of the one nor the content of the other remained a closely guarded secret. Indeed, the ministers of the Kirk very naturally took exception to James's stringent remarks on their political aspirations, and when a second edition of *Basilikon Doron* was issued at the time of James's accession to the English throne, these and other controversial passages had been omitted. The second edition of *Basilikon Doron* became a best-seller, enthusiastically read by James's new subjects, who found in his high ideals of kingly behaviour a hopeful augury for the new reign.

Yet, in the meantime, his reputation as 'one of the most secret princes of the world' remained intact, and this was justified; what he revealed, he chose to reveal, and what he wished to keep secret, he protected from discovery with consummate success.

It is evident from verbal descriptions that James possessed a façade of bonhomie; he delighted in merry jests, as Sir Henry Wotton recalled. But this aspect of his character is not revealed in his portraits. Painted likenesses, which required hours of stillness from the sitter, were unlikely to capture any of his transitory moods. Certainly no genius capable of such an achievement painted King James vi; but a portrait of him which bears the date 1595 captures the 'secrecy' imputed to him by Wotton. The brooding immobility of the face, the suspicious watchfulness of the heavy-lidded eyes, hint at a mind full of concealed and private thoughts. If such a man laughed and talked freely, the laughter was superficial, the freedom more apparent than real.

How adept King James was at concealment is well illustrated by the extraordinary episode of 'the Gowrie Plot' of 1600, which has retained its mystery to the present day.

The facts of the story survive only from the King's version of it; for of the principal persons involved, only he lived to tell the tale.

In brief, in the early morning of 5 August 1600, the King rode out of Falkland Palace to hunt. Outside the palace he was met by Alexander, Master of Ruthven, the younger brother of the second Earl of Gowrie, who had a strange story to tell him. (Alexander was a member of the Queen's household, but he was not then in attendance on her, for he had ridden to Falkland from his brother's residence of Gowrie House in Perth.)

He told the King that the previous night he had found a man about to bury a pot of gold coins, in the fields outside Perth. The inference was that the King might claim the treasure. Had it been found buried, it would indeed have been forfeit to the Crown as treasure trove; Alexander argued that the man's intention to bury it placed it in this category. James was impatient to enjoy his hunting, and he needed time to think the matter over. He ordered Alexander Ruthven to follow the hunt.

After the kill, the King, accompanied by Ludovic, Duke of Lennox, the Earl of Mar and other courtiers, rode to Perth. On their arrival at Gowrie House it became clear that they were not expected. They were kept waiting while a moorfowl, a shoulder of mutton and a chicken were cooked. The King was served apart from the others, to show him honour.

After he had dined, he sent the Earl of Gowrie to drink his health with the courtiers and accompanied Alexander Ruthven upstairs, to interview the man who had been found with the treasure. The King said afterwards that Alexander had locked several doors behind them.

When the courtiers had finished their meal, they were led out into the gardens of Gowrie House, where they ate cherries while they waited for the King to return. But they did not see him descending in a dignified manner with the Master of Ruthven; instead they glimpsed him at a turret window and heard him shout, 'I am murdered! Treason! My Lord Mar, help! help!' They rushed into the house, not following the same route as the King and Alexander but running up the turnpike stair of the tower in which the King had been seen. They were headed by a youth named John Ramsay, who found the King struggling with Alexander Ruthven. The King shouted, 'Fy, strike him high because he has a chain doublet upon him!' Ramsay stabbed Alexander in the neck, and he fell down the stair, pushed and slashed by others and dying with the words, 'Alas, I had no wyte [blame] of it!'

The Earl of Gowrie, who in the meantime had left the courtiers and sent to tell them that the King had departed without them, at the sounds of combat ran up the turnpike stair to be despatched by Ramsay in his turn. James was left to explain to his rescuers what had happened.

He told a story which has never commanded entire belief. He said that there had been no pot of gold. The tower chamber had contained a man in armour, who had been there apparently to aid Alexander Ruthven to overpower the King, though in the event he had taken no action. Alexander had threatened James with death, in revenge for the execution of his father, the first Earl of Gowrie, in 1585. James had first reasoned with Alexander and then struggled with him sufficiently successfully to reach the window and call for help. The ensuing rescue had resulted in the death of both the Ruthvens.

The young Earl and his brother had enjoyed great popularity in Perth, and the violent events which led to their deaths stirred up the populace to a frenzy of anger against the King. A crowd gathered under the windows of Gowrie House, shouting, 'Come down, thou son of Seigneur Davie!' – a humiliating reminder of the old scandal concerning Mary, Queen of Scots and David Riccio.

This echo of the past would have served to awaken James's old suspicions of the Ruthvens, which he had so far forgotten as to accompany Alexander to Perth without anxiety. With the young Ruthvens dead at his feet, and the populace yelling its insults under the window, he would have remembered the old story of how Patrick, Lord Ruthven, had endangered his life while he was still in the womb, on the night of Riccio's murder. He would have remembered that Patrick's son, the first Earl of Gowrie, had been the ringleader of the Raid of Ruthven, which had unpardonably offended his fledgling sovereignty and robbed him of Esmé Stuart. Unless he had some private knowledge of the explanation of the events of that day, James would have had little difficulty in believing that Alexander Ruthven had decoyed him to Perth with the intention of doing him to death. (Spurious evidence was later produced of the Ruthvens' intention of handing him over to the Queen of England, though whether Elizabeth would have wished to hold captive the most obvious inheritor of her kingdom may be doubted.)

Many attempts, ingenious, scholarly and merely specious, have been made to explain the events of 5 August 1600.[1] None has been wholly satisfactory, because to find a perfect solution is as impossible as to complete a crossword puzzle with an incomplete set of clues. It has been suggested that the Ruthvens' death is explained by the fact that the Crown owed the family £80,000 from the time when the first Earl of Gowrie had held office as Treasurer and had borne a deficit of that sum.[2] But it is unlikely that James would have resorted to murder, and endangered his own life in achieving his end, merely to rid himself of creditors. When he desired a man's death, he secured it by trial and execution; from the death of Morton in 1581 to that of Raleigh in 1618 he showed a preference for the forms of legality.

Another flimsy explanation has been sought in the faint whispers of scandal which linked the names of Alexander Ruthven and Anne of Denmark, but to that suggestion the same objection applies. Yet another hypothesis has been that James committed an indecent assault on Alexander Ruthven and invented the odd account of what happened in the tower room to conceal the shameful cause of the tragedy which followed;

but this is wholly out of character with all that is known of James's relations with any of his favourites.

To the present author it appears perfectly feasible that the Ruthven brothers plotted to avenge the death of their father and used the story of the pot of gold to decoy the King to Perth. Upon this hypothesis, the Earl of Gowrie had no meal prepared because he did not expect the King to bring his hunting party. The arrival of the attendant courtiers meant that the Ruthvens, prevented from merely seizing and murdering the King, were obliged to arrange impromptu entertainment. Alexander endeavoured to achieve the vengeance unaided (or with one accomplice who failed to act), while the Earl tried to get rid of the courtiers by telling them that the King had left alone. When Alexander met unexpected difficulties and the Earl's ruse failed, the *dénouement* was inevitable.

The simplest explanation may be the nearest to the truth, and the official version the product of guesswork rather than of disingenuousness; but if the official story of the 'Gowrie Plot' concealed any secret which was discreditable to the King, that secret remained concealed.

More interesting perhaps than fruitless speculation is the way in which James managed to turn the aftermath of a dubious episode to his advantage. Quick to recognize the power of propaganda, James published his own version of the affair, which was entitled *Gowries Conspiracy: A Discourse of the Unnaturall and vyle Conspiracie, attempted against the Kings Majesties Person, at Sanct-Iohnstoun* [Perth], *upon Twysday the Fifth of August, 1600. Edinburgh, printed 1600, cum Privilegio Regis*. James followed this publication by commanding the ministers of Edinburgh to offer public thanksgiving for his deliverance from a regicidal conspiracy. Five of the ministers refused to offer thanks in the words which the King required; four eventually agreed to do so, the exception being Robert Bruce, who was banished to the north of Scotland.[3]

The ministers' reluctance was caused both by scepticism of the official story and by unwillingness to think ill of the Ruthvens, who had been constant supporters of the Kirk. James, however, forced public acceptance of the official version and in so doing demonstrated his authority over the ministry. For the rest of his life thanks were given for his deliverance every

5th of August. John Ramsay, the slayer of both the Ruthven brothers, was not only knighted but, after James's accession to the English throne, created Earl of Holderness; on every anniversary of the occasion an appropriate sermon was preached, and any favour which the Earl of Holderness chose to request was granted.

'One of the most secret princes of the world' knew how to keep a secret, if such an exercise were required, or how to reward a service if such a reward had been deserved.

Whatever the exigencies imposed by the events of 5 August 1600, the most sustained exercise in concealment ever achieved by James vi was that which accompanied his efforts to ensure that he would succeed to the English throne on the death of Elizabeth i.

From the viewpoint of posterity, his succession appears to have been inevitable; but at the time it seemed by no means so certain. To Elizabeth herself, despite her silence, to her ministers and to the majority of the English people, James was the most obviously desirable heir. He was an experienced ruler, whose accession would unite two kingdoms which had a long history of enmity and thereby bring them peace. But such advantages were mere ornaments to the firm structure of his hereditary claim, which was indubitably the best, though there were others, which for various reasons could be canvassed.

Lady Arbella Stuart, as previously mentioned, had a claim inferior to James's own in the same line, though she enjoyed the advantage of having been born in England, where theoretically James, as an 'alien', could not inherit so much as a farm.

Then, if the Will of Henry viii were taken into consideration, the Stuart line was excluded; the descendants of Henry's sister Margaret being eliminated in favour of those of his younger sister Mary, who had been married first to Louis xii of France, by whom she had no issue, and then to Charles Brandon, Duke of Suffolk. At the end of the sixteenth century the representatives of the Suffolk line were Edward Seymour, Lord Beauchamp, and Ferdinando Stanley, Lord Derby (see genealogical table at back).

These claimants were not seriously considered by Elizabeth's chief minister, Sir Robert Cecil, who knew as her reign drew to its end that upon him would devolve the responsibility of arranging a peaceful succession; but the mere existence of an assortment of claimants of English birth, who might possibly command a following, was sufficient to agitate the mind of James.

The most important outsider, who had some support in Catholic Europe and among English Catholic exiles, was Philip II's daughter, the Infanta Isabella Clara Eugenia, whose claim as a descendant of Edward III had been put forward as a pretext for the sailing of the Spanish Armada.

Strangely enough, Elizabeth's last favourite, Robert Devereux, Earl of Essex, was also tenuously descended from Edward III, but the measure of how unseriously this ancestry was regarded is that James conducted a cautious intrigue with Essex, while the latter was abusing his sovereign's confidence in Ireland, and certainly did not regard him as a competitor for the English throne. Essex undoubtedly intended to profit from King James's favour after the ageing Queen's death.[4]

Essex has often been compared with Francis, Earl of Bothwell, and certainly, in their instability and self-dramatization, the two men resembled each other. Essex was a flamboyantly handsome man and a vainglorious and impetuous soldier. But apart from his brilliant if meretricious personal qualities, he had an influential claim to Elizabeth's favour in being the stepson of the dead Earl of Leicester, who perhaps had been the only man that Elizabeth had ever loved.[5]

The Queen's ill-judged favour gave Essex supreme command of her army in Ireland. The result was a mismanaged campaign against the rebellious Earl of Tyrone, a dishonourable and unauthorized peace between the two Earls and the unbidden return of Essex to England. Early one morning in September 1600 he forced an entry into the Queen's bedchamber, ostensibly to justify his conduct, possibly with the thought of forcing her to maintain him in favour (as Bothwell had hoped, in similar circumstances, to coerce James). The arrest of Essex inevitably followed, but unlike the situation which had existed between Bothwell and James, that between Essex and Elizabeth was complicated by the Queen's affection. Essex remained under house arrest while Elizabeth awaited his abject suing for her favour; the proud Earl, who had no intention of abasing himself, fretted with inaction and brooded on his wrongs.

On Christmas Day 1600 he wrote to James, referring to Sir Robert Cecil and the latter's supporters: 'Now doth not only their corrupting of my servants, stealing of my papers, subborning of false witnesses, procuring of many forged letters in my name, and other such like practises against me appear; but their ... juggling with our enemies, their practice for the Infanta of Spain, and their devilish plots with your Majesty's own subjects against your person and life. ...'[6]

Essex thus succeeded in convincing James that Cecil (to whom James himself referred as 'Mr Secretary, who is King there in effect') favoured the Infanta's claim and might have had a hand in encouraging the 'Gowrie Plot'.

Early in February 1601 Essex rebelled and, confident of his popularity, endeavoured to raise the city of London, ostensibly to overthrow the Cecilian régime but also with the intention of forcing the Queen to appoint him Lord Protector of England. The rebellion was the supreme folly of Essex's career, and retribution was swift: on 8 February Essex rebelled, and on the 25th he was executed.

In the meantime an embassy had been dispatched from Scotland. It was headed by the Earl of Mar and Edward Bruce, Commendator of Kinloss, with a suite of forty attendants. King James was undoubtedly cognizant of Essex's intentions, for his embassy was expected by Essex, who hoped for his support.[7] But the embassy, which travelled slowly in bitter winter weather, arrived to find Essex already dead and an urbane Cecil desirous of established secret contact with the King of Scots.

At his trial Essex had been obliged to confess that his statements that Cecil favoured the Infanta's claim had been baseless, and therefore James was presently reassured that, where he had supposed there lurked a serpent of enmity, his ambassadors had encountered a dove of peace.

With the initial connivance of the Scottish ambassadors, a correspondence between James and Cecil was established, in which Cecil sought to reassure James of the certainty of his succession, and with the utmost discretion to advise and instruct him in preparation for it. His letters were written in such terms that, should they fall into Elizabeth's hands, she would find no treasonable matter in them. He referred to James's impending accession as 'that natural day . . . wherein your feast may be lawfully proclaimed (which I do wish may be long deferred) . . .', and went on: 'I do herein truly and religiously profess before God, that if I could accuse myself to have once imagined a thought which could amount to a grain of error towards my dear and precious sovereign . . . I should wish with all my heart, that all I have done, or shall do, might be converted to my own perdition.'[8]

He also encouraged James to trust Elizabeth's tacit goodwill towards him, and discreetly advised him not to indulge in any intrigues which might alter her attitude without improving his position: '. . . This I dare say for the present (and that upon good experience) that as long as we see our horizons clear from lively apparitions of anticipation, your Majesty may *dormire securus*.'[9]

Cecil took into his confidence Lord Henry Howard, to share with him the task of advising, encouraging, instructing and warning the future King of England. On behalf of them both Cecil wrote: 'We do neither presume to indent with you for future favours . . . because we think it not ingenious to recommend to Honour itself the things which Honour requireth, with which conclusion I humbly kiss your royal hands.'[10] They could scarcely have indented with James for future favours more directly, whatever the orientalism of the language.

Sir Robert Cecil was the younger son of Elizabeth I's great minister Lord Burghley. The elder son inherited the title; the younger, who had a greater measure of his father's statesmanship, inherited his political position. Sir Robert Cecil was a small man, five feet three inches in height, and hunchbacked; if he was not quite dwarfish, he had the misfortune to be a slightly grotesque figure of a man. He had long, delicate hands, a high white forehead and eyes of almost reptilian brilliance. He was a man who lacked the attributes to become the King's favourite and possessed the abilities to become a whole government in his own person.

It was fortunate for James VI that he was not to inherit those of Elizabeth's ministers who had been most closely connected with the execution of his mother: Lord Burghley and Sir Francis

Walsingham. Burghley's son perhaps deliberately turned to a member of a family which had been closely and tragically connected with Mary, Queen of Scots, when he sought the favour of Mary's son. Mary's last suitor, Thomas Howard, Duke of Norfolk, had been executed in 1572 for intriguing to marry her; Lord Henry was his younger brother, 'an elderly and penurious nobleman, who had never had success with Queen Elizabeth'.[11] He was the cleverest member of a family of stately English grandees, a group which Cecil judged would appeal to King James more than the coterie of bellicose malcontents which had followed the standard of Essex. Also to be excluded from James's future favour was that arrogant and scholarly warrior-poet Sir Walter Raleigh, who now appears to have been the quintessential Elizabethan hero, though his contemporaries detested him as 'a person who most religious men do hold Anathema'.[12]

The correspondence between Cecil, Lord Henry Howard and the King of Scots hid the identities of the participants behind numerical ciphers: they were 10, 3 and 30 respectively, a mathematical relationship which itself is probably significant.[13] Lord Henry Howard wrote letters which James described as 'Asiatic and endless volumes', in which he warned the King against Sir Walter Raleigh and, more circumlocutively, against the curiosity and possible interference of Anne of Denmark.

Queen Anne had become a convert to the Church of Rome, possibly under the influence of Henriette, Marchioness of Huntly, who was her close friend. Apparently the Marquis of Huntly introduced a Jesuit, Father Robert Abercrombie, to give her instruction.[14] To King James's English correspondents, Anne therefore represented a security risk; to James himself, it has always been said, her conversion was at least an irritant, at worst a political liability. But there were few liabilities which James could not turn to advantage. He may have despised his wife for her inability to make the right choice between what he saw as Romish superstitions and Calvinist truths; but that did not prevent his finding a use for her new Catholic affiliations which might assist him to approach the English throne by a back door, should the main portal be closed against him at the last.

In 1599 King James had written to Pope Clement VIII a letter which began with the address 'Beatissime Pater', and which the King concluded by signing himself the Pope's 'Obedientissimus Filius'. It was a letter unimportant in itself, a request that William Chisholm, the Scottish Bishop of Vaison in France, be appointed a Cardinal. The implication was that the King was seeking to advance a Scottish Catholic churchman, and his form of address was one appropriate to a Catholic monarch. After he had used this decoy to win Clement's favourable opinions, James could go no further without making embarrassing commitments. Accordingly, he brought his converted Queen into the correspondence. She wrote to the Pope and to Cardinal Borghese, announced her own conversion, declared that she wrote on behalf of James as well as of herself and used the royal plural with sufficient ambiguousness to give the Court of Rome hopes of James's conversion. The intended result of this sleight of hand was that the Pope allowed James's claim to the English throne to go unchallenged and did not support the claim of the Spanish Infanta.[15]

James also received cautious support from Henri IV of France who, though he had turned Catholic to win his throne, preferred the prospect of a friendly Protestant monarch on the English throne to that of an inimical, though Catholic, Spaniard. Less successful were James's attempts to win the support of other Catholic powers: the Venetian republic refused to enter an anti-Spanish alliance with him, and Ferdinand I, Grand Duke of Tuscany, while he conducted a friendly correspondence with James, refused to give one of his daughters in marriage to Prince Henry.[16]

In the long run, James's foreign diplomacy was far less influential in securing the English succession than was his correspondence with Sir Robert Cecil and Lord Henry Howard. From the moment of its inception, the event which would follow the death of Elizabeth was never again in doubt: in Cecil's words, 'Your ship shall be steered into the right harbour, without cross of wave or tide that shall be able to turn over a cockboat.'[17]

While James impatiently awaited the day on which he would come into his inheritance, he laboured assiduously at the task of ruling his native kingdom. Sir Henry Wotton, in 1601, described him as 'patient in the work of government', and probably he was never so patient in it as he was during the years after he had lost Maitland of Thirlestane and before he gained Sir Robert Cecil, both of whom were indefatigable in the exercise of delegated power.

Maitland died on 3 October 1595, and the King wrote a graceful tribute to him, in the form of a sonnet, which was carved on a marble memorial tablet above his tomb in Haddington Church:

> Thou passenger that spies with gazing eyes
> This trophie sad of death's triumphant dart,
> Consider when this outward tombe thou sees,
> How rare a man leaves here his earthly part:
> His wisdom and his uprightness of heart,
> His piety, his practice of our state,
> His quick engine,* so verst in every art,
> As equally not all were in debate†
> Thus justly hath his death brought forth of late
> An heavy grief in prince and subjects all
> That virtue love, and vice do bear at hate,
> Though vitious men rejoyces at his fall.
> So for himself most happy doth he die
> Though for his prince it most unhappy be.[18]

However, as he had matured, James had found an irksome didacticism in Maitland's relationship with him. Probably his sorrow at losing a good servant was tempered by a certain sense of liberation. He was reported to have remarked after Maitland's death that he would 'no more use chancellor or other great men in those his courses, but such as he might convict and were hangable'.[19]

The King may have spoken in jest, but, true to his words, he did not replace Maitland with a single omnicompetent, or even multi-competent, minister. Maitland's place was taken by a group of ministers, who, since they were eight in number, were nicknamed 'the Octavians'. They were James Elphinstone, Lord Balmerino, and Walter Stewart, Lord Blantyre; Sir David Carnegie of Colluthie and Sir John Skene of Curriehill; Thomas Hamilton, Lord Drumcairn (better known by the King's nick-

*intelligence
†So well-balanced that his talents did not contend with one another.

name for him, 'Tam o' the Cowgate', and later to become successively Earl of Melrose and Earl of Haddington); John Lindsay, Lord Menmuir; Sir Alexander Seton, later Earl of Dunfermline; and Sir Peter Young, who had enjoyed the King's favour ever since he had been his kindly young tutor.

The Octavians were originally appointed to put the King's finances in order; some of them had served the Queen and had made her more solvent than her husband. Archbishop Mathew observed that they were 'appointed almost by chance' and added that, 'They had been known to their master throughout his lifetime and . . . there were no feuds among them. . . .'[20] Perhaps the element of chance was more apparent than real; James would have appreciated a group without internecine enmities.

A somewhat amorphous opposition to the Octavians was provided by 'the Cubiculars', a group of courtiers who enjoyed the King's favour and in varying degrees his intimacy but who did not receive official appointments at the same time as the Octavians. The nicknames of these groups are unimportant except insofar as they illustrate the ethos of the Court and the development of political rivalries which did not have to be expressed in the form of deadly feuds.

The Octavians held office as a group of financial experts for only a few months, but thereafter individually they continued to hold office as ministers of the Crown. Because they were essentially professional Crown servants, it has often been assumed that the Octavians were of middle-class origins; in fact, they were members of lairdly and aristocratic families, and 'Tam o' the Cowgate', despite his proletarian-sounding nickname, was a kinsman of the royally-connected Hamiltons.

James's government was personal, and his relationships with his ministers were informal; at times one gains the impression that the results were remarkably haphazard. An undated letter survives, written by James, in obvious fury, to the Lord Justice Clerk, Curriehill:

I have been Friday, Saturday and this day waiting upon the direction of my affairs, and never man comes. Them of the Exchequer that were ordained to take the accounts, never one. The affairs of the household should have been ended this day, no man comes down. I sent for the advocate both Friday and Saturday –

never met no answer. . . . In short, no tryst or meeting is kept. What is spoken this night is forgot the morn. . . . [21]

Yet, despite such collective lapses, the result of James's labours during the later years of his reign in Scotland was beyond expectation. His abiding preoccupation was to bring his country law and order, which, from the death of James v in 1542 until approximately 1586, it had never known except in the form of the short-lived efforts of James v's widow Marie de Guise, of Mary, Queen of Scots, and of the Regents Moray and Morton, none of whom had succeeded in giving the kingdom more than brief respites from the convulsions of disorder.

After James vi had reached the age of twenty, his power had steadily increased, and the ensuing decade of hard work brought long-lasting benefits: in Professor Donaldson's words, 'From the riot in Edinburgh of 17 December 1596 to another riot in Edinburgh on 23 July 1637 there stretched forty years of unprecedented tranquillity.'[22]

This great achievement represented a triumph over daunting problems, of which perhaps the most basic and intractable was that of imposing peaceful habits upon an armed society. The swords and daggers which men habitually carried could turn any quarrel into a lethal affray; the increasing use of firearms during the sixteenth century made murder easy. Furthermore, the conventions of the 'deadly feud' or vendetta imposed on its participants the obligation of exacting a life for a life.

Against casual violence and barbarous custom, James strove to establish the usages of civilized behaviour. He executed the Lords Maxwell and Sanquhar for murder, in 1608 and 1612 respectively, and in 1615 he executed his cousin, Patrick Stewart, Earl of Orkney, after the latter had been imprisoned upon complaints of his tyrannous rule in his earldom, and armed rebellion on his behalf had been raised by his son.[23] But the problem of the administration of criminal justice throughout the kingdom was in fact much greater than that of making examples of a few high-ranking offenders. James had written in *Basilikon Doron* that the 'greatest hinderance to the execution of our laws' was the existence of 'heritable sheriffdoms and regalities, which being in the hands of great men, do rack the whole country'.[24] The words 'heritable sheriffdoms' are self-

explanatory; 'regalities' possessed 'a system of legal administration reproducing in miniature that of the kingdom; its courts
might have power to deal with all crimes except treason.'[25]
These courts limited the scope of royal justice and, because of
local vested interests, frequently failed to act impartially.

James admitted the existence of the problem and also recognized that there was no easy remedy. So far as the heritable
sheriffdoms were concerned, James could only recommend
'taking the sharper account of them [the sheriffs] in their offices
... and ever as they vaike [become vacant] for any offences
committed by them, dispone them never heritably again' (i.e. 'do
not grant them heritably again').[26] Following his own advice, in
1599 James summoned before the Council the sheriffs of Rox-
burgh, Berwickshire, Selkirk and Peebles, for 'sharper account'.
Though James had argued that the King was above the law, he
did not force his argument to its logical conclusion and use the
power which he claimed to abolish a system he disliked. He was
too wise to offend a multitude of local interests; his preference
was to work quietly towards the reduction of their powers.
More than one lifetime of patience was required, for heritable
jurisdictions remained part of the Scottish legal system until
1747.

King James, however, endeavoured to increase the scope and
efficiency of royal justice, by increasing the frequency of
'Justice Ayres,' itinerant courts of criminal justice which
travelled the country to deal with offences which were not
sufficiently serious to be brought before the Justice General in
Edinburgh. In 1609, after he had had the opportunity of observing the English system of Justices of the Peace, James attempted
to introduce it into Scotland[30]; but the existence of the heritable
jurisdictions prevented it from successfully taking root. Nonetheless, the fact that the country grew more peaceable is itself
indicative that James made both the royal courts and the local
jurisdictions function more efficiently than before.

There were certain problem areas, in which the imposition of
law and order was far more difficult than it was throughout the
country as a whole: these areas were the Highlands, the Isles
and the Borders.

Taken together, the Highlands and the Northern and Western
Isles lie beyond the wavering diagonal of the 'Highland Line'

which bisects Scotland from north-east to south-west. Long ago King Alexander III, who died in 1286, had come near to uniting all the subjects of the Crown of Scots, who then included English, Norman-French and Gaelic speakers, in a common loyalty which in time would have created a homogeneous nation. Unhappily, the Wars of Independence which followed Alexander's death provided an opportunity for a geographical dichotomy to assert itself, and, when Scotland emerged from the struggle for independence as a free nation, it had already become a divided nation, with two cultures, Gaelic-speaking in the Highlands and Isles, and Scots- (or Anglo-Scots) speaking in the Lowlands.

James I of Scotland had endeavoured to break down the division by holding his Court at Perth, which could have become a capital for both Highlands and Lowlands; but after his death in 1437 the political centre of Scotland gravitated to the un-compromisingly Lowland city of Edinburgh. The later Stewart Kings looked to France, the Low Countries and Scandinavia for their political alliances, and with England indulged in frequent enmity and occasional alliance. The political attention of Scotland was thus directed increasingly eastward and southward, and the north-west of the kingdom was left too much to its own devices.

The last Scottish King to have spoken Gaelic had been James IV, who had died on Flodden Field in 1513. His great-grandson, although he was a gifted linguist, did not trouble to learn Gaelic (nor had the European learning of George Buchanan taken cognizance of the need). In consequence James VI wrote of his Gaelic-speaking subjects in the following words: 'As for the Highlands, I shortly comprehend them all in two sorts of people: the one that dwelleth in our main land, that are barbarous for the most part, and yet mixed with some show of civility: the other, that dwelleth in the Isles, that are alluterly barbares [utterly barbarian] without any sort of show of civility.'[28]

With this view, James had no wish to bridge the gulf between the pastoral and heroic society of the Highlands and the agrarian and trading communities of the Lowlands; the latter, being more law-abiding, appeared to him to be unquestionably superior, and he desired to impose Lowland culture on the Highlands and Isles.

James's policy in controlling the turbulence of the High-landers followed that of his fifteenth- and early-sixteenth-century predecessors: in the north he relied on the Gordons to keep their neighbours in order, and in the Western Highlands the Campbells had a similar responsibility. This policy might have its own efficacy, but it made the Crown reliant on the loyalty of the families whose power was enhanced by the powers which the Crown delegated to them. In 1610 the near-destruction of the MacGregors by the Campbells brought about the solution of a problem of disorder at the cost of many lives and of the inception of unforgotten resentment.

A different policy was attempted for the taming of the Isles, where James hoped to implant Lowland culture by colonization. The experiment was a failure, for, of the colonists who were established in Lewis, 'far from influencing the Islesmen, those who stayed were absorbed into Gaelic society.'[29]

More instrumental in achieving the pacification of both the Highlands and the Isles was the application of the principal of the 'general bond', by which a chief accepted responsibility for the conduct of his clansmen. This was not a device invented by James VI, but it was employed during his reign with a new efficiency, and with rewarding results.

James's most effective deputy in the pacification of the Western Isles was Bishop Andrew Knox, who in 1609 induced an influential group of chiefs to pledge themselves to uphold 'the Statutes of Iona',[30] which among other provisions, forbade the carrying of firearms and required that heirs to substantial properties should receive their education in the Lowlands. After 1616 no man who could not read, write and speak English was permitted to inherit property in the Isles.[31] There was tragedy in the fact that peace and a mortal blow to the Gaelic language, with its rich tradition of poetry, came hand in hand. James VI, who rightly desired to give his subjects the blessings of peace, could not be blamed that his own education had not taught him to honour the achievements of Gaelic culture.

The role of Bishop Andrew Knox in the Western Isles was complemented by that of Bishop James Law in Orkney. He it was who broke the power of Earl Patrick Stewart and after the latter's execution became the King's 'Commissioner, Sheriff and justice' in the Northern Isles.[32] The activities of these two Bishops as deputies of the Crown in problem areas of Scotland adds extra point to James's dictum, 'No Bishop, no King.'

The stormy history of the Borders ended almost spontaneously with the accession of James to the throne of England. One of the last of the Border incidents which for centuries had furnished the material of heroic ballads, is one of the best remembered, though when it occurred it had already the character of an isolated event.

On a 'Day of Truce' in 1596, a party of Englishmen, riding homeward from a Border parley, laid hands on Willie Armstrong of Kinmont, a valiant Scottish ruffian who belonged in spirit to the violent past, carried him prisoner to Carlisle Castle and put him in the custody of Lord Scrope, the English Warden of the West March. And out of the apparently impregnable English stronghold, the Laird of Buccleugh daringly spirited 'Kinmont Willie' away, to the delight of the Scottish borderers and the perturbation of the English authorities. Lord Scrope gave chase, as Kinmont Willie, still loaded with chains, swam his horse across the Eden Water to safety :

> All sore astonish'd stood Lord Scroope.
>   He stood as still as rock of stane;
> He scarcely dared to trew his eyes,
>   When through the water they had gane.
>
> 'He is either himsell a devil frae hell,
>   Or else his mother a witch maun be;
> I wadna have ridden that wan water
>   For a' the gowd in Christentie. . .'

The dramatic exploit, which might have belonged to any decade of three centuries of strife, proved to be almost a postscript to the story of Border warfare. The uproar which followed it, the Anglo-Scottish governmental recriminations, died down, and 'King James's Peace' – the forty years' tranquillity which outlasted his lifetime by more than a decade – settled upon the Borders as upon the other areas of his realm.

The achievement of the last King of Scots who ruled a separate kingdom, before the destinies of Scotland and England were inextricably interwoven by the Union of Crowns, has been well summed up by a modern Scottish historian:

James VI was outstandingly successful in Scotland not ... because he solved all his Scottish problems but because he understood and acted on a policy of co-operation and practical common sense. He governed his country conscientiously and effectively, using traditional methods to do so, and using them successfully because he was a realist who knew very well both his powers and his limitations ... he was, in terms of Scottish politics, the last and greatest exponent of the old style of Scottish kingship.[33]

That style was, and had always been, personal. It had always depended on the monarch's ability to secure the support of powerful individuals, of influential groups or institutions and of disparate interests within the kingdom, for the Crown of Scots had never possessed the means of coercion. James VI had been the heir of a monarchy weakened by the circumstances of the Reformation and by the political causes of the fall of Mary, Queen of Scots. His subsequent success is the measure of his personal ability, his adaptability in adjusting his theories of kingship to the exigencies of contemporary events, and his capacity to tap the rich resources of the cumulative experience of his dynasty.

At last the long-awaited Union of Crowns approached. Queen Elizabeth I, who, James had once complained, seemed likely to outlive the sun and moon, began to display the ineluctable symptoms of mortality: 'Time's victory was apparent. The tallest of ruffs could not conceal it, the most glittering of diamonds could not overpower it; voice, action, attitude disclosed it. ...'[34]

Once, towards the end of her reign, chance almost revealed to the failing Queen the secret correspondence between Sir Robert Cecil and the King of Scots. According to Sir Henry Wotton:

The Queen, having for a good while not heard anything from Scotland, and being thirsty of news, it fell out that Her Majesty, going to take the air towards the heath (the Court being then at Greenwich), and Master Secretary Cecil then attending her, a post came crossing by and blew his horn. The Queen, out of curiosity, asked him from whence the despatch came, and being answered 'from Scotland' she stops the coach and calls for the packet. The Secretary, though he knew there were in it some letters from his correspondents, which to discover were as so many serpents, yet made more show of diligence than of doubt to obey, and asks some one that stood by (forsooth in great haste) for a knife to cut up the packet (for otherwise he might have awakened a little apprehension); but in the meantime approaching with the packet in his hand, at a pretty distance from the Queen, he telleth her it looked and smelt ill-favouredly, coming out of a filthy budget, and that it should be fit first to open and air it, because he knew she was averse from ill scents. And so, being dismissed home, he got leisure by this seasonable shift to sever what he would not have seen.[35]

In the opinion of her recent biographer, Neville Williams, Elizabeth was 'too shrewd to be unaware that the careful Cecil had long been making plans, even though she knew not the details'.[36] With that knowledge, or even that shrewd supposition, she could afford to maintain her resolute silence concerning the succession, even on her deathbed. No doubt she was confident that James would succeed her peacefully and satisfied that her successor would be a kinsman and a king and neither a nonentity nor an invader. She died in the small hours of the morning, on Thursday 24 March 1603, the eve of Lady Day, in the Palace of Richmond.

Later in the morning Sir Robert Carey, who had long ago been the bearer of Elizabeth's unhappy excuses for the execution of Mary, Queen of Scots, to King James, set out from Richmond to bear the King news of another death. This time he could be confident that he was the bringer of welcome tidings; he had, indeed, previously promised the King that he would bring them.

Sir Robert Carey had made his preparations; relays of horses were stationed in readiness on the route north. It was mid-morning when he left London, and he covered 162 miles before he slept that night at Doncaster. Next day he mercilessly galloped horse after horse another 136 miles along the well-worn, ill-kept track which linked the capitals of two kingdoms. He spent the night at Widdrington in Northumberland, which was his own northern home. The next day, probably bemused with weariness, he set out again; the conclusion of his journey is vividly described in his own words:

Very early on Saturday I took horse for Edinburgh and came to Norham about twelve at noon, so that I might well have been with the King at supper time : but got a great fall by the way, and my horse with one of his heels gave me a great blow on the head that made me shed much blood. It made me so weak that I was forced to ride a soft pace after, so that the King was newly gone to bed by the time that I knocked at the gate. I was quickly let in and carried up to the King's chamber. I kneeled by him, and saluted him by his title of England, Scotland, France and Ireland. He gave me his hand to kiss, and bade me welcome. . . .[37]

Welcome indeed! James knew that official news would follow, and in a few days he could begin his preparations to enter into his inheritance. That night, he lay in his great bed in Holyroodhouse savouring the sweet taste of fulfilled ambition; he had waited almost all his conscious life to hear himself hailed by the sonorous titles with which Sir Robert Carey had greeted him.

In the meantime the English Privy Council, which had disapproved but failed to prevent Sir Robert Carey's precipitate departure, acted with the measured stateliness of Elizabethan officialdom.

On the morning of Queen Elizabeth's death, when Carey had been galloping northward for an hour or more, 'At the west side of the High Cross in Cheapside . . . were assembled the most part of the English princes, peers, divers principal prelates and extraordinary and unexpected numbers of gallant knights and grave gentlemen of note well mounted, besides the huge numbers of common persons; all which, with great reverence, gave attention unto the Proclamation, being most distinctly and audibly read by Mr Secretary Cecil. . . .'[38]

That diminutive and immensely powerful man, who had engineered the peaceful succession, declared :

Forasmuch as it has pleased Almighty God to call to his mercy, out of this transitory life, our Sovereign Lady the high and mighty Princess Elizabeth, late Queen of England, France and Ireland, by whose death and dissolution the Imperial Realms aforesaid are come absolutely, wholly and solely to the high and mighty Prince James the Sixth, King of Scotland; who is lineally and lawfully descended from Margaret, daughter of the high and renowned Prince Henry the Seventh, King of England, France and Ireland, his great-grand-father. . . .

We, therefore, the Lords Spiritual and Temporal, being here assembled, and assisted with those of her last Majesty's Privy Council . . . are resolved by the favour of God's holy assistance, and in the zeal of our conscience (warranted by certain knowledge of his undoubted right, as has been said before), to maintain and uphold his Majesty's person and estate, as our only undoubted Sovereign Lord and King, with the sacrifice of our lives, lands, goods, friends and adherents, against all the force and practice that shall go about, by word or deed, to interrupt, contradict, or impugn his just claims, his entry into this kingdom at his good pleasure, or disobey such royal directions as shall come from him, to all which we are resolved to stand to the last drop of our blood . . . beseeching God to bless his Majesty and his Royal posterity, with long and happy years to reign over us. God save King James.[39]

The assembled crowd returned a thunderous echo, 'God save King James!'

With Cecil's words the relationship between Scotland and England, as his hearers had known it, and as many generations of their ancestors had known it, was instantaneously changed. During the Middle Ages it had seemed probable that an English king would conquer Scotland (Edward I had indeed come near to doing so). Generations of Englishmen had been schooled to regard the Scots with hatred, and those living had only recently learned to adopt a more temperate attitude of slightly hostile suspicion. But so great had been the general fear that civil disorder or foreign invasion would follow the death of the childless Queen, that the reversal of historical probability, the accession of a Scottish king to the throne of England, was greeted with national rejoicing.

Appendix

James VI instructs the Master of Gray to plead for the life of Mary, Queen of Scots.

'Instructions by James vi to the Master of Gray', 17 November 1586

Ye shall in our name signify to our dearest sister the Queen of England that we marvel not a little of the late preposterous and strange proceedure against the Queen our dearest mother, who being a sovereign princess, and in all degrees of the best blood in Europe, has been by subjects judged both in life and title, a dangerous precedent for all princes, and without any approved example in any age or kingdom, and so contrary to our honour as hardly could anything have fallen out so prejudicial there-unto.

We doubt not but our said dearest sister has been sufficiently advertized how the restraint of our dearest mother has been commonly interpreted, she being the prince in the world most near unto her both in blood and vicinity, having reposed her chief worldly esperance in her amity often confirmed by many friendly promises, and by her advice and persuasion demitted the government of this realm, and in her greatest extremity had her refuge unto her, *tan [quam] ad sacram anchoram*, looking for nothing less than captivity or imprisonment, but that *jura sanguinis gentium et hospitii* (*[quae] semper sacrosancta sunt habita*) should have availed as mickle [i.e., much] at her hand as could have been expected of a generous and pitiful princess, near cousin and kindly affected friend. And though her restraint was by the most part thought strange, yet it would have been construed by many to the better part if this more strange proceedure had not ensued. Ye shall desire our dearest sister to consider advisedly how all men may conceive of so uncouth and rare a form, so repugnant to the immediate supremacy granted by God to sovereign princes, whose ordinances will not permit sacred diadems to be profaned nor his higher power in any his anointed be subject to inferiors, nor their lives, crowns or kingdoms to be judged or disposed upon at the appetite or subjects, and that such proceedure may be thought the more strange that by no law, specially within this isle, very subjects' selves be judged otherwise but by the most part their peers and of equal rank and estate.

Ye shall also declare unto our said dearest sister that, having made special choice of her amity and in affection preferred her to all others, and with the loss of our nearest and well affected friends continued in all sincerity towards her, omitting no part of a well-devoted friend and brother, we did always expect and good desert have merited the like correspondence and reciproc[al] kindness on her part, whereby she might have been moved to a friendly consideration how such proceedure might concern us, as well in honour as otherwise, to have abstained from all things importing our dishonour and prejudice.

Ye shall desire our dearest sister to consider what construction can be made of this pretended process and what primices [?] this same may be thought of our so strict amity lately contracted, no part of the said pretended process having at any time been imparted unto us, either by letter or message, but the whole deduced without our knowledge or privity, notwithstanding the special interest we had therein so well known to her, which and the sincere observation of our so strait friendship could not permit us to be overseen or neglected in a matter of so great weight and dangerous sequel. And if the same had been timously signified unto us we should have so satisfied her in honour and surety for them both that she could not have needed to have had recourse to any so dangerous remedies and hard effects as are likely to fall out.

Ye shall expone to our said dearest sister with what just grief we have heard of the rigour against our dearest mother, and that nothing this world is more dear unto us than her life by whom we received life, and what duty we owe unto her both by the inviolable law of God and the straitest bond of nature between us, wherein we would rather yield our own life nor [i.e. than] offend in a point so carefully recommended unto us by God and so highly touching us in honour, heartily desiring her to enter in deep consideration both what becometh us of duty and nature, and what she herself would do, being in our place. Ye shall therefore most earnestly deal with her and in our behalf intercede with all instance that our said dearest mother's life (all ways so dear unto us) may be spared, that we may thereby have the better occasion to continue in our good devotion towards our said dearest sister and reap that fruit of our deserts and expectation, remonstring therewithal what a blemish it would be to her reputation to deborde [i.e. depart] so far from her accustomed clemency and natural mildness of her sex as to embrue herself with her own blood, by taking the life of her nearest cousin, being also of the like calling and sex to herself, beside the miscontentment of many great princes, who may be moved thereby, and divers other inconvenients that such rigour may breed, which will not import that surety to her own person and estate that some would persuade her may be confirmed by extremity [i.e. extreme measures].

If it shall be objected unto you that the preservation of our dearest mother's life carries with it an apparent danger to our dearest sister the Queen of England, for albeit our said dearest mother may be kept under restraint, and perhaps stayed from practising moyen and intelligence, yet that will be but gaining of time unto her, and neither her own esperance nor the hope of her partisans thereby removed, who for preferment, revenge or pretended religion are about to conspire against our said dearest sister, but will be still lying in wait attending opportunity and occasions to attain their designs ye may answer – her dealing and alleged attempts (if any have been) seems to have proceeded of a despair our said dearest mother had conceived by long and strait imprisonment and a womanly fear deeply apprehending danger of her life, and, as all captives naturally reclaiming liberty, has solicited such as she might move and has been induced by some of a contrary disposition to our dearest sister to shun her peril and seek her delivery. The most fit and sure expedient for the indemnity of our said dearest sister and quiet of this whole isle shall be by putting her to liberty out of the realm of England upon security and joint obligations of the princes of her kin, friendship and alliance, that nothing shall be directly or indirectly attempted by her or any her adherents or favourers against our dearest sister or her estate. So shall both and will and power to annoy be removed; and the cause ceasing, so shall the effect.

If it shall be objected that the sparing of our dearest mother's life shall breed peril to the true Christian religion and professors thereof ye may answer – it must needs produce the very contrary effect, and chiefly within this isle; for that such as indeed mean the subversion of the true religion would aid themselves in their enterprises by pretexing quarrel for her restraint and danger, and for her respect look to be assisted by her favourers within this isle, which they account their most importing force if our countenance or oversight [i.e. patronage] might be procured in any sort – so by her preservation and liberty their quarrel and chief moyen shall be removed, and consequently more surety and quiet to the whole isle shall ensue. And by the contrary, by her death a more just quarrel may be thereby pretexed, and they and their adherents and favourers more eagerly enflamed to a more cruel desire of revenge wherein they would assure themselves of our aid and concurrence, who have the chief interest and shame by her death.

If it be objected that the preservation of our dearest mother's life after the pretended condemnation will either argue the iniquity of the sentence or a fear in our dearest sister, whereby she is moved to abstain from putting the same to further execution, ye may answer – it will breed infinite praise and immortal name to our said dearest sister for her prudency, mildness and natural clemency, proceeding only of her own accord, beside and against the advice and deliberation of them who seeking by blood to settle her estate gives occasion of greater unquietness thereunto, and will breed to her a number of enemies and common misreport. And if our dearest mother's life be taken, it will plainly appear to proceed of fear and passion, and be deemed of all men *potius vindicta quam justitia*.

If the oath and the danger of the associates be opposed, ye may answer – that *functi sunt officio*, and though our dearest mother being alive may be thought formidable unto them, she shall be altogether gained by the clemency of our dearest sister, whose so great praise, as she shall acquire thereby, and surety of our person, we are assured they will prefer to their own particular dread or any future event specially by occasion of her who by nature cannot have long continuance.

If it be objected that by the death of our dearest mother factions or such as carry boldened hearts shall lack a head on whom to depend, ye may answer – her death by likelihood will rather incense nor terrify and rather stir up nor quench factions, and move and inflame than settle or mitigate boldened hearts. And if force and faction do remain it will be easy for them to find out a conductor more to be redoubted than an afflicted woman of unsound health and weak and diseased body, who (upon good security and capitulations, being out of the realm of England), is no ways to be feared, and apparently will have no desire, and possibly no power, to annoy.

Ye shall also inform our dearest sister (*quae sunt nobis undique angustiae et quam ancipiti cura distrahimur*), our natural duty and honour pressing us on the one part, and the care we have of our dearest sister (to whom we are entirely devoted) on the other, and above all, our zeal to true religion, whereupon both our states are settled, which and our dearest sister's person and estate may by all likelihood be put in full surety by joint and several bonds, obligations and pledges of such princes as will interpone their faith and security with our dearest mother and us, that she being delivered to one who will be always answerable upon his faith and peril of the hostages, that she shall neither directly nor indirectly deal, practise or attempt against our dearest sister's person and estate; so although she would violate her faith and forget the benefit of her liberty and life (which we cannot suspect she will, being denuded of all force and moyen, and lacking the assistance and goodwill of them of whom she expects most aid and are best affected to her), she shall be able to do no harm by herself, and shall incur the wrath of all such as has given their faith and hostages for her; and consequently our dearest sister's person shall be in surety and her realm freed from practices and attempts, and the dangerous designs prevented of such as affect the change of religion within this isle.

If our dearest sister shall not like of our dearest mother's liberty, she may avoid all peril by her sure restraint and strait bond and oath, no ways to practise against our dearest sister nor her estate, containing a provision that in case she shall violate her faith she shall be willingly subject to whatsoever ignominy or punishment may be inflicted to a rebel, renouncing in that case all rank and privileges of a sovereign prince, and by caution and obligations of the said princes to be interposed, who may be bound for her sincere observing of her oath or otherwise to allow of whatsoever proceedure against her.

If neither of the overtures foresaid be thought sufficient, ye shall with all instance press our dearest sister to set down by advice of her wisest and best affected counsellors such form of security as she and they shall think sufficient, or possibly or conveniently may be craved, whereunto we will not only yield for ourselves, but also do our best endeavour to obtain the performance thereof of all others with whom she will capitulate in this behalf, protesting before God the life of our dearest sister is no less dear unto us in all respects than the life of our dearest mother or our own.

The following note precedes the transcript of the Instructions in *King James's Secret* by Robert S. Rait and Annie I. Cameron: 'They have been printed in *Papers of the Master of Gray*, pp. 120–25, from Harleian MSS No. 1579, fol. 75. The document in the "Warrender Papers" is a copy. Part of the edge is worn away, and words have been supplied from the text in P.M.G. That text, however, contains many obvious errors and omits an important paragraph.' (Note p. 107; text pp. 107–15.)

The text given in *King James's Secret* (Warrender Papers, Vol. B. fol. 327) amended as described above, has here been anglicized by the author.

Bibliographies

A : WRITINGS BY KING JAMES VI

B : COLLECTIONS OF STATE PAPERS, LETTERS AND OTHER DOCUMENTS

C : CONTEMPORARY AND SEVENTEENTH-CENTURY WRITINGS

D : SELECT BIBLIOGRAPHY OF LATER WORKS

[All works listed are published in either Scotland or England unless otherwise stated; volumes which form part of a series – i.e. 'Edinburgh History of Scotland' – are thus specified.]

A : WRITINGS BY KING JAMES VI

  i) *The Essayes of a Prentise in the Divine Art of Poesie* (1584)
 ii) *Ane Fruitfull Meditatioun . . .* (1588)
iii) *Ane Meditatioun upon the First Buke of the Chronicles of Kings* (1589)
 iv) *His Maiesties Poeticall Exercises* (1591)
  v) *Daemonologie* (1597)
 vi) *The Trew Law of Free Monarchies* (1598)
vii) *Basilikon Doron* (1599)

see also Craigie, J. (ed.), *The Poems of King James VI of Scotland* (2 vols., Scottish Text Society, 1948, 1952) The second volume contains the poems which were not published during the King's lifetime.

B : COLLECTIONS OF STATE PAPERS, LETTERS AND OTHER DOCUMENTS

Calendar of State Papers relating to the Affairs of the Borders of England and Scotland (abbreviated as *CSP* [Border])

Calendar of State Papers (*Scottish*) (abbreviated as *CSP* [Scot])

Calendar of State Papers relating to English Affairs preserved principally in the Archives of Simancas (abbreviated as *CSP* [Simancas])

Correspondence of Robert Bowes (Surtees Society, 1842)

Correspondence of King James VI of Scotland with Sir Robert Cecil and Others . . ., ed. John Bruce (Camden Society, 1861)

Documents relative to the Reception at Edinburgh of the Kings and Queens of Scotland, 1579–1650 (1822)

Letters of Queen Elizabeth and King James VI of Scotland, ed. John Bruce (Camden Society, 1849)

Papers Relative to the Marriage of King James VI of Scotland with the Princess Anne of Denmark (Bannatyne Club, 1828)

Register of the Privy Council of Scotland

Papiers d'État . . . relatifs à l'histoire de l'Écosse au XVIᵉ Siècle, ed. A. Teulet (3 vols., Bannatyne Club, 1852– 60)

Scottish Historical Documents, ed. Gordon Donaldson (1970)

Source Book of Scottish History, eds. W. Croft Dickinson, Gordon Donaldson, Isabel Milne (1953)

Warrender Papers, ed. Annie I. Cameron (2 vols., Scotish History Society, 1931–2)

C: CONTEMPORARY AND SEVENTEENTH-CENTURY WRITINGS

BANNATYNE, GEORGE, *The Bannatyne Manuscript, Writt in Tyme of Pest, 1568*, ed. W. Tod Ritchie (4 vols., Scottish Text Society, 1928–33)

BIRREL, ROBERT, *Diarey of Robert Birrel . . . 1532–1605* (printed in Dalyell's *Fragments of Scottish History*, see below)

BUCHANAN, GEORGE, *A Detection of the Actions of Mary, Queen of Scots* (*Detectio Mariae Reginae Scotorum*) (anon., trans. 1721)

BUCHANAN, GEORGE, *De Jure Regni apud Scotos* (anon., trans. 1721)

BUCHANAN, GEORGE, *History of Scotland* (2 vols., anon., trans. 1751–2)

CALDERWOOD, DAVID, *History of the Kirk of Scotland* (8 vols. Wodrow Society, 1849)

DALYELL, JOHN GRAHAM (ed.), *Fragments of Scottish History* (1798)

Diurnal of Remarkable Occurrents, 1513–1575 (Bannatyne and Maitland Clubs, 1833)

HACKET, JOHN, *Scrinia Reserata: A Memorial Offer'd to the Great Deservings of John Williams, D.D.* (1692)

HERRIES, LORD, *Historical Memoirs of the Reign of Mary, Queen of Scots, and of King James the Sixth* (Abbotsford Club, 1836)

Historie and Life of King James the Sext (anon.) ed. Thomas Thomson (Bannatyne Club, 1825)

HUME, DAVID, OF GODSCROFT, *The History of the House and Race of Douglas and Angus* (1748)

KNOX, JOHN, *History of the Reformation*, ed. David Laing (2 vols. of Complete Works. Wodrow Society, 1846, 1848)

Maitland Folio Manuscript, ed. W. A. Craigie (2 vols., Scottish Text Society, 1919, 1927)

MELVILL, JAMES, *The Autobiography and Diarey of Mr James Melvill* (Wodrow Society, 1842)

MELVILLE, SIR JAMES, *Memoirs of His Own Life* (Bannatyne Club, 1827; also published in modernized editions by Chapman and Dodd, 1929; and as *The Memoirs of Sir James Melville of Halhill*, ed. Gordon Donaldson, by the Folio Society, 1969)

MONTGOMERY, ALEXANDER, *Poetical Works*, ed. J. Cranstoun (Scottish Text Society, 1887)

MOYSIE, DAVID, *Memoirs of the Affairs of Scotland, 1577–1603* (Bannatyne Club, 1830)

SANDERSON, WILLIAM, *A Compleat History of the Lives and Reigns of Mary, Queen of Scots and her son and successor James the Sixth* (1656)

Satirical Poems of the Time of the Reformation, ed. J. Cranstoun (Scottish Text Society, 1891)

SPOTTISWOODE, JOHN, *History of the Church of Scotland* (3 vols., Bannatyne Club and Spottiswoode Society, 1847–51)

D : SELECT BIBLIOGRAPHY OF LATER WORKS

AKRIGG, G.P.V., *Jacobean Pageant: The Court of King James I* (1962)

ANDERSON, WILLIAM, *The Scottish Nation* (3 vols. 1863)

ASHLEY, MAURICE, *The Stuarts in Love* (1963)

ASHTON, ROBERT, *James I by His Contemporaries* (1969)

BELLESHEIM, A., *History of the Catholic Church in Scotland*, trans. D.O. Hunter-Blair (4 vols. 1887–90)

BINGHAM, CAROLINE, *The Making of a King: The Early Years of James VI and I* (1968)

BINGHAM, CAROLINE, *The Stewart Kingdom of Scotland 1371–1603* (1974)

BLACK, J. B., *The Reign of Elizabeth, 1558–1603* (Oxford History of England, 2nd ed. 1959)

BROUGHAM, ELEANOR M., *News out of Scotland* (1926)

BROWN, JENNIFER M., *Scottish Politics, 1567–1625*, in *The Reign of James VI and I*, ed. Alan G. R. Smith.

CHAMBERS, ROBERT, *Biographical Dictionary of Eminent Scotsmen* (4 vols. 1885)

CHAMBERS, ROBERT, *Domestic Annals of Scotland* (3 vols. 1874)

CHAVBRIÈRE, COISSAC DE, *Les Stuarts* (Paris, 1930)

COOK, E. THORNTON, *Their Majesties of Scotland* (1930)

COWAN, IAN B., *The Enigma of Mary Stuart* (1971)

CRUDEN, STEWART, *The Scottish Castle* (1960)

CUST, LADY ELIZABETH, *Some Account of the Stuarts of Aubigny in France, 1422–1672* (1891)

DICKINSON, W. CROFT, *A New History of Scotland: Earliest Times to 1603* (1961)

Dictionary of National Biography

DONALDSON, GORDON, *Mary, Queen of Scots* (1973)

DONALDSON, GORDON, *The Reformation in Scotland* (1960)

DONALDSON, GORDON, *Scotland: Church and Nation through Sixteen Centuries* (1960)

DONALDSON, GORDON, *Scotland: James V to James VII* (Edinburgh History of Scotland, vol. III, 1965)

DONALDSON, GORDON, *Scottish Kings* (1967)

G

DONALDSON, GORDON, AND MORPETH, ROBERT, *Who's Who in Scottish History* (1973)

DRUMMOND, HUMPHREY, *Our Man in Scotland: Sir Ralph Sadleir, 1507–87* (1969)

DUKE, JOHN A., *A History of the Church of Scotland to the Reformation* (1957)

DUNBAR, SIR ARCHIBALD H., *Scottish Kings: A Revised Chronology of Scottish History, 1005–1625* (1899)

DUNLOP, GEOFFREY A., *John Stewart of Baldynneis, the Scottish Desportes* (*Scottish Historical Review*, XII, 1915)

ELLIOTT, KENNETH, AND RIMMER, FREDERICK, *A History of Scottish Music* (1973)

FARMER, HENRY GEORGE, *A History of Music in Scotland* (1947)

FERGUSSON, SIR JAMES, *The Man Behind Macbeth* (1969)

FORBES-LEITH, WILLIAM, *Narratives of the Scottish Catholics under Mary Stuart and James VI* (1889)

FRASER, LADY ANTONIA, *King James VI of Scotland I of England* (1974)

FRASER, LADY ANTONIA, *Mary, Queen of Scots* (1969)

FRASER, SIR WILLIAM, *The Douglas Book* (4 vols. 1885)

FRASER, SIR WILLIAM, *The Lennox* (2 vols. 1874)

GENT, FRANK, *The Coffin in the Wall: an Edinburgh Castle 'Mystery'* (pamphlet reprinted from *Chambers' Journal*, Sept–Oct. 1944)

GORE-BROWN, R. F., *Lord Bothwell* (1937)

GRANT, I. F., *The Social and Economic Development of Scotland before 1603* (1930)

HARRISON, G. B. (ed.), *Daemonologie* and *Newes from Scotland* (Bodley Head Quartos, 1924)

HENDERSON, T. F., *James I and VI* (1904)

HENDERSON, T. F., *The Royal Stewarts* (1914)

HENDERSON, T. F., *Scottish Vernacular Literature* (1910)

HUME-BROWN, P., *George Buchanan, Humanist and Reformer* (1890)

HUME-BROWN, P., *History of Scotland* (3 vols. 1908–9)

INNES OF LEARNEY, SIR THOMAS, *Scots Heraldry* (2nd ed. 1956)

KENYON, J. P., *The Stuarts: A Study in English Kingship* (3rd ed. 1966)

KINSLEY, JAMES, *Scottish Poetry: A Critical Survey* (1955)

LANG, ANDREW, *History of Scotland* (4 vols. 3rd ed. 1903–7)

LANG, ANDREW, *James VI and the Gowrie Conspiracy* (1902)

LAW, T. G., *English Jesuits and Scottish Intrigues, 1581–2* (*Edinburgh Review*, Jan–April 1898)

LINDSAY, IAN GORDON, *The Cathedrals of Scotland* (1926)

MCELWEE, WILLIAM, *The Wisest Fool in Christendom: the Reign of King James VI and I* (1958)

MCILWAIN, C. H., *Political Works of James I* (Harvard, 1918)

MACKENZIE, AGNES MURE, *Scottish Pageant, 1513–1625* (1948)

MACKIE, J. D. (ed.), *Negotiations between King James VI and I and Ferdinand I, Grand Duke of Tuscany* (1927)

Bibliographies

MACKIE, J. D., *Scotland and the Spanish Armada* (*Scottish Historical Review*, XII, 1915)

MCLAREN, MORAY, *The Wisdom of the Scots* (1961)

MACQUEEN, JOHN, AND SCOTT, TOM (eds.), *The Oxford Book of Scottish Verse* (1960)

MASSON, ROSALINE, *Scotland the Nation* (1934)

MATHEW, DAVID, *James I* (1967)

MATHIESON, W. L., *Politics and Religion* (2 vols. 1902)

MATTINGLY, GARRETT, *The Defeat of the Spanish Armada* (1959)

MAXWELL, SIR HERBERT, *History of the House of Douglas* (2 vols. 1902)

MENZIES, GORDON (ed.), *The Scottish Nation: A History of the Scots from Independence to Union* (1971)

MICHEL, FRANCISQUE (François-Xavier Michel) *Les Écossais en France: Les Français en Écosse* (2 vols. 1902)

MITCHISON, ROSALIND, *A History of Scotland* (1970)

NEALE, J. E., *Queen Elizabeth I* (reprint, 1952)

NICHOLS, J., *The Progresses, Processions and Magnificent Festivities of King James the First . . .* (4 vols. 1828)

NOTESTEIN, WALLACE, *The Scot in History* (1946)

Peerage of Scotland (2nd ed. 1813)

PURVEY, FRANK, *Coins and Tokens of Scotland* (Seaby's Standard Catalogue of British Coins, 1972)

RAIT, ROBERT S., *Lusus Regius* (1901)

RAIT, ROBERT S., AND CAMERON, ANNIE I., *King James's Secret: Negotiations between Elizabeth and James VI relating to the Execution of Mary, Queen of Scots* (1927)

READ, CONYERS, *Lord Burghley and Queen Elizabeth* (1960)

READ, CONYERS, *Mr Secretary Walsingham and the Policy of Queen Elizabeth* (3 vols. 1925)

ROUGHEAD, WILLIAM, *The Riddle of the Ruthvens* (1919)

ROUTH, C. R. N., *Who's Who in History, 1485–1603* (1964)

ROWSE, A. L., *The Expansion of Elizabethan England* (1955)

SCHIERN, F., *Life of James Hepburn, Earl of Bothwell*, trans. the Rev. David Berry (1880)

SCHWARZ, MARC L., *James I and the Historians: Toward a Reconsideration* (*Journal of British Studies*, XIII, May 1974)

SHIRE, HELENA MENNIE, *Song, Dance and Poetry of the Court of Scotland under King James VI* (1969)

SMITH, ALAN G. R. (ed.), *The Reign of James VI and I* ('Problems in Focus' Series, 1973)

STAFFORD, HELEN GEORGIA, *James VI of Scotland and the Throne of England* (American Historical Association, 1940)

STAIR-KERR, ERIC, *Stirling Castle: Its Place in Scottish History* (1913)

STEEHOLM, C. AND H., *James I of England* (1938)

STEWART, I. H., *The Scottish Coinage* (1955)

STRICKLAND, AGNES, *Lives of the Queens of Scotland . . .* (8 vols. 1850–58)

THOMSON, DUNCAN, *Painting in Scotland, 1570–1650* (1975)

TRANTER, NIGEL G., *The Fortalices and Early Mansions of Southern Scotland, 1400–1650* (1935)

TYTLER, PATRICK FRASER, *History of Scotland* (4 vols. 1873–77)

WARNER, G. F., *The Library of James VI . . . 1573–83* (Miscellany of the Scottish History Society, I, Edinburgh, 1893)

WARRACK, JOHN, *Domestic Life in Scotland, 1488–1688* (1920)

WESTCOTT, ALLAN F., *New Poems by James I of England* (Columbia University Press, 1911)

WILLIAMS, CHARLES, *James I* (1934)

WILLIAMS, ETHEL CARLETON, *Anne of Denmark* (1970)

WILLIAMS, NEVILLE, *Elizabeth, Queen of England* (1967)

WILLSON, D. H., *King James VI and I* (1956)

Notes and References

PROLOGUE: THE METAMORPHOSIS OF A KINGDOM

1 Knox, *History of the Reformation*, Vol. II, pp. 268–9.

2 *Maitland Folio Manuscript*, Vol. I, p. 37.

3 *Bannatyne Manuscript*, Vol. II, p. 235.

CHAPTER ONE: THE ROYAL CHILD

1 The reasoning behind this view was that as Elizabeth was the daughter of Henry VIII's second wife, Anne Boleyn, she was illegitimate. In Catholic eyes, neither Henry's divorce from Catherine of Aragon nor his marriage to Anne Boleyn could be accepted as valid.

2 Knox, *op. cit.*, II, p. 162.

3 Prose translation: 'The turtle-dove does not suffer more sorrow for her mate than I do for the sake of the lady who has my heart in her keeping. Until death my heart shall be dedicated to the service of that chaste lady who is the very fount of womanhood.' Professor John MacQueen observes: 'The poem is presumably addressed to Queen Mary before her marriage to Darnley on 29 July 1565' *Ballatis of Luve: The Scottish Courtly Love Lyric, 1400–1570*, p. 133.

4 The opinion of Argyll and Moray, *cit.* Donaldson, *Mary, Queen of Scots*, p. 97.

5 Melville, *Memoirs* (1929 ed.), p. 102.

6 This account of the murder of Riccio is taken from the *Diarey of Robert Birrel*, which is printed in Dalyell's *Fragments of Scottish History*, a book without continuous pagination.

7 Fraser, *Mary, Queen of Scots*, p. 304.

8 Herries, *Historical Memoirs*, p. 77.

9 *Ibid.*, p. 79.

10 *Ibid.*

11 Frank Gent, *The Coffin in the Wall: an Edinburgh Castle 'Mystery'*,

p. 28. This pamphlet is essential reading on the subject, as it successfully demolishes the fantastic theories based upon this 'mystery'.

12 McKerlie's Account No. 1, *cit.* Gent, *op. cit.*, p. 8; McKerlie's subsequent accounts, *ibid.*, pp. 10–14.

13 Geddie, *Romantic Edinburgh*, pp. 88–9.

14 Woodgate, *Reminiscences of an Old Sportsman*, p. 349.

15 *Ibid.*, pp. 349–50. Chapter XVI of this book, pp. 349–64, is entitled *The Mystery of James I (or VI)*. Unfortunately this agreeable memoirist has been guilty of a horrible mélange of errors and unwarrantable hypotheses. Its only importance is the part it has played in leading others astray.

16 Fraser, *Mary, Queen of Scots*, pp. 321–2 (fn). Lady Antonia Fraser's opinion of the find itself, expressed at the end of a long and interesting footnote, is that 'the little skeleton in the wall – if child it truly was, and this point was never officially stated at the time of the discovery – is far more likely to be the sad relic of a lady-in-waiting's peccadillo, than a Queen's conspiracy' (i.e. conspiracy to substitute a living infant of the Erskine family for her own dead baby). However, the present author inclines to the opinion of Grant R. Francis, in *Scotland's Royal Line*, p. 61 : 'It does not appear unlikely, however, that the so-called "coffin" was merely a reliquary wrapped in part of a vestment, and that the whole was hidden during the Reformation after Mary's departure from Edinburgh.' If this hypothesis is correct, and the object was a holy relic, it could equally well have been hidden in 1688, at the time of the Revolution against James VII and II. The relic theory would account for the initial J or I as part of the Holy Name monogram JHS or IHS. If there was a G also, it could be accounted for as the first letter of '*Gloria in excelsis Deo*'. Both the monogram and the gloria appear in ecclesiastical embroidery.

17 A recent examination of the subject is *The Casket Letters* by M. H. Armstrong Davidson (1965).

18 Calderwood, *History of the Kirk of Scotland*, Vol. III, p. 560.

CHAPTER TWO : A PATTERN FOR PRINCES

1 Donaldson, *Scotland: James V to James VII*, p. 159.

2 Douglas Young, *St Andrews*, p. 178.

3 Buchanan, *Epigram*, ii, 27, trans. P. Hume-Brown, *George Buchanan, Humanist and Reformer*, p. 254.

4 Trans. by James Michie, *cit.* Fraser, *Mary, Queen of Scots.* p. 221.

5 Melville, *Memoirs* (FS), p. 103.

6 Killigrew to Walsingham, 30 June, 1574; *CSP* (*Scot*), Vol. V, p.13.

7 Melville, *Memoirs* (FS), p. 103.

8 Mathew, *James I*, pp. 20–21.

9 Richard Bannatyne, *Journal of the Transactions in Scotland during the Contest between the Adherents of Queen Mary and those of her Son, 1570, 1571, 1572, 1573* (1806), pp. 246–7, 257; Calderwood, Vol. III, p. 136; *Historie and Life of King James the Sext*, p. 143 — in this narrative the story is told with a slight difference: the young King sees a hole in the tablecloth on a nearby table, not in the roof of the building.

10 Melville, *Memoirs* (FS), p. 96.

11 *Ibid.*, p. 101.

12 Peter Young's record of James's daily routine was printed by Dr Thomas Smith in *Vitae Quorundam Erudentissimorum* (1707), *cit.* George F. Warner, *The Library of James VI*, in *Miscellany of the Scottish History Society*, Vol. I, p. xiii, fn 3.

13 The pronunciation and speaking of the classical languages are notoriously subject to fashion, and Ben Jonson presented the English viewpoint when he told the Scottish poet William Drummond of Hawthornden that, 'He said to the King, his master M[r] G. Buchanan, had corrupted his ear when young, and learned him to sing verses when he should have read them' (*Ben Jonson's Conversations with Drummond of Hawthornden*, ed. and introd. R. F. Patterson, 1923, p. 46). Perhaps it is pardonable to wonder if Jonson spoke to the King as bluntly as he claimed to have done; some of the verses which he addressed to him were models of sycophancy.

14 *Cit.* Warner, *The Library of James VI*, in *Misc. Scot. Hist. Soc.*, Vol. I, p. xviii.

15 *Ibid., passim*. The comment on the ratio of French to English books is made by Mathew, *James I*, p. 26.

16 *Apophthegmata Regis*, recorded by Peter Young on the flyleaves of the notebook in which he listed James's books (BM Add. MSS. 34, 275) printed by Warner, *op. cit.*, pp. lxxii – lxxv.

17 Buchanan, dedication to *History of Scotland*, Vol. I.

18 *Basilikon Doron*, McIlwain, *Political Works of James I*, p. 18.

19 Archbishop Mathew invented the expression 'a regal Calvinist' to define James's personal religion, *James I*, p. 127.

20 *Register of the Privy Council of Scotland*, Vol. II, p. 164.

21 Mathew, *op. cit.*, p. 33.

22 *Apophthegmata Regis*, Warner, *op. cit.*, p. lxxiv.

CHAPTER THREE: 'MY PHOENIX RARE'

1 Robert S. Rait, *Lusus Regius*, pp. 24–7.

2 Shire, *Song, Dance and Poetry of the Court of Scotland under King James VI*, p. 73.

3 Description of Edinburgh in 1598 from the *Itinerary* of Fynes Morison, cit. Agnes Mure Mackenzie, *Scottish Pageant, 1513–1625*, pp. 16–17.

4 Moysie, *Memoirs*, p. 25.

5 Calderwood, Vol. III, p. 458.

6 *Ibid.*, p. 459. A puncheon may measure from 72 to 120 gallons; on either reckoning the people of Edinburgh were not ungenerously provided with wine.

7 Duncan Thomson, *Painting in Scotland, 1570–1650*, pp. 20–21.

8 Shire, *op. cit.*, pp. 83–4.

9 Moysie, *Memoirs*, p. 26.

10 Hacket, *Scrinia Reserata*, p. 30. John Aubrey's life of Camden hints at the origin of this piece of gossip, which does not display Bishop Hacket in a very wholesome light: 'Sir William Dugdale tells me that he has minutes of King James's life to a month and a day, written by Mr William Camden. . . . Sir William Dugdale had it from John Hacket, Bishop of Coventry and Lichfield, who did filch it from Mr Camden as he lay a-dying' (Aubrey, *Brief Lives*, ed. O. Lawson Dick, 1949, pp. 150–1).

11 *CSP (Border)*, Vol. I, p. 82.

12 Calderwood, Vol III, pp. 460–61.

13 *Ibid.*, p. 460.

14 Mathew, *James I*, p 35

15 Calderwood, Vol. III, p. 468.

16 *Ibid.*, p. 569.

17 *Ibid.*, p. 559.

18 Donaldson, *Scottish Historical Documents*, pp. 150–53.

19 Melville, *Memoirs* (1929 ed.), p. 145. Melville reported that Gowrie was informed by Drumwhasel that Lennox intended to 'slay him at first meeting'. However, Professor Donaldson points out that Gowrie, as Treasurer, was carrying a heavy deficit; Lennox's regime was extravagant, and in a few months the deficit had risen from £36,000 to £45,000 (Scots). This gave Gowrie a realistic reason for changing sides, without the influence of rumoured threats of violence. Donaldson, *Scotland: James V to James VII*, p. 178.

20 Melvill, *Diarey*, p. 95.

21 *BM. Cott. Calig. C VII. fol. 100*, original French translated by author. *CSP (Scot)* Vol. VI, pp. 223–4, another translation of full text.

22 This refers to *The Testament of the Papyngo* by Sir David Lindsay of the Mount, the leading poet at the Court of King James V. Lindsay appears to be the only one among the earlier Scots poets with whose works James VI was familiar.

23 *The Poems of King James VI of Scotland*, ed. J. Craigie, Vol. I, pp. 40–59. The true subject of *Phoenix* was revealed by a prefatory verse which appeared in *The Essayes of a Prentise in the Divine Art of Poesie*, first in the form of a votive column, and on the next page as a verse of four quatrains and a couplet. The base of the column is

i)   The column:

A Colomne of 18 lynes feruing for a Preface
to the Tragedie enfuying.

```
    1           Elf           1
      2     E c h o     2
        3   help, that both   3
          4   together      we,   4
            5   Since caufe there be, may   5
              6   now lament with tearis, My   6
                7   murnefull yearis.      Ye furies als   7
                  8   with him, Euen Pluto grim, who duells   8
                    9   in dark, that he, Since chief we fe him   9
                      10   to you all that bearis The ftyle men fearis of   10
                        11   Diræ, I requeft, Eche greizlie gheft that dwells   11
                          12   beneth the fee, With all yon thre, whofe hairs are fnaiks   12
                          12   full blew, And all your crew, affift me in thir twa:   12
                        11   Repeit and fha my Tragedie full neir, The   11
                      10   chance fell heir. then fecndlie is beft, Deuills   10
                    9   void of reft, ye moue all that it reid,   9
                  8   With me in deid lyke dolour them   8
                7   to griv', I then will liv' in   7
              6   leffer greif therebj. Kyth   6
            5   heir and try your force   5
          4   ay bent and quick,   4
        3   Excell      in   3
      2   fik   like   2
    1           ill,           1
            and murne with
          me. From Delphos fyne
        Apollo cum with fpeid: Whofe
      fhining light my cairs will dim in deid.
```

ii)   The verse:

The expanfion of the
former Colomne.

E	If Echo help, that both together w	E
(S	ince caufe there be) may now lament with tear	S
M	y murnefull yearis. Ye furies als with hi	M
E	uen Pluto grim, who dwels in dark, that h	E
S	ince cheif we fe him to you all that beari	S
T	he ftylé men fearis of Diræ: I requef	T
E	che greizlie gheft, that dwells beneth the S	E
W	ith all yon thre, whofe hairis ar fnaiks full ble	W
A	nd all your crew, affift me in thir tw	A
R	epeit and fha my Tragedie full nei	R
T	he chance fell heir. Then fecoundlie is bef	T
D	euils void of reft, ye moue all that it rei	D
W	ith me, indeid, lyke dolour thame to gri	V
I	then will liv', in leffer greif therebi	I
K	ythe heir and trie, your force ay bent and quic	K
E	xcell in fik lyke ill, and murne with m	E

From Delphos fyne Apollo cum with fpeid,
VVhofe fhining light my cairs wil dim in deid.

formed by the couplet with the addition of four words from line sixteen; the upper part of the column is formed by the first fifteen-and-a-
half lines. It contains a cryptogram on Lennox's name and title. When
the column is resolved into verse, the first and last letters of each
line of the quatrains read, downwards, ESMÉ STEWART DUIKE (sic).
Since U and V were interchangeable, and W was printed as either UU
or VV, the liberties taken with the spelling of the word 'duike' would
not in the sixteenth century have appeared to be liberties at all.

24 Cust, *Some Account of the Stuarts of Aubigny in France, 1422–1672,*
   pp. 95–6.

CHAPTER FOUR : 'HOW TO MAKE VERTUE OF A NEED'

1 James V had asserted his authority when he was sixteen, in 1528;
   James IV at about the same age, shortly after his accession in 1488;
   James III when he was eighteen, in 1469, and James II when he was
   nineteen, in 1449.

2 Calderwood, Vol. III, p. 678.

3 Donaldson, *Scotland: James V to James VII*, p. 180.

4 *Cit.* Tytler, *History of Scotland*, Vol. III, p. 143.

5 Maxwell, it may be remembered, had been created Earl of Morton; but for the sake of clarity he will continue to be referred to as Maxwell.

6 James Melvill made the following comment on the privations which Lennox suffered at Dumbarton:

> [He] remained in Dumbarton, at the West Sea, where...he was put to as hard a diet as he had caused the Earl of Morton to use there, yea, even to the other extremity that he had used at court. For, whereas his kitchen was so sumptuous that lumps of butter were cast in the fire when it burned low, and two or three crowns were spent on dressing a head of kale, [now] he was glad to eat of a thin goose scorched with barley straw.

Diarey, p. 96 (language modernized).

7 Melville, *Memoirs* (FS), pp. 110–11.

8 *Ibid.*, p. 111.

9 *Ibid.*

10 *The Historie and Life of King James the Sext*, p. 198.

11 An excuse for the grant was found in the fact that Arran's grandmother was Châtelhèrault's half-sister.

12 Hoby to Burghley, 15 August 1584, *cit.* Tytler, Vol. III, p. 164.

13 Fergusson, *The Man Behind Macbeth*, p. 32. The work quoted is a biographical essay which provides an excellent sketch of Arran's personality and career. The author also advances the view that his character and that of his wife could have provided Shakespeare with the prototypes of Macbeth and Lady Macbeth.

14 Melville, *Memoirs* (FS), p. 109.

15 Lady March was Elizabeth Stewart, daughter of John, sixth Earl of Atholl.

16 After Knox's death Margaret Stewart married Ker of Fauldonside, previously mentioned as one of the murderers of Riccio. *Supra* p. 16.

17 Walsingham to Elizabeth I, 11 September 1583: *CSP* (*Scot*), Vol. VI, p. 603.

18 Davidson to Walsingham, 27 March 1584, *cit.*, Tytler, Vol. III, p. 156; *CSP* (*Scot*), Vol. VII, pp. 155–59.

19 Mathew, *James I*, p. 41. The author applies the same description to Lennox, observing: 'They [Lennox and Arran] were not in fact submissive to their youthful sovereign.' Lennox, however, had especially endeared himself to James by adopting a submissive style of address.

20 Donaldson, *Scotland: James V to James VII*, p. 181: 'nearly a score'.

21 *CSP (Scot)*, Vol. VII.

22 Montgomerie refers to Esmé, Duke of Lennox, as his 'umquhyle Maister' (i.e. 'late master') in a sonnet in which he laments the wreck of his fortunes in Scotland. The circumstances are conjectural, but the poem leaves the desperate nature of his circumstances in little doubt:

> Adew, my King, Court, cuntrey, and my kin:
> Adew, swete Duke, whose father held me deir:
> Adew companiones, Constable and Keir:
> Thrie trewar hairts, I trow, sall never twin.
> If byganes to revolve I suld begin,
> My tragedie wald cost you mony a teir
> To heir how hardly I am handlit heir,
> Considring once the honour I wes in.
> Sirs, ye haif sent me griter with his Grace,
> And with your umquhyle Maister, to, and myne,
> Quha thoght the poet somtyme worth his place,
> Suppose ye sie they shot him out sensyne.
> Sen wryt, nor wax, nor word is not a word,
> I must perforce ga seik my fathers sword.

The 'swete Duke' was Esmé's son, Ludovic, second Duke of Lennox; Constable was Henny Constable, the English poet, and Keir was Henry Keir, Duke Esmé's Scottish secretary.

23 Shire, *op. cit.*, p. 90.

24 *Ibid.*, p. 85.

25 This conjecture is suggested by the following paragraph, in Shire, *op. cit.*, pp. 8–9:

> In the course of these studies here are some of the questions I am interested to ask. . . How were the songs made and how presented? Were they sung and listened to as in a modern concert performance, the interest being primarily musical? Or was the meaning of the words of greater pertinence, the intention of the performance of more serious import? Did the performers simply sing or did they 'act in song' – sing with gesture and significant movement? When the music was music of the dance, were the songs danced by the singers or danced by a courtly company to the singers' music? (All three modes of performance are noticed by Bacon as in use in the 1580s. . .).

26 The 'Spenserian' sonnet first appeared in England in a prefatory sonnet to Spenser's *Faerie Queen* (1590). The fact that both James VI and Alexander Montgomerie had published 'Spenserian' sonnets in

1584 was first noticed by Dr Allan F. Westcott, in *New Poems by James I of England*, introd., pp. l–li:

> The rhyme scheme of the Spenserian sonnet abab, bcbc, cdcd, ee, was used by both Alexander Montgomerie and James. The first appearance of this form in print was one of Montgomerie's dedicatory sonnets in the *Essayes of a Prentise* in 1584. Spenser first published a sonnet in this form in the dedicatory verses at the opening of the *Faerie Queene* in 1590 . . . by this time he would have been familiar with the King's reputation as a patron, and doubtless also with his verse. It is not in any case a matter to be settled by the relative merits of the writers concerned. Either James or Montgomerie, with their fondness for intricate and frequent rhyming, might have invented the scheme by following Gascoigne's statement that 'the first twelve [lines] do ryme in staves of four lines by crosse meetre, and the last two ryming togither do conclude the whole'.

27 Shire, *op. cit.*, pp. 98–9.

28 It was at Fauldon Kirk that Sir Edward Hoby met Arran and wrote the description quoted on p. 71, *vide supra*, note 12.

29 Tytler, Vol. III, p. 165.

30 Even the previous year Fontenay had written in this letter to Nau: 'I do not know what to say of Monsieur de Arran. Everyone hates him like the Devil' CSP (*Scot*), Vol. VII, p. 275.

31 Fergusson, *op. cit.*, p. 52.

32 Lee, *Maitland of Thirlestane*, p. 86.

33 *Cit.* D. H. Willson, *King James VI and I. CSP* (*Scot*), Vol. VIII, pp. 43–6; 491–2 illustrates the development of the situation.

CHAPTER FIVE: 'WE DEAL FOR A DEAD LADY'

1 Courcelles, *Negotiations in Scotland*, pp. 3, 9, *cit.* Rait and Cameron, *King James's Secret*, p. 25.

2 Master of Gray to Archibald Douglas, *cit.* Rait and Cameron, *op. cit.* p. 23.

3 Moysie, *Memoirs*, p. 152 (in 'Various readings'. The expression of opinion quoted does not appear in the main text, on p. 57, where Douglas's return to Scotland is recorded).

4 Rait and Cameron, *op. cit.*, p. 34.

5 *Warrender Papers*, Vol. I, pp. 235–6; Rait and Cameron, *op. cit.*, p. 35. In the ensuing notes references are given both to the *Warrender Papers* and to Rait and Cameron, *op. cit.* In the *Warrender Papers*

résumés of the letters are provided; Rait and Cameron quote the original texts. Quotations have been modernized by the author.

6 Labanoff, *Lettres et Mémoires de Marie, Reine d'Ecosse*, Vol. VII, p. 36; Maxwell-Scott, *Tragedy of Fotheringhay*, p. 31; Fraser, *Mary, Queen of Scots*, p. 596.

7 Chantlauze, *Bourgoing's Journal*, cit. Fraser, op. cit., p. 600.

8 *CSP (Scot)*, Vol. IX, pp. 152–4.

9 Douglas to Gray, 22 November 1586, *Warrender Papers*, Vol. I, pp. 236–7; Rait and Cameron, op. cit., pp. 48–51.

10 Gray to Douglas, 23 November 1586; Rait and Cameron, op. cit., p. 55.

11 James VI to William Keith, 27 November 1586: *Ibid.*, pp. 60–62. The editors have added an [s] to James's reference to King Henry VIII's reputation being 'prejudged' in nothing but in the beheading of his bedfellow. Henry VIII beheaded two of his queens, Anne Boleyn (2) and Catherine Howard (5); but James obviously intended the singular 'bedfellow' to have its full force in referring to Queen Elizabeth's mother alone.

12 *Instructions by James VI to the Master of Gray*: for full text, see Appendix.

13 James VI to Leicester, 15 December 1586, *Warrender Papers*, Vol. I, pp. 248–9; Rait and Cameron, op. cit., pp. 101–2.

14 George Young to Maitland of Thirlestane, 10 January 1587: *Warrender Papers*, Vol. I, pp. 255–8; Rait and Cameron, op. cit., p. 144.

15 Gray to James VI, 12 January 1587: *Warrender Papers*, Vol. C, printed in *Illustrations of Scottish History*, ed. Margaret Warrender (1899) and cit., Rait and Cameron, op. cit., pp. 145–50.

16 Courcelles, *Negotiations*, pp. 31–2.

17 Tenlet, *Relations Politiques*, Vol. IV, pp. 166–7.

18 BM Add. MSS. 48027 f644b, cit. Conyers Read, *Lord Burghley and Queen Elizabeth*, p. 367. In Note 121 to Chapter XVIII Conyers Read notes that Walsingham approved Paulet's refusal to arrange the secret murder of Mary, Queen of Scots.

19 Elizabeth to James VI, 14 February 1587: *Warrender Papers*, Vol. II, p. 11; Rait and Cameron, op. cit., p. 194–5.

20 James VI to Elizabeth, *Letters of Queen Elizabeth and King James VI of Scotland*, ed. J. Bruce, p. 46. The letter is undated, but the editor's conjecture is that it was written in March. The text survives in the form of a fair copy in James's handwriting.

21 Calderwood, Vol. IV, p. 611.

22 Ogilvie of Powrie to Archibald Douglas, *cit.* Rait and Cameron, *op. cit.*, p. 191.

CHAPTER SIX: 'THE GREAT FLEET INVINCIBLE'

1 In a letter to Mendoza (20 May 1586) Mary stated that she intended to make a Will ceding her right to the English Succession to King Philip '*en cas que mon dit fils ne se réduise avant ma mort à la religion Catholique*' ('in case my son should not return to the Catholic religion before my death'). This Will, however, was never made. See *Scot. Hist. Rev.*, XI, pp. 338–44; J. B. Black, *The Reign of Elizabeth*, p. 390 fn.

2 *CSP (Simancas)* Vol. IV, p. 16: Philip II to Count of Olivares, 11 February 1587.

3 *CSP (Scot)*, Vol. IX, pp. 557–8.

4 *Vide* Mathew, *James I*, Select Chart Pedigrees, No. 4, p. 329.

5 *CSP (Scot)*, Vol. IX, p. 699–706.

6 Mathew, *op. cit.*, p. 54.

7 Melvill, *Diarey*, p. 271.

8 *Ibid.*, p. 260.

9 *CSP (Simancas)*, Vol. IV, p. 200.

10 Calderwood, Vol. IV, pp. 648–9.

11 J. B. Black, *The Reign of Elizabeth*, p. 396.

12 *Ibid.*

13 Lee, *Maitland of Thirlestane*, p. 170.

14 Sanderson, *A Compleat History of the Lives and Reigns of Mary, Queen of Scots and of her son and successor James the Sixth*, p. 141.

15 J. B. Black, *op. cit.*, p. 402.

16 *CSP (Scot)*, Vol. IX, p. 588.

17 J. B. Black, *op. cit.*, p. 404.

18 *CSP (Scot)* Vol. IX, p. 596.

19 Gray to Douglas, 14 December 1588: *Ibid.*, p. 649.

20 Lee, *op. cit.*, p. 174

21 *Ibid.*

22 *CSP (Scot)*, Vol. IX, p. 644.

23 *Ibid.*, p. 635.

24 *Ibid.*, p. 640–41.

25 Calderwood, Vol. IV, pp. 694–5.

CHAPTER SEVEN : HERO AND LEANDER

1 Calderwood, Vol. V, pp. 7–8.

2 *CSP (Scot)*, Vol. IX, pp. 699–700.

3 *CSP (Scot)*, Vol. X, p. 3.

4 Melville, *Memoirs* (FS), p. 143.

5 *Ibid.*, p. 144.

6 Stafford, *James VI of Scotland and the Throne of England*, p. 52.

7 *CSP (Scot)*, Vol. X, p. 129.

8 Ashby to Walsingham, 24 September 1589 : *Ibid.*, p. 157.

9 James VI to Anne of Denmark, c.2 October 1859 : *Warrender Papers*, Vol. II, pp. 109–10. Original French and trans. Quotation in text, author's trans.

10 E. C. Williams, *Anne of Denmark*, pp. 16–17.

11 *Discourse of James VI on taking his Voyage, CSP (Scot)*, Vol. X, pp. 174–5.

12 *Ibid.*, p. 76. The *Discourse* is also printed in *Register of the Privy Council of Scotland*, Vol. IV, pp. 127–9, and in *Papers Relative to the Marriage of King James VI*, pp. 12–16.

13 Lee, *Maitland of Thirlestane*, p. 203.

14 E. C. Williams, *op. cit.*, pp. 19–20.

15 Ashby to Elizabeth I, 23 October 1589 : *CSP (Scot)*, Vol. X, pp. 180–81.

16 Westcott, *New Poems by James I of England*, p. 24.

17 E. C. Williams, *op. cit.*, p. 23.

18 Westcott, *op. cit.*, p. 26.

19 E. C. Williams, *op. cit.*, p. 30.

20 *Ibid.*, p. 31.

21 Westcott., *op. cit.*, p. 2.

22 Goodman, *The Court of King James the First*, pp. 167–8.

23 *CSP (Border)*, Vol. I, pp. 31, 34.

24 Westcott, *op. cit.*, pp. 12–19.

CHAPTER EIGHT : 'DEBELLARE SUPERBOS'

1 The outburst [of witch-hunting] came with the accession of a
Scottish King, who, though he rejected the best part of the spirit of
Knox, was crazed beyond his English subjects with the witch-mania
of Scotland and the continent.
G. M. Trevelyan, *England under the Stuarts* (1904; reprint 1965), pp.
28–9.

Owing to the lurid attractiveness of the more awesome portions of
the Scriptures, this dark and degrading delusion [belief in witch-
craft] was now, in Scotland, at the zenith of its potency. James had
studied with avidity the sixteenth-century literature on the subject. . . .
Under his auspices witch trials were therefore instituted in different
districts, over which he, deeming himself a special adept in witch-
finding, often presided.
T. F. Henderson, *The Royal Stewarts*, p. 173.

It is worth noting that the type of witchcraft which was associated
with the countryside appears to have aroused but little interest in
King James's mind. . . . One would wish to curb a tendency towards
the fanciful, but it sometimes seems to me that King James's concern
with the devil was part of the interest which he showed in the Dark
monarchy. . . . He would perhaps see the Prince of Darkness as
another kind of ruler who would exercise his sway over the King of
Scotland's subjects.
Matthew, *James I*, p. 76.

2 Christina Larner, *James VI and I and Witchcraft*, in *The Reign of
James VI and I*, ed. Alan G. R. Smith, pp. 74–90.

3 Larner in Smith, *op. cit.*, p. 74.

4 Mathew, *op. cit.*, p. 76

5 Melville, *Memoirs* (FS), p. 155.

6 *Ibid.*

7 *Ibid.*

8 *Ibid.*

9 James VI, *Daemonologie*, p. 2.

10 *Ibid.*, p. 81.

11 Mathew, *op. cit.*, p. 57.

12 Westcott, *New Poems by James I*, p. 30.

13 Calderwood, Vol. V, pp. 225–6.

14 *Vide supra*, p. 73–4, 82.

15 Mathew, *op. cit.*, p. 64.

16 *Ibid.*

17 *Ibid.*, p. 70: 'In some respects King James was from the Presbyterian point of view a perfect ruler and had it not been for the theocratic outlook of the leading ministers the relationship would have been entirely peaceful.'

18 Melvill, *Diarey*, pp. 370–71.

19 Elizabeth I to James VI, 6 July 1590, *CSP (Scot)*, Vol. X, pp. 349–50.

20 Donaldson, *Scotland: James V to James VII*, p. 200.

21 Calderwood, Vol. V, p. 669.

22 *Ibid.*, p. 681.

23 Donaldson, *op. cit.*, p. 194.

CHAPTER NINE : THE KING'S BOOKS

1 *Trew Law of Free Monarchies*, McIlwain, *Political Works of James I*, p. 53 (spelling modernized in this and all ensuing quotations).

2 *Ibid.*, pp. 54–5.

3 The sixteenth-century Scots believed that their first King had been Fergus I, who came from Ireland in 330 BC. In reality, there was an historical Fergus who ruled in the small kingdom of Dalriada (Argyll) in about AD 500. The union of the Picts and the Scots under Kenneth MacAlpin in 843 created the beginnings of the later kingdom of Scotland. The strength of the Scottish monarchy derived less from a sense of hereditary descent (though there was a continuity in the successive royal Houses) than from a profound belief in the extreme antiquity of the monarchy as an institution.

4 *Trew Law of Free Monarchies*, McIlwain, *op. cit.*, pp. 63–4.

5 *Ibid.*, p. 70.

6 *Vide supra*, p. 30–31.

7 Westcott, *New Poems by James I*, introd. p. lii.

8 *Basilikon Doron*, McIlwain, *op. cit.*

9 *Ibid.*, p. 4.

10 Buchanan, introd. to *Baptistes, cit.* Hume Brown, *George Buchanan*, p. 24.

11 *Basilikon Doron*, McIlwain, *op. cit.*, p. 12.

12 *Ibid.*, pp. 18–19.

13 *Ibid.*, p. 23.

14 *Ibid.*, p. 24.

15 *Ibid.*, pp. 24–5.

16 *Ibid.*, p. 26.

17 *Ibid.*, p. 26–7.

18 *Ibid.*, p. 20.

19 *Ibid.*, p. 36.

20 *Ibid.*, p. 37.

21 *Ibid.*, p. 41.

22 Charles Williams, *James I*, p. 299.

23 *Basilikon Doron*, McIlwain, *op. cit.*, p. 29.

24 *Ibid.*

25 *Ibid.*, p. 40.

26 *Ibid.*, p. 43.

27 *Ibid.*, p. 43–4.

28 *Ibid.*, p. 44.

29 *Ibid.*, pp. 45, 47.

30 *Ibid.*, p. 48.

31 *Ibid.*, p. 52.

32 Jennifer M. Brown, *Scottish Politics, 1567–1625*, in *The Reign of James VI and I*, ed. Alan G. R. Smith, p. 26.

33 *Vide infra* p. 153ff.

34 L. Pearsall Smith, *Life and Letters of Sir Henry Wotton* (1907), Vol. I, pp. 314–15.

35 Jennifer M. Brown, *op. cit.*, p. 36.

CHAPTER TEN : 'ONE OF THE MOST SECRET PRINCES OF THE WORLD'

1 Mathew, *James I*, p. 89 n : The period of most active discussion was at the end of the last century. Andrew Lang, *James VI and the Gowrie Mystery*, was printed in 1902, and W. N. Roughead, *The Riddle of the Ruthvens and Other Studies*, in 1919. A more recent analysis of these events by W. F. Arbuckle appears in *Scottish Historical Review*, XXXVI.

2 Archbishop Mathew, *op. cit.*, p. 90, is incorrect in stating that 'the Earl of Gowrie owed a very large sum of money, about £80,000, to the Crown dating from the period when his father had held the office of lord treasurer of Scotland'. The debt was in fact the other way

about, owed by the Crown to the first Earl of Gowrie's heirs. *Vide* Donaldson, *Scotland: James V to James VII*, p. 203.

3 Donaldson, *op. cit.*, p. 203.

4 *Correspondence of King James VI of Scotland with Sir Robert Cecil and Others* . . ., ed. J. Bruce, introd. *passim*.

5 Robert Devereux, second Earl of Essex, was the second cousin of Elizabeth I. Both were descended from Thomas Boleyn, Earl of Wiltshire, who had two daughters, Anne and Mary. Anne married King Henry VIII and was the mother of Queen Elizabeth. Mary married William Carey, and there were two children of this marriage: Henry Carey, Lord Hunsdon, and Mary Carey, who married Sir Francis Knollys. They were the parents of Lettice Knollys, who married Walter Devereux, first Earl of Essex: the son of this union was Robert Devereux, who succeeded to his father's title and was the Queen's favourite. After the death of her first husband, Lettice Knollys secretly married Robert Dudley, Earl of Leicester, the Queen's earlier favourite, who was thus the stepfather of the second Earl of Essex.

6 Essex to James VI, Christmas Day 1600, *cit.* Stafford, *James VI of Scotland and the Throne of England*, p. 215

7 *Correspondence of King James VI* . . ., introd. pp. xxviii–xxix.

8 *Ibid.*, p. 4.

9 *Ibid.*, p. 5.

10 *Ibid.*, p. 6.

11 Mathew, *op. cit.*, p. 97.

12 *Correspondence of King James VI*, p. 19.

13 Numerical ciphers were chosen to represent the participants in the correspondence, their confidants and persons who were frequently mentioned. John Bruce, the editor of the *Correspondence of King James VI of Scotland with Sir Robert Cecil and Others* . . ., listed the ciphers as follows:

> 0 was the Earl of Northumberland
> 2 was Sir Walter Raleigh
> 3 was Lord Henry Howard
> 7 was Lord Cobham
> 8 was Mr Edward Bruce
> 9 was Mr David Foulis
> 10 was Sir Robert Cecil
> 20 was the Earl of Mar
> 24 was Queen Elizabeth
> 30 was King James
> 40 was a Colleague of Cecil's, but who has not been discovered.

Correspondence..., Introd. pp. xxxv–xxxvi. H. G. Stafford, in *James VI of Scotland and the Throne of England*, added: 'The "40" of the cipher used, which Bruce failed to identify, was probably Nottingham', p. 255 fn.

14 Forbes-Leith, *Narratives of the Scottish Catholics*, Vol. I, pp. 63–5.

15 D. H. Willson, *King James VI and I*, pp. 146–7. The *Beatissime Pater* letter had an embarrassing sequel. In 1608, after James's accession to the English throne, its existence was discovered and divulged by an English Catholic. James blamed it on his Scottish Secretary of State, Lord Balmerino, saying that the latter had inserted it among letters for his signature, which he had signed in haste before going hunting. It was less compromising to appear as a negligent ruler than as an intriguer with the Papacy.

16 The story of James's diplomatic relations with Ferdinand I has been followed in all its ramifications in *Negotiations between King James VI and I and Ferdinand I, Grand Duke of Tuscany*, ed. J. D. Mackie (St Andrews University Publications XXV, 1927).

17 *Correspondence of King James VI*, p. 23.

18 Westcott, *New Poems by James I*..., Appendix II, poem iii, pp. 63–4.

19 *CSP* (*Scot*), Vol. XII, p. 117.

20 Mathew, *op. cit.*, p. 65.

21 *Cit.* Brown, *Scottish Politics, 1567–1625, op. cit.*, pp. 34–5. Dr Brown writes: 'I am indebted to Dr G. G. Simpson of the University of Aberdeen for drawing my attention to this letter. The text given here is a translation of the Scots original, which has an even stronger flavour of violent fury, indeed parts of it almost defy understanding,' p. 229 n.

22 Donaldson, *Scotland: James V to James VII*, p. 212.

23 Earl Patrick Stewart was a grandson of King James V; his father, Lord Robert Stewart, was an illegitimate son of the King by Euphemia Elphinstone, one of his many mistresses. Patrick was born after 1561 and was educated by Sir Patrick Vaus of Barnbarroch, who played some part in negotiating the marriage of James VI with Anne of Denmark. Earl Patrick's character and conduct are controversial; his indisputably excellent taste in architecture is witnessed by the palace which he built at Kirkwall in Orkney, and by his castle at Scalloway in Shetland. On the controversy concerning the oppressiveness or otherwise of his rule, see G. Donaldson, *Shetland Life under Earl Patrick* (1958).

24 *Basilikon Doron*, McIlwain, *op. cit.*, p. 26.

25 Donaldson, *Scotland: James V to James VII*, p. 5.

26 *Basilikon Doron*, McIlwain, *op. cit.*, p. 26.

27 *Scottish Historical Documents*, pp. 169–171.

28 *Basilikon Doron*, McIlwain, *op. cit.*, p. 22.

29 Brown, *Scottish Politics 1567–1625*, *op. cit.*, p. 31.

30 *Scottish Historical Documents*, pp. 171–5.

31 *Ibid.*, pp. 178–9.

32 Donaldson, *op. cit.*, p. 233.

33 Brown, *Scottish Politics, 1567–1625*, *op. cit.*, p. 38–9.

34 *Correspondence of King James VI* (1907), introd. p. v.

35 Sir Henry Wotton, *Reliquiae Wottonianae* (1672), p. 169.

36 Neville Williams, *Elizabeth, Queen of England*, p. 352.

37 Sir Robert Carey, *Memoirs*, cit. John Nichols, *The Progresses, Processions and Magnificent Festivities of King James the First*, Vol I, p. 34.

38 Howes (continuator of *Stowe's Chronicle*), cit. Nichols, *op. cit.*, Vol. I, p. 26.

39 *Ibid.*, pp. 27–30.

Index

Index

The English Succession

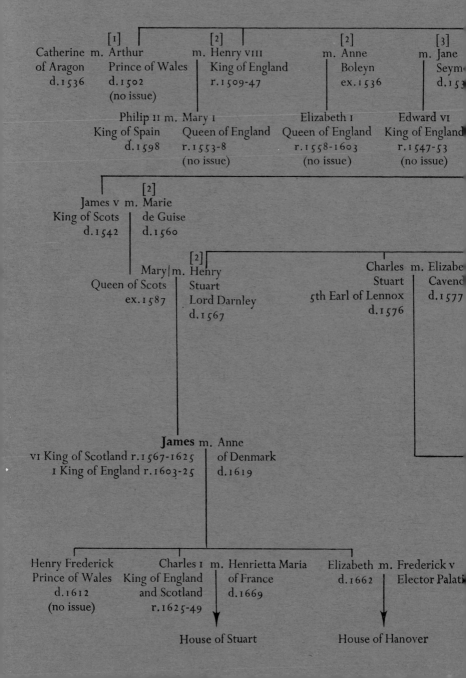

[1] Catherine m. Arthur
of Aragon   Prince of Wales
d.1536   d.1502
(no issue)

[2] m. Henry VIII
King of England
r.1509-47

[2] m. Anne
Boleyn
ex.1536

[3] m. Jane
Seym
d.153

Philip II m. Mary I
King of Spain   Queen of England
d.1598   r.1553-8
(no issue)

Elizabeth I
Queen of England
r.1558-1603
(no issue)

Edward VI
King of England
r.1547-53
(no issue)

James V m. [2] Marie
King of Scots   de Guise
d.1542   d.1560

Mary | m. [2] Henry
Queen of Scots   Stuart
ex.1587   Lord Darnley
  d.1567

Charles m. Elizabe
Stuart   Cavend
5th Earl of Lennox   d.1577
d.1576

James m. Anne
VI King of Scotland r.1567-1625   of Denmark
I King of England r.1603-25   d.1619

Henry Frederick
Prince of Wales
d.1612
(no issue)

Charles I m. Henrietta Maria
King of England   of France
and Scotland   d.1669
r.1625-49

Elizabeth m. Frederick V
d.1662   Elector Palati

House of Stuart   House of Hanover